New York

ON $500 A DAY

•

ALSO BY
FERNE KADISH AND KATHLEEN KIRTLAND

London on $500 a Day

Los Angeles on $500 a Day

Paris on $500 a Day

New York
ON $500 A DAY *

Ferne Kadish
Kathleen Kirtland
Gladyce Begelman

COLLIER BOOKS
A Division of Macmillan Publishing Co., Inc.
New York

COLLIER MACMILLAN PUBLISHERS
London

* Before lunch

Copyright © 1977 by Ferne Kadish and Kathleen Kirtland

All rights reserved. No part of this book may be reproduced or transmitted in any form or by any means, electronic or mechanical, including photocopying, recording or by any information storage and retrieval system, without permission in writing from the Publisher.

Macmillan Publishing Co., Inc.
866 Third Avenue, New York, N.Y. 10022
Collier Macmillan Canada, Ltd.

Library of Congress Cataloging in Publication Data
Kadish, Ferne.
New York on $500 a day* (*before lunch)
Includes index.
1. New York (City)—Description—1951–
—Guidebooks. I. Kirtland, Kathleen, joint author.
II. Begelman, Gladyce, joint author. III. Title.
F128.18.K32   1977b   917.47'1'044   77-12029
ISBN 0-02-097740-9

First Collier Books Edition 1977

New York on $500 a Day is also published in a hardcover edition by
Macmillan Publishing Co., Inc.

Designed by Jack Meserole

Printed in the United States of America

TO NEW YORK,
WITH LOVE!

To all our friends in the Big Apple:
we salute you for being so fast-moving
that dozens of exciting places
will have opened between the time we write
and the time you're reading; for being
so unique that we're sure to have walked
right by some of your most innovative
restaurants and shops; and for being
so friendly and stimulating that
we just can't wait to get back!

●

For all the out-of-towners: the area code
of all phone numbers listed in New York City is 212.
In the case of a few out-of-town numbers,
the area code is included.

Contents

INTRODUCTION ix

I. TRANSPORTATION   New York Knows How
   to Get Around   1
   GETTING THERE IS HALF THE FUN, 1
   Car Services, 2   Creative Coaches, 5

II. HOTELS   Don't Go Away Till You Know Where
   to Stay   8

III. NEW YORK RESTAURANTS AND CLUBS
   Food for Thought   21
   RESTAURANTS, 22
      Out of Town, 95
   CLUBS, 96

IV. EATING IN   Adventures in Food Shopping   102
   BAKERIES, 103
   GOURMET FOOD STORES, 111
   CANDY, NUTS, CONFECTIONS, 116
   CATERERS, 119

V. RAGS FOR THE RICH   124
   DEPARTMENT STORES, 125
   BOUTIQUES/TAILORS/ACCESSORIES, 136
      For Men and Women, 136   For Women, 146
      For Men, 170   Furs, 178   For Children, 180

CONTENTS

VI. NEW YORK JEWELRY   It's Sparkle City   183

VII. MANHATTAN   Anything Goes!   196
 FLOWERS, 196
 CRYSTAL, 199
 HOME DECORATIONS AND FURNITURE, 201
 LEATHER, 205
 LINENS, 206
 POTPOURRI ELÉGANT, 210
 STATIONERY, 215

VIII. ANTIQUES AND GALLERIES   Growing Old
   Gracefully in Manhattan   217
 ANTIQUES, 217
 GALERIES, 228

IX. THE NEW YORK BEAUTY SCENE   Pretty Is
  as Pretty Does   235
 BODY TONING, 235
 HAIR, 243
 SKIN, 248
 TOILETRIES, 253

X. THE SPORTING LIFE   256

NEW YORK   We Don't Want to Say Goodbye   265

INDEX   267

INTRODUCTION

New York is my town—and I share every Comden-and-Greene sentiment about it, from the Bronx to the Battery. I've learned the city's alphabet from Azuma to Zabar—from the nuances of its neighborhoods to the flavors of its food—from the good time of a New York nighttime to the adventure of Fifth Avenue shopping. I'm familiar with New York's names and faces and places—where to go for what and when. And how to get there, and whom to ask for. In short, I'm a typical know-it-all New Yorker.

This book has taken me down several pegs and put me quite properly in my place. The Mesdames Kadish, Kirtland, and Begelman not only have a fix on New York that most full-time residents might well envy—they've come up with a clutch of well-kept secrets which have escaped even devoted denizens like me.

What's more, their rundown of Manhattan life on the lush side is breezy, easy, and informative. Their know-how about wheels is a revelation. Their analysis of hotels and restaurants has style and savvy. They've caught the character of sizeable stores and small shops with sharp-eyed accuracy. What this trio of big-time travelers has done is to cover the well-heeled waterfront in everything the town has to offer when it comes to comfort, clothes, and cachet. And—whether New York on $500 a day is a fact of your life or just a high number on your list of fantasies—they've made it fascinating fun to read about.

—Geraldine Stutz

New York

ON $500 A DAY

•

I. TRANSPORTATION
New York Knows How to Get Around

We've heard that things are getting simply horrid on the subways. Now all we want to know is... what's a subway?

Traffic may be terrible, and flight schedules into the city a perfect mess, but we've managed to find ways for you to get into and around town (or out of town if you prefer) without disturbing one Kenneth-coiffed hair. What with chauffeurs and helicopters at your disposal, subways are better left unexplored anyway.

Of course we should start with first impressions... they're so important, aren't they! And think how good an impression you'll make when you slip into New York in your own Lear jet.

GETTING THERE IS HALF THE FUN

Executive Jet Aviation	(614) 237-0363 OR TELEX 245495

America's scheduled airlines fly into a total of 507 airports; Executive Jet Aviation can land in 11,500. Enough said? Besides, on your private jet you can order anything from Rice Krispies to fresh caviar and find it waiting on board when those hunger pangs strike somewhere over the Rockies. And food is *so* important, isn't it!

With clients like the Whitneys and the Guests, Executive Jet Aviation is truly the Rolls-Royce of air travel. It has about twenty planes, and lands more of them at LaGuardia than at any other airport in the country.

If you're coming from Los Angeles to New York, you'll want a six-passenger Lear Jet, which should run you about $6,000 one-way. But on shorter hops, you're better off with a smaller aircraft at a lower price. After all, we wouldn't want you to be wandering around without a sou when you land in the Big Apple.

Just call or TELEX Bruce Sundlun, and let him know what time you're planning to hop in or out of New York. Your jet will be ready and waiting, which is comforting when you consider that after 9 or 10 P.M. in New York, scheduled flights are few and far between. Whatever would you do without Executive Jet if you decided to make a last-minute trip to the Kentucky Derby or Cape Cod? Bunny Mellon uses them as often as George C. Scott does. Barbara Walters used them to fly slides across the country; and Isaac Stern used Executive Jet to fly to Washington for a concert. And we're sure that you'll use them to equally good purpose.

By the way—once you find out what fun it is flying Executive Jet, you'll probably want to snap up one of their 100,000-mile contracts. When you pay for 100,000 miles at once, Executive Jet will promise to pick you up anywhere in the world within four hours. What power!

For a dear friend you might consider a 5,000-mile contract, which will guarantee their being picked up anywhere in the United States within eight hours. And for a not-so-good friend it's always good to remember that you can send them away to any spot on the globe at just $2.50 per mile—with a minimum of 300 miles.

Car Services

How anyone manages in New York without a chauffeur is beyond our comprehension. Not that it's so difficult to drive your own car—it's just impossible to park it! And cabs have the nastiest habit of disappearing just when you need them the most, like at five in the afternoon or at the first sign of rain. Besides, you look ever so much better pulling up in front of Orsini's in black.

Chauffeurs	310 WEST END AVE. 10023
Unlimited	362-5354

Edward Klanit offers a rather special service—his chauffeurs will drive your own car for you. For about $5.40 per hour, with a minimum of two and a half hours, they will pick up the car at your garage, pick you up at wherever, make sure you meet every appointment during your busy day, then drop off the car when you're finished.

Drivers range from actors and opera singers to policemen and firemen, and frankly, during the last couple of years we've noticed a lot of the Wall Street executives we used to see sitting next to us during dinner at La Grenouille. Oh, well, at least they know their way to every good restaurant in town!

All are required to wear charcoal-gray jackets and pants with white or blue shirts, and a hat and gloves to match, so do be sure that your car is dressed in a similarly understated fashion if you're planning to have them drive it.

If you don't happen to have an extra car sitting in your garage, Chauffeurs Unlimited will also provide you with a limousine. Of course, that's $14 an hour or 60 cents a mile, rather than the $5.40 you were paying when you brought your own. But that's the way executives of CBS, Union Carbide and NBC prefer it, and you might, too.

Dave-el Livery	625 W. 51ST ST. 10019
	541-4747

We can understand why rock stars love driving in David Klein's stretched-out white Lincoln Continental with custom-built sun roof, stereo and bar . . . they're just kids at heart. But Leonard

Bernstein? Oh, well, undoubtedly he requested the slightly (but not much) more conservative version in dark blue or black. He *would* make a bit of an impression pulling up in front of Carnegie Hall in a snow-white block-long Continental, wouldn't he!

For the *real* wallflowers, David keeps an unobtrusive brown Cadillac limousine, but don't count on getting it when we're in the city—it's the one for which we always put in a reservation.

Now a word of caution: among David's drivers you'll find everything from would-be opera stars to has-been rock stars who used to ride in the passenger section of the Continental in which you're riding. So be sure to request someone with experience, or you might find yourself trying to help find the 59th Street Bridge, which is a bit much at $18 an hour.

Harvey Limousine 9–15 115TH ST.
Service COLLEGE POINT, N.Y. 11356
LE 9-4600

Harvey Crook, professional chauffeur, went into business over twenty years ago ... so who should know better what clients look for in a limousine service? To Harvey's way of thinking, they're looking for someone who'll satisfy their every whim, whether they want a simple ride to the airport, a steak for cooking in their hotel suite, or an ice cream soda from Rumpelmayer's (in the St. Moritz Hotel). That's right, it *was* one of Harvey's boys you saw running across the lobby of the Regency holding aloft a slightly dripping chocolate soda! To say the least, it's a very personalized and efficient service.

Harvey has about thirty-five cars, including limousines, station wagons, and mini-vans. One hundred chauffeurs are on call over a twenty-four-hour period, our favorite and regular driver being Peter Borodin. If you're going to Connecticut, Harvey will call on one of the hundred drivers familiar with the area. If you're on your way to the Hamptons, he'll find a driver who knows the difference between East and West. And if you're just going to stay in the city, he'll find someone who (miraculously) seems to be familiar with any place you might want to shop or eat. Just $18 an hour or 60 cents a mile will buy you this perfection in driving. He's proven his worth by serving everyone from Henry Fonda and Kirk Douglas to the presidents of Bethlehem Steel and Allied Chemicals, not to mention most of the studio executives of Columbia and Paramount.

By the way, when we tell you that Harvey is cooperative, we mean he's as cooperative *before* you arrive as he is after. You want your refrigerator filled with Mountain Valley water, orange juice, cottage cheese or pâté when you arrive? Just call Harvey at his office and tell him of your heart's desires... and as quickly as he can say "Go shopping, Peter," things will be waiting for you in perfect order upon your arrival. Think about it: how many limousine services do you know of that are as polite to a bag of groceries as they are to its owner?

Rollston Livery Service / Rollston Motor Services Ltd. 442 E. 92ND ST. 10028
427-6155

Of course there's a reason why it's the most expensive car service in the city—it's the most unusual. Rollston is probably the only service in the city which will be able to rent you a Rolls-Royce Phantom. Forty dollars an hour might seem a bit much, but compared to a trip to London when you want to enjoy this kind of high camp, it's a positive bargain. So put down your passport, dial 427-6155, and be prepared to don a top hat and morning suit for a minimum of three hours. After all, you wouldn't want to underdress for your car, would you?

Creative Coaches

Carey Limousine 41 E. 42ND ST. 10017
937-3100

We can't say that we're in love with their limousine service, but we *are* in love with the idea of having them rent us a bus for that next trip to Shea Stadium. After all, what better way to make a trip to Long Island than with an open bar and forty friends? A bus that holds forty-one people is just $75 an hour for a minimum of three hours (if you can get them to finish a game in less time than that, you're a miracle worker), and $20 for every hour thereafter. If you have quite a few intimate friends in New York, you'll want the fifty-three-passenger model at $105 per hour. And do be forewarned that if you're going out for a terribly long drive (you know, anything beyond the East Side), you'll be paying an additional 85 cents per mile for gas.

Carey usually requires about one week's notice to have a bus ready; the caterer might require a bit more!

Island Helicopters, Inc. 421 E. 60TH ST.   10021
751-5978
HELIPORTS: 34TH ST. & EAST RIVER DR.
895-5372
WALL ST. HELIPORT
895-5372

Running a touch late for that Kennedy flight? Wouldn't be so bad if it weren't snowing? Well, don't fret—just call the Timechopper. Island Helicopter has thirty-five two- to twelve-passenger choppers waiting to run you out to Kennedy, LaGuardia, or a neighborhood shop if you should so desire. Just ante up $550 per hour (that's for the S58J, but something a bit more modest would run around $140) and don't keep them waiting—that costs an extra $100 an hour. But why bother yourself with adding; let's book it for the day at $2,000. And don't worry about running a tiny bit overtime. They'll wait for you forever at $500 an hour!

Of course, if you're going to limit yourself to an airport run, addition becomes simpler. There's a set fee of $105 from the downtown heliport at Wall Street to Kennedy. And if you'd rather deal in round figures, save yourself $5 by going to either East 60th or 34th Street and taking the $100 flight. These charges for trips out to the airport do include your landing fee and a fifteen-minute no-charge waiting period, which should give you ample time to unload that matched set of Hermes. You might even have the good fortune to find a copy of the *New York Times* still hot from the hands of Frank Sinatra, Sammy Davis, Jr., Ed McMahon, Arthur Godfrey, or Liza Minnelli—they're all Time-chopper fans.

Wait a moment. Are you telling us that you're having such a good time in New York that you have no intention of going to the airport? That's no reason to pass up Island Helicopter. Just call General Manager Reid Philips or New York City Manager Ken Johnston, and tell him that you want to look Miss Liberty right in the eye. A six-minute skyline trip costs $8 per person, a twelve-minute ride $16, and the super-duper all-around-town trip is a $64 forty-minute ride. It's a thrilling way to see New York City, from a peek at the secretaries in the United Nations Building to a survey of the skyscrapered horizon.

You're right. It's such a good, quick way to get around town without looking for parking places that it's truly habit-forming. But if you like it so much, don't worry. Island Helicopter even has a flight school. A lot depends on you, but if you want a private pilot's certificate, they can start you off using an Enstrom S28, and give you fifty classes of ground school instruction and five solo and thirty duo classes, at the cost of $5,000 to $10,000. Of course, that still doesn't include the helicopter.

On second thought, that $2,000 a day doesn't look so bad anymore, does it!

II. HOTELS
Don't Go Away Till You Know Where to Stay

THERE'S NO PLACE like home... is that what you say? How right you are! We have no intention of putting you anywhere that even *remotely* resembles home! Of course we *do* have a few places in mind where you might run up a one-night bill that's equal to your house payment. But then that's not really the same, is it?

The first thing to remember in choosing a New York hotel is location... from some you can see both Harry Winston *and* Tiffany's. *That's* what we call a good hotel!

Next, consider service. No matter how hard you try, your room service waiter won't be as dear to you as that wonderful houseman you left back home. But he *will* be one of hundreds—just consider it an adventure to see who will show up with your next order.

And finally, remember that with the schedule we've planned for you in New York, your room is going to be more of a place to store your luggage than a place to stow yourself!

The New York	1335 AVE. OF THE AMERICAS 10019
Hilton	586-7000

We might as well admit it from the start... we're really not numbered among the Hilton Hotel chain's biggest fans. Admittedly, closed-circuit TV for security, fancy bathroom accessories, and an electronic gadget which allows the switchboard to awaken dozens of groggy hotel guests with the same 7 A.M. phone call might impress some. But we'd rather have a kindly manager who remembers that we want four pillows rather than two in our bed when we arrive in New York. Just sweet old-fashioned girls... that's us.

The New York Hilton, however, *has* managed to pull us in on occasion. But then we're just suckers for a $750-a-day hotel suite, and this is no exception. Besides, the New York Hilton has two beautiful duplexes to choose from, so that even if Queen Elizabeth happens to be in town, there should still be a suite available for you. And the fact that the two penthouse suites have private elevators which are not open to guests in the other 2,000 rooms allows us to retain just enough of that elitist feeling to get us through the Hilton's front doors.

The last time we booked the West Penthouse (let's see, it was to celebrate the last good truffle season, wasn't it?), it was a simple matter of ringing up manager Jorgen Hansen and it was ready for us within hours. But you might want to try writing ahead if you're afraid of its slipping through your fingers. Consider enclosing a copy of your latest Dun & Bradstreet rating just in case.

We think you'll like the West Penthouse best. Not only does it have an oriental theme running through everything from the Ming altar table in the living room to the bamboo motif in the bedroom (excuse us, *one* of the three bedrooms), but it also has a perfectly tuned grand piano. As you can see, it's just a fabulous place to spend an evening—once you get tired of trying out all those new wok recipes you mastered after your last trip to Peking, you can go right out into the living room and render a chorus of "Sidewalks of New York."

If, unfortunately, the West Penthouse is booked, settle for the East. But *do* bring sunglasses. Bill Pahlmann was in a rather vibrant mood when he worked out the parrot-green and mandarin-orange color scheme. Don't worry. If it gets to be too much, you can always wander over to one of the floor-to-ceiling windows and comfort yourself with a view of New York—the whole state.

You wouldn't want to miss that, so do be sure to set aside $750 for a night on the town... on *top* of the town, that is.

The Lombardy   111 E. 56TH ST.   10022
                 753-8600

As much as we admire originality, the fact that the Lombardy Hotel doesn't own any of its rooms seemed a touch *too* original at first glance. But then manager Norman King explained and calmed us down immediately. You see, the Lombardy is a co-op, each room or apartment owned by a different private owner, with about half of the space in the hotel available for rental to transient guests.

One of the joys of this hotel—aside from room service by Laurent—is that each apartment is decorated differently by the individual owner, which gives you limitless possibilities for exploration. There's a new surprise in store on each return trip. Naturally everyone eventually chooses favorites—it might be a good idea to ask Mr. King to show you a selection before you commit yourself to unpacking.

Our favorite is the triplex penthouse, with its private elevator, library, three bedrooms, maid's room and five baths for a paltry $600-a-day price tag. If you're not feeling quite that expansive, ask for the duplex—also three bedrooms—and hope that its Parisian owner won't be using it.

Other possibilities range from one to seven rooms, and might include a one-bedroom apartment in beige, black, and brown with antique baker's rack (Room 1407 at $100), or a two-bedroom, two-bath apartment with leather-upholstered furnishings, fabric-covered walls and antiques (Room 1404 at $140). If a poor cousin is coming to town book him in Room 712 at $65 and hope he doesn't object to being squeezed into a sitting room with a sofa bed.

But if he does, remind him that a Continental breakfast is a complimentary part of the price of the room. In New York that might well be a $10 saving, which should perk him up immediately.

When Richard Burton played in *Equus,* he enjoyed the relative quiet of the Lombardy's side-street location. Ingrid Bergman loves it, too. If you think it's just right for you, call Cathleen in reservations.

Mayfair House   PARK AVE. & 65TH ST.   10022
288-0800

When the legendary real-estate tycoon William Zeckendorf, Jr. was living at the Mayfair House, he decided he'd rather be staying at a place like London's Connaught. So he and co-owner Sheldon S. Wilson simply hired Frank Bowling away from the Connaught. How simple can things be?

Mr. Bowling brought with him that fabulous Connaught card system which tells him if you're the visitor who prefers to have ice water in your room or a super-hard mattress. Just tell him once, and it will be yours forever.

The only problem is that since the hotel is primarily residential, only 140 apartments are available for transients like us and the waiting line can get a bit long. Fear not—once in the hotel, you'll probably be in one of the 112 suites.

Is it Marisa Berenson Randell who likes Suite 407's particular combination of beige and brown with the black-checked floor? Or is it Rex Harrison? No . . . he's the one who prefers Suite 1506, isn't he? Restful blues with a wonderful combination of French and English furniture accented by Chinese lamps, and high enough to be above the street noise. How perfect!

You might just run into Christopher Plummer or Claudette Colbert in the elevator, too. They all love it at the Mayfair, and they don't even blink at the $200 top tab for a two-bedroom suite. It's no wonder. There's none of that tiring New York hustle and bustle in the lobby of the quiet Mayfair—just a staff which has worked together for years and likes doing it. Telephone operators learn your name immediately and even (miracle of miracles) get your telephone messages straight. Frank Bowling is a miracle worker who can lay his hands on a pair of tickets to any show in town. The bell captain, Tommy, has been there for forty years—if rain is falling at a rate that makes you want to book a cabin on Noah's Ark, Tommy can still find you a cab. How far would you go to get the right starch in your collars?

Two thousand miles? Sounds unlikely—until you've met the Mayfair's wonderful Sadie, that is. And truth to tell we do have one friend in Beverly Hills who air freights hers to New York regularly just to get Sadie's gentle touch. She's really that special.

Sadie hand-finishes the dry cleaning when it returns to the hotel, and hand-washes simply everything (shirts from a mere $2.50—let's see, with air freight that will run you around $5). In case of emergency you needn't panic; she lives right on the premises to make sure that your whites are white and your colors are bright. We've known people's laundry bills to run as high as $163 for a single day's visit, but we suspect they'd been saving their dirty clothes through three cities and a few charity balls.

Now you know why some corporations keep suites at the Mayfair year-round. At $24,000 a year, it's a bargain. But if you don't think you'd use one quite so often, feel free to take one for a shorter period. Just cable MAYHOUSE and leave the rest to Mr. Bowling. And if he happens to be booked, you can always call Mr. Fernandez at the Regency, right down the street.

Hotel Pierre   FIFTH AVENUE & 61ST STREET
TE 8-8000

Now that you've been spoiled by the service in London and catered to by the chef of Paris' Plaza-Athénée, you must be longing to find a good European hotel in Manhattan (you know, one where they actually remember not only your name but whether you prefer Vichy to Perrier, too). How nice that we've discovered the Pierre. From the moment you hear about Andre de Beauharnais, you know you've come to the right place!

Andre is the only concierge in New York City, and all those little extras you grew to love in Europe, he'll procure for you right in mid-Manhattan. Tickets to that sold-out show? No problem, darling. The best table at the best restaurant in New York? Don't worry about it at all. Andre is a member of Les Clefs d'Or, and when a member of the International Fraternity of Concierges can't get you a table at Regine's ... no one can!

Does the Pierre's manager, M. Manassero, look familiar to you? Think back to the Carlton Hotel in Cannes. Or did you meet him the last time you golfed at Gleneagles? Or was it in Dublin or Bremen? Maybe it was at the Plaza-Athénée in Paris. Whichever, he's the one who looked over that VIP list and allotted the proper tribute of fruit, flowers, candy, or champagne to you. He's doing it still, right at the Pierre. If you find them all in your room, it means that you made an indelible impression on him during one of your European visits.

By now it's no surprise to you that the crème de la crème of Europe and America frequents the Pierre. The atmosphere makes them feel right at home immediately. The hotel's card index can tell you whether the Duke of Bedford prefers twin beds or a kingsize, and let you in on which room Henry Kissinger is particularly fond of. The likes and dislikes of everyone from Yves St. Laurent to Pierre Cardin, from Valentino to Madame Rochas, from Liv Ullmann to Sean Connery, are recorded and adhered to. Rest assured you'll be no exception. If it's vodka you request in your suite on your first visit, vodka will be waiting for you each time you return.

As large as the hotel looks, a reservation isn't automatic. To begin with, 150 of the hotel's suites are permanent residence apartments. As for the remainder of the rooms, the demand is so great that you'd be a fool not to call well ahead for your reservation. If you call even further ahead, you can get our favorite suite, number 3901-4. Of course you could book just a portion of it, but really the decision as to which rooms to give up is more than we can make!

You certainly wouldn't want to sacrifice that dramatic living room overlooking the Hudson and Central Park, would you? Or give up the 17th-century English secretary and backgammon table? You wouldn't want to sacrifice the marble bath with its Sherle Wagner porcelain sinks and handy wall-mounted magnifying mirror for shaving. And who would give up those bedrooms with electrically controlled drapes that you can open from your bed to reveal a nightime view of the city at just the perfect moment. It's all so wonderful, why not keep it all? Anyway, what's a mere $700 for a day of luxury?

Well, even the best of us might not want to spend quite *that* much if we have a lot of shopping in mind, so if your budget doesn't stretch that far, have Peter Buse arrange a double room for you (from $100), or opt for a small suite (about $200). Then take the extra money you've saved and head downstairs. After all, you wouldn't want to leave a hotel that has Bulgari jewels in the lobby without picking up at least *one* little trinket, would you?

Plaza Hotel   FIFTH AVE. & 59TH ST.   10022
                          759-3000

If you have an Eagle Scout's sense of direction and can find your way through not one but two lobbies, and if you happen to thrive on chaos... you may want to stay at the Plaza.

Be prepared, though: if the population of mainland China is increasing at the rate of 1,000 a minute, the number of people to be found in the lobby of the Plaza Hotel is growing at a rate dangerously similar. In fact, by the time you trip your way through the luggage of three tour groups and waste fifteen minutes standing in line to register, minutes which could be spent window-shopping on Madison Avenue, you know you've become part of a population explosion. Which is perfectly all right for mainland China, but does it have to affect us while we're lugging around three Vuitton trunks?

The Plaza, of course, does have all the modern conveniences. Each room has individually controlled air-conditioning, as well as color television with first-run movies in case you plan on spending a good deal of time in your room. And from the looks of the lobby you probably *will* be safer there, in which case you'll be happy to learn that the Plaza has 24-hour room service. There won't be a second of any day in which fresh caviar isn't available to you. Good news... *n'est-ce pas?*

If you do stay there, you'll probably want Suite 1401, a one-bedroom suite done in oranges and browns which rents at just $210 per night. (Like all of the 01 suites, it faces the park.) It was originally decorated for a shah, who found upon his arrival that he had a kitchen and even a stove, though his butler was forbidden to use it—no fires are allowed in the hotel. (If you want to know what real frustration is, try booking a suite for your next rendezvous that has two, not one but two, fireplaces, only to be told that you can't light them.) He also had a wonderful dome-ceilinged bathroom, relic of a day when the hotel was the luxurious home-away-from-home for the cream of New York society.

If the shah happens to be in town during your next stay you might find yourself relegated to suite 1435: it's also done in browns, and overlooks a wonderful view of Fifth Avenue. Bring binoculars and you'll know beyond a doubt which of your friends visits Tiffany's most often. This particular suite is just $160, but frankly we'd recommend that you stick to one just a bit lower in the hotel. The ceilings are quite a bit higher from the fourteenth floor down and give you a rather stately feeling, despite the fact that you're liable to walk right into a leftover room-service cart as you exit into those endless hotel corridors.

One of the nicer high-ceilinged suites is 523, which is a corner suite (important since these have wide areas between bedroom and living room which can be opened for cocktail parties) and which rents for just $180.

Despite the drawbacks of the Plaza, there *is* one bit of charm there which will never be replaced. Since 1907 ladies have been enjoying tea in the Palm Court quietly seated amid antique Chinese urns and sedately glimmering chandeliers. Heaven only knows how many proposals have been serenaded by the Palm Court violins during an apres-theater brandy. And having Sunday brunch there is as much a New York tradition as finding a twenty-four-hour ticket scalper. Be sure to ask Joseph to find you a table next to the pastry cart.

Though you may not want to stay there, it's worth taking note that the Plaza has been designated one of the landmarks of New York, so take a quick trip through the lobby for a glimpse of its crystal chandeliers, marble and mahogany.

The Sherry-Netherland	781 FIFTH AVE. (AT 59TH ST.) 355-2800	10022

The Sherry is one of those wonderful little European-style hotels in which the elevator operators have memorized your name and floor within hours of your arrival, messages arrive without fail at your door, and the management stands ready to order anything from diapers to a grand piano should you so wish.

If you want to stay at the Sherry-Netherland, a sure way to get a reservation is to buy one of the Tower Apartments. Just $400,000 and you're guaranteed a room of your own—in fact, a floor of your own. That's room enough for the butler, the maid, the helicopter pilot and the chauffeur, with a bit left over for you. True, the floors of the Sherry are a touch smaller as you go above the sixteenth, but if you feel a little cramped, you're within walking distance of Central Park, Fifth Avenue, Madison Avenue. How stifled can a person feel with a few million dollars' worth of shopping and a dozen horse-drawn cabs available within a five-minute walk?

On the off-chance that the Tower Apartments are sold out, call manager Philip Landeau for a regular reservation; something along the lines of a two-bedroom park parlor suite, perhaps, at around $250. The butler's still useful there, since many of the rooms have facilities for preparing and serving meals. By the way, unless you know someone at the hotel they simply won't guarantee you a park view, so *do* drop Mr. Landeau's name as often as possible.

If Mr. Landeau is out, call Miss Ertracher in reservations. You might want to ask her for Suite 305, a rather pretty one in gold and blue, with the wonderful ability to add on up to three bedrooms according to your whim of the moment. It can fulfill your every desire ... antiques, a fireplace and a lovely little conversation area for the cocktail hour. Just $325 and it's yours.

If you're not in the mood for largess, how about a one-bedroom suite for just $165? They're really simpler to get unless it's "the season." From September through December and from mid-March through June, try to make reservations at least two weeks in advance.

The hotel houses the Sherry-Netherland Grill, which is an institution in the city second only to the Statue of Liberty. (You'll find it in the restaurant chapter.)

The Tuscany	120 E. 39TH ST. 10016
Hotel	686-1600

How terribly thoughtful. How really kind. The Tuscany has a Dow Jones ticker tape right in the lobby to let you know where you stand. If there's a late fade in electronics and you can't really afford the suite you booked before you caught your flight, you'll be aware of it before the damage is done. If, on the other hand, you're looking at a bull market, you can immediately demand a suite on the twelfth floor. Expensive, but well worth it!

In either case, talk to manager Peter Schwartz, who caters to the personal tastes of everyone from Rod Laver to Mr. Brioni of Italy. If he doesn't have a card made out for you yet, be sure to let him know about your little idiosyncrasies (we all know no one's perfect) and you'll find the grapefruit juice or skim milk you simply must have each morning waiting in the refrigerator on arrival.

By the way, every room *does* have a butler's pantry with its own refrigerator, so if you don't feel like facing those gray walls in the Tuscany dining room at breakfast (a bit bleak if you're not awake yet), you can fix your own.

The hotel's on a quiet, leafy section of East 39th Street, close enough to Seventh Avenue to guarantee your seeing the top brass from Hathaway or Aquascutum trading fashion tips. The Mets stay here and enjoy the clubby atmosphere of the downstairs bar, so book your lunch reservations early if you intend to eat there. And from 5 to 8 P.M. you're going to have to fight your way in!

The Tuscany is such an impeccable blend of American hospitality and European flair that you'll find that many Europeans who are relocating in New York are making it their first stop. Ike, the bell captain, won't hesitate to tell you if he thinks you're not going to be dressed warmly enough to brave the weather, and if you argue, he may just send you up to your room to change.

By the way, try to make that room Suite 1100. With two bedrooms, two TV sets, an outdoor terrace for breakfast, and a bar, it's a steal for $150.

The Tuscany. What it lacks in immediately obvious posh, it makes up for in comfort.

The United Nations Plaza Hotel 1 UNITED NATIONS PLAZA 10017
355-3400

Now, as you know, we've never been particularly attuned to the idea of replacing the old traditional graces with brash newness. Why, the last innovation we were really enthusiastic about was the Lear Jet! As for the new hotels, they've managed to get along without us, while we've managed to get along without them. But all that was before we discovered that there was a sparkling fresh hotel that didn't insist on having Muzak piped into every nook and cranny. Ah, blessed relief... they built the U.N. Plaza!

Since you're up above 27 stories of offices, you can forget about being bothered by the noise of traffic or the idiosyncrasies of lobby loiterers. It follows that the views are spectacular. And since there's no ballroom, there's no need to pick your way through hordes of partygoers in the lobby. As if that weren't enough, the shag carpeting in the suites is rich enough to tempt you to spend your nights on the floor instead of the bed. But then that would be wasting that upstairs bedroom, wouldn't it! Ah yes... the $300 suites are duplexes, complete with lush, plush modern furniture; you'll have a suspended circular staircase, and a baby grand piano, and even a glass-topped dining-room table for those tête-à-têtes you're planning to have catered by the Four Seasons.

You'll be pleased to hear that the staff speaks 27 languages among them (you know how you've been dying to practice that Berlitz French!), and manages to be polite beyond all New York standards.

But the thing we most like about the U.N. Plaza is that it's planned for night owls... what could be more fun after dancing till 2 A.M. at Le Club, then coming home for a quick set of doubles on the 24-hour tennis court? Why not? With 24-hour room service available, you'll be kept in fresh tennis balls and fresh caviar till the wee hours of the morning!

The Waldorf-Astoria	PARK AVE. AT 50TH ST. 10022
	355-3000

One square block, 1,900 rooms, and 42 floors. As one observer so aptly put it, "What a nice way to bring exclusivity to the masses." Since we were never one for masses ourselves, the Waldorf isn't our cup of tea. But it is nice to know that there's one spot in New York which will grant any request you might possibly have—and we *do* mean any!

You can safely arrive without your pajamas, shaving kit, or cosmetics, and know beyond a shadow of a doubt that the Waldorf will have your size ready and waiting. Food's no problem, either. Fried ice cream is a snap. Recipes along the line of young lamb stuffed with boned pheasant which in turn has been stuffed with boned quail stuffed with *pâté de foie gras* takes a bit longer. Still, they managed to whip it up for the Shah of Iran and, no doubt, still remember how to make it in case you'd like room service run a snack up to your suite.

By the way, make sure that that suite's in the Waldorf's "Towers." You'll be assured of an exclusive entrance, a 24-hour concierge system, and a reasonable proximity to the Duchess of Windsor, who still keeps an apartment there. You'll also be assured of a bill of at least $550 per day if you order the three-bedroom suite with two maid's rooms, living room and sitting room. The Waldorf Towers extends from the 21st to the 42nd floor of the hotel, and has been the official residence of the U.S. Ambassador to the United Nations, the home of General Douglas MacArthur, and the site of inspired songwriting by Cole Porter. Of the Tower Apartments, most are permanent residences, with only one-quarter available for temporary guests. If there's a question of availability, call manager Eugene Scanlan and test your powers of persuasiveness on him.

He still says the Tower Apartments are all booked? Pity! Well, settle for one of the Tower Suites, ranging from the 21st to the 27th floors. Beyond that, rebel and move on.

The Waldorf is perhaps the most international of New York's hotels. In order to encourage the patronage of multinational travelers and diplomats, the hotel maintains an international department with a staff speaking 30 different languages. The director alone speaks six fluently. How handy to have all the correspondence you've been receiving from Paris and Tokyo translated at no extra cost. And if you want to prove your savoir faire, feel free to request menus and laundry lists printed in Japanese.

III. NEW YORK RESTAURANTS AND CLUBS
Food for Thought

IT'S BEEN perfectly obvious to us for years that the privileged of New York are more privileged than anywhere else. They've enjoyed it more, too! And why shouldn't they—New Yorkers can daily make that painful choice between satisfying their yearnings at one of Manhattan's four-star symbols of in-ness (Christ Cella, La Caravelle, Le Cygne, Maxwell's Plum, or Parioli Romanissima), or taking a few moments longer to search for something as offbeat as that miniature restaurant row on 58th between Second and Third (11 restaurants in a row the last time we counted, including Jacques and Katja). There's just never any end to the restaurants you can find in New York!

We've heard that some traditionalists bemoan the loss of such landmarks as the Spanish Pavilion, Le Pavillon, and The Forum of the Twelve Caesars, but really, how bad can it be when there's still La Côte Basque, La Grenouille, Le Madrigal and Lutèce to fall back on in a pinch? In fact, there are so many chic "le's" and "la's" left in mid-Manhattan, you might even be lucky enough to be able to book a table without calling days in advance! But don't fret; even if you're *not* that lucky, New York has a solution for your problem (how can they say it's a city without a heart!); James A. Beard's cooking classes are so popular that some students travel all the way in from Philadelphia after work just to learn how to smooth a mousse from the master. Do try it at least once—even if you don't like the idea of seeing yourself in an apron, you'll love his stories of the Gritti Palace in Venice.

Of course, one solution to booking a table is to buy it. Some of New York's chicest tables are at her private clubs. From Régine to Le Club, there's as much emphasis on ambiance as on good cuisine. And as soon as *they* close for the night (even maitre d's have to have *some* sleep, you know) you can move on to the all-night danceathon at Le Jardin, Infinity Studio 54, or New York, New York.

New York... the possibilities are endless; the solutions are only as limited as your own imagination!

RESTAURANTS

Alfredo's　　　　125 SEVENTH AVE. SOUTH　　10014
Settebello　　　675-4630

From those wonderful folks who brought you Trattoria da Alfredo (with its wonderful in-house wine store) Café Alfredo and the Tavola Calda... a new sensation, Alfredo's Settebello. Even bigger, and sometimes even more fun than the other three! Alfredo Viazzi has organized a traveling band of card readers, musicians, and cabaret entertainers to wander from table to table keeping you amused between mozzarella and tomatoes and the perfectly *al dente* pasta. And for those who'd rather entertain *themselves,* Alfredo is providing tea dancing during cocktail hours.

The service is amiably casual; the dress is the same. After all, if the waiters can wear blue jeans, how could they possibly expect *you* to wear a tie? While the tortoise-patterned tabletops may be mere formica, the food is merely divine! All the dishes that Alfredo lovers learned to know and love at his other three Greenwich Village gathering places can be found here, with a few additions to spice the mix.

Our favorite Alfredo appetizer is Carpaccio Alfredo—how could it be bad when super-thin slices of raw prime sirloin steak are served with tangy mustard mayonnaise? Add a glass of wine from the list (26 vintages that range from superb to passable), then follow it with Ravioli al Ragu, with wild mushrooms and sausages at $3.75, or with scalloppine Settebello, nice veal with a light, fresh vegetable and ham sauce at $6.50. You can get a half bottle of Soave Bolla for just $4 and save your budget to splurge on fresh berries, fruits, and ice cream for dessert. Or maybe that card reader will tell you that you're about to come into an inheritance, so that you can splurge on every single course. Just one lucky conversation like that and you'll surely know why Alfredo named his newest restaurant after the winning card in the game of Scopa!

Ballato   55 E. HOUSTON ST.   10002
                226-9683

In 1957 John Ballato rose to the challenge when his fellow restaurateurs and friends said it was impossible to open a successful restaurant on the lower East Side. He's still going strong today. Frankly, it doesn't surprise us one bit. Anyone who's ever tried his veal scallopini would understand perfectly how he's managed to do it.

The restaurant holds just twelve tables, so each dish is prepared to order. Besides the veal scallopine, there are six other variations of veal. Veal piccata and veal marsala with mushrooms are our favorites. None should go unaccompanied by fettucine verde.

Ballato is near Soho, the artists' colony in New York, so the sight of gallery owners such as Leo Castelli entertaining Jasper Johns or Roy Lichtenstein is hardly a rarity. And as for Andy Warhol, he's been frequenting it ever since he gave up that fetish for Campbell's soup!

Expect lunch to run $8–$12 per person, dinner $12–$20 per person, plus wine ($6.75–$12 a bottle).

The Box Tree   242 E. 50TH ST.   10022
                     758-8320

To think we used to drive all the way to Purdy to enjoy The Box Tree! But no longer—not since Augustin opened a Manhattan branch right across the street from Lutèce. Granted it's a bit different picking your way through brownstones and garbage cans to get to the front door instead of walking up a wooded path, but perhaps that's what makes you *need* a little jewel like The Box Tree even more. Some say the fact that Lutèce's own André Soltner drops by so often proves that The Box Tree's a bit of perfection. (Others say he's just stopping by to give the waiters French lessons.)

Luckily, Augustin's food is more French than his help. His brownstone on East 50th features French haute cuisine, mixing a beautiful blend of formal and informal. For those casual moments, asparagus spears served without even the hint of a sauce to disturb their natural essence. Your formal moods might call for anything from the finest smoked trout mousse to *vacherin* Box Tree, a mélange of ground hazelnuts, Grand Mariner, fresh raspberries, and meringue. Though the small kitchen tends to keep the menu somewhat limited, regular changes every four to six weeks let you repeat visits to the Box Tree without getting bored. And *whenever* you arrive, you'll find yourself selecting from the sort of nonconformist haute cuisine which chef Paul Bocuse has been making famous—a bit lighter, a bit better for you, and yet still delicious. One taste of Augustin's Bayonne ham accompanied by fresh pear will be enough to convince you that nonconformity could become a way of life! Particularly when it includes such non-New York specialties as *fraises de bois* flown in to JFK and delivered right over by messenger just in time for your dessert.

Augustin is as handsome, soft-voiced, and Old World as his restaurant. Don't let the London accent fool you, he's more Bulgarian than British. But it was during his London life that he came up with the idea of importing the spirit behind that city's famous Box Tree restaurant to the States. It was obviously a good idea; though the tiny restaurant seats only 18, everyone you talk to in New York will claim to have been there at least once. In a city of millions, we can't imagine how Augustin does it. It's certainly not by rushing his patrons through dinner—he books only two seatings each night. And it's not by serving them at private parties. It's so popular that you have to reserve the restaurant four to six weeks in advance if you want to take it over for a group of friends. We suspect that more than a few New Yorkers are exaggerating when they claim Augustin's acquaintance.

Well... don't *you* be one of them. Be sure you actually go to the restaurant. After all, you'll describe it so much better after spending a few hours there. And what with Augustin's $40,000 worth of stained glass, as well as his exquisite Lalique crystal, 18th- and 19th-century tableware and Christofle silverware set on perfect Queen Anne tables, you'll want to be accurate. The restaurant has such a sweet spirit that you'll not only find a bud vase on your table, you'll receive one more bloom with your check to soften the blow. Which, incidentally, will be based on a prix-fixe menu ranging from $10–12 for lunch, and from $17.50 to $19.50 for dinner. Of course the tab does jump a bit when you add on a few bottles of Corton Charlemagne '71 at $50... but if you want to keep the evening underpriced there's always a passable Chateau Pétrus '64 at $7 to look forward to.

Experienced Box Tree patrons will tell you that arriving early for the second seating will only lead to the discomfort of being jammed into a sea of coats in the minuscule foyer until the first seating has finished its meal, or the embarrassment of being sent away to have a drink at some other neighborhood restaurant until the tables are cleared. One way to avoid this discomfort is to request the early seating, but really, no one who counts will be there and they do sometimes rush you to finish your meal. Another is to arrive just a few minutes late and let *them* wait for *you*.

Café des Artistes 1 W. 67TH ST. 10023
877-3500

Owner George Lang is the kind of man who struggles over how to invent a bathtub made of soap and ponders the significance of channeling a carpet's static electricity to run the family's electric toothbrush. Obviously it was no great feat for him to renovate the Café des Artistes and turn it into one of the city's most interesting restaurants. Nobody else in the city could have done it with such flair, but for George it was just another of life's little challenges.

Before he opened the nostalgic eatery that has always boarded at the Hotel des Artistes, he promised honest French home cooking at absurdly low prices. Considering that the prix fixe is only $9.50, we think he surpassed even the absurd. For those who want to spend more, George has included other dinner possibilities, but with a prix-fixe choice like bluefish with anchovy butter, who needs to opt for roast sirloin or pork cassoulet?

Even if the food weren't delicious, it would be worth the prix fixe to sit and just marvel at the Howard Chandler Christie murals that decorate this 1917 landmark. Christie was famous for painting kings, queens, and nudes, but he decorated the café sans royalty. Though the walls may have been the World War I answer to *Penthouse,* they seem pleasantly innocent today. The only thing about Café des Artistes that could be considered the least bit obscene is the mouth-watering pecan pie with real whipped cream that George gets from that nice Mrs. Rosenberg down the street. You'll find different desserts each day, as people in the neighborhood whip up their specialties for Café des Artistes.

What was once the haunt of Valentino, Al Jolson, and Edna Ferber—who all lived in the hotel—is now a favorite spot for John Lindsay, Zero Mostel, and Alexis Smith; but only ex-Mayor Lindsay lives that close today. They enjoy all the Langisms: candles housed in hurricane chimneys, Swiss warming plates, Italian cheese graters, serious tea services with two pots—one for water, one for tea—all the touches that have turned this New York bistro into an instant institution.

Most of the staff is the same as it was before George Lang added his finishing touches to the café. In fact, you'll still be greeted by Charlie Turner, who has been welcoming guests for 38 years. Just like the Christie murals, Charlie is a permanent fixture. If you long for the old New York, ask Charlie to tell some of the stories about the days when Noel Coward and Lawrence Tibbett came in almost every day. If you start to get nostalgic, do go to the bar and have a Chambraise Strawberry Vermouth—it will bring you back to the present and whet your appetite for some modern cuisine. If George happens to be there, though we doubt that, do ask him about his next New York restaurant (we hear it will have coed saunas and feature pizza with caviar). Be prepared for a long, spicy and pretentious reply, as George takes his cue from Goethe: "Only the good-for-nothings are modest."

La Caravelle	33 W. 55TH ST. 10019
	586-4252

If, like Nelson Rockefeller, you decide that this is your favorite restaurant, don't be wary of coming in two, three, even four times a week. The menu changes daily just for you creatures of habit. Only the table d'hôte $23.75 per person remains the same.

Proprietors Fred Decre and Robert Meyzen live by the strictest rules of French haute cuisine. They wouldn't consider serving turbot unless it was flown in fresh from France; as far as they're concerned, no caviar is worth its salt unless it's Beluga, and no customer is worth his dinner unless he pays cash. Of course they *will* consider personal checks if your face has become familiar—no wonder Nelson takes the trouble to stop in so often! If it's not a fresh turbot day, feel safe with any of the veal dishes. And if veal kidneys bordelaise are on the menu, count your blessings!

John Fairchild, the top brass from *Gourmet* magazine, and ever so many ladies who lunch love to snuggle down among those red velvet chairs, wall murals and mirrored columns midday nibbling entrecôte and fruit tarts. But though La Caravelle is high on the list for the luncheon circuit, we suggest that you reserve this treat for dinner. After all, there are only five restaurants in the whole city that rate four stars from the *New York Times,* and this is the best of the quintet. Besides, what could look better than baskets of fresh flowers and a plate of Caravelle's wonderful smoked trout at the end of a tough day in Manhattan? Dinner it must be! Be sure Fred saves you that B.P. front table and one of chef Roger's delectable soufflés.

When Prentice and Denise Minnelli Hale are in from San Francisco, they love to take over the back room of the restaurant and have dinner for 45 of their closest East Coast friends. Joe Kennedy used to do that, too, when Caravelle first opened. Though some say this French treasure might have gone undiscovered but for Joe's recommendation, we don't see how that could possibly be true since everyone who tastes one of those marvelous soufflés immediately runs out and tells six friends. Don't come to Caravelle in blue jeans. Ladies might choose Adolfo for lunch; Halston wouldn't be out of place at dinner. And when you call in advance for that front table, do give our best to Fred and Robert.

Café Carlyle   35 E. 76TH ST.   10021
                                  744-1600

If the glitter of Régine's has become a bit much for you, try reviving your taste for café society with a visit to Café Carlyle and Bobby Short. Plushly dressed young ladies pose in various stages of enjoyment next to murals by Ertès. But they're both eclipsed by Bobby's renditions of Cole Porter, Gershwin and Rodgers and Hart. The ambiance of the Carlyle is wonderful, assuming you don't make your plans to drop in to coincide with one of those unfortunate weeks when Bobby's fulfilling his concert dates in San Francisco, Los Angeles, or Houston.

Call ahead ... Bobby's soloist-in-residence status at the Carlyle since 1968 has allowed him to amass an incredible number of followers. Not only will your table require a $7.50 per person cover charge (once you order the Dom Perignon it's merely symbolic), it will require a bit of cooperation on the part of maître d' Ambrose. Though he's only been in charge of the Carlyle since the early seventies, you can remind him that you've known him since the years when he was growing up there as a busboy. That's always sure to do the trick. Then just settle down, request a few favorites, and enjoy Bobby Short. Bnt don't learn to love him too much. After all, if you stay for two shows, you'll have to pay a double cover!

Chez Pascal   151 E. 82ND ST.   10028
                                  249-1334

That's not good old upholstery fabric ... it's Ultrasuede by Halston. When even the banquettes dress this chicly, you just know it's bound to cost you a bundle, and in the case of Chez Pascal, you couldn't be more right. The suggestions de jour, the chef's own choice of hors d'oeuvre, entree, green salad, and pastry, will cost you $18.50 *before* you remember the waiter and captain who made it all possible. And if you order à la carte and find suitable wine to keep that duck with green peppercorns company, the price of *your* next Geoffrey Beene will be eaten up before you leave for home.

It's a small restaurant: just one long narrow room in a brownstone, bordered by brick walls and complete with oaken plank floors, a tile ceiling, false oak fireplace and a small standup bar for waiting if you happen to be badly timed for that 7:30 or 9:30 seating. There are good paintings, fresh flowers, and helpfully soft indirect lighting bounced off the ceiling or by candlelight. The chic, pinstriped clientele might include Governor Carey sampling sausage *en croûte* with Anne Ford Uzielli's dad, Henry Ford. Or her mother, Mrs. Deane Johnson, nibbling delicious asparagus vinaigrette with daughter Charlotte. You might see the lobster salad, a wonderful arrangement of small claws, green beans, and truffles, being slipped in front of Eileen Ford, while Alan King tries desperately to decide between the veal in mustard sauce or the fresh bass and fennel in butter sauce with mushrooms.

As for us, our favorite is the grilled sole with mushrooms, colorfully presented on painted pottery plates, and surrounded by fresh beans, carrots, potatoes, and tomatoes with watercress. The well-dressed country French feeling of the plates is just a continuation of the tone that was set with the menu written on flower-bedecked glass and the waiters in blazers and ascots. Naturally no meal is complete without at least one slice of that iced lemon mousse pie that Pascal has shipped in from La Mousse in Los Angeles. It's so good that West Coasters have been known to ask him to ship one home with them, little suspecting that by the time it reaches their front door, that lemon mousse will be as well-traveled as they are!

The restaurant is owned by Robert Escanes, but for all you see of Robert it might as well be the property of Pascal Chevillot, whose family owns the Hotel de la Poste in the capital of Burgundy. Closer to home, his uncle owns La Petite Ferme, which is even smaller, and even *more* difficult to get a table at.

Pascal is as chic as those Halston booths. Rumored to be on the tender side of thirty, he slips into those cut-to-the-body French suits each day just in time to share lunch with the Fords or Niarchoses. These days he's spending a good part of his time slipping into ski clothes, too, in order to take care of the newest Pascal creation, a Sun Valley restaurant, Chez Paul, owned in conjunction with Paul Anka. How nice! Now the Harrimans, Kennedys, Onassises, Fords, and Hiltons can take to the slopes without sacrificing their nicely sculpted bass *en croûte*.

Pascal's 7:30 seating tends toward the chairmen-of-the-board types, with the 9:30 seating being the one for which the truly Beautiful People report before heading over to Pascal's new club on East 67th Street. But whichever you choose, rest assured of one thing—one serving of that Tourinois, their cake of chocolate and chestnut purée layered with Grand Marnier and whipped cream and covered by chocolate mousse—and even at Chez Pascal you'll have come up with a menu whose calorie count exceeds the check!

Christ Cella   160 E. 46TH ST.   10017
                    697-2479

There's no denying you can get a wonderful steak at The Palm. But if you're in the mood to get that wonderful steak and still be able to hear what your dining companion is saying, it's time for you to call Christ Cella. Compared to the rowdy, good-sport atmosphere of most New York steakeries, Christ Cella's dignified waiters, spare yet stylish decor, and courteous, efficient service make for a welcome island of calm.

Richard Cella stopped flying to carry on the tradition started by his father and mother in their two-story brownstone. The steaks, chops, lobster, seafood, potatoes and salads are every bit as good as they were when Robert Morley first started frequenting their counter. Today clients, like Flying Tigers' president Bob Prescott, sit in a slightly more glorified atmosphere of butcher-block tables and hardwood floors, and find the four-star food so agreeable that they call from as far away as Los Angeles to make sure that special table in the kitchen or bar is ready for them when they arrive in Manhattan. Naturally they make it a point not to arrive on Sunday, the day Christ Cella is closed!

Do call ahead—the regular "lunch club" of ad execs, Wall Street brokers and bankers fills up those precious few tables far in advance. If Richard is out when you phone up, ask for maître d' John, and even if he tells you they're full don't worry about missing this rare steak treat. Just call ahead, book one of the private dining rooms upstairs, and use that blessed peace and quiet to figure out how you're going to come up with enough traveler's checks to cover that $20–$30 per person tab you can expect.

Le Cirque 58 E. 65TH ST. 10021
794-9292

Le Cirque was originally a doctor's office located off the lobby of the Mayfair Hotel. Decorator Helen McCluskey decided to trade waiting room white for terracotta chairs and tan suede banquettes and voila ... a fine French restaurant was born. The partners in Le Cirque include Joe, who is just the perfect man to call for that special table, Sirio, who serves as maitre d' during lunch and dinner, and executive chef Jean Vergnes.

Some of the things that Jean is busy whipping up are *pâté de campagne*, fettuccine al prosciutto, and duck with lemon, apples and raisins. He also does a marvelous seafood crepe, as well as a delicious stroganoff. Finish it off with a generous helping of coupe Le Cirque, and you'll be lucky to find the energy just to get yourself back upstairs to a room in the Mayfair, much less to deal with anything so strenuous as getting into a limo to go back home.

As for the crowd, we've heard it referred to as the great gray fringe ... the simple act of lowering your eyes and looking around the room at ear level will tell you why. There's hardly a head there which isn't graying around the temples. If this leads you to believe that this is the perfect place to frequent once you've become a moderately mature and highly successful businessman, you're correct. But if you're looking for the young and beautiful crowd, look elsewhere.

Le Cirque's attention to detail is so great that even the small murals which decorate the walls were executed by hand. Look carefully and you'll see that they're of monkeys; but think even more carefully before you let that lead you to believe that the place is inhabited by swingers!

The Coach House   110 WAVERLY PLACE   10011
777-0303

What do you mean you refuse to pick at your pâté on the same ground where the Wanamakers' horses used to be kept? Really, it's been cleaned up since then! In fact, the Coach House today is a wonderful blend of clubby red brick walls and rich red carpet, cerise tablecloths, beamed ceilings, and brass containers filled with fresh flowers. Why, Dobbin and Prince wouldn't even recognize it. Many gourmets claim the Coach House is the best restaurant in the city; you owe it to yourself to eat there at least once.

If there's one thing Leon Lianides believes in, it's patriotic cooking. His fame in the preparation of our national dishes has spread to such an extent that when France's most famous chefs visited America, they requested a meal at the Coach House. Now you might have a bit of trouble persuading Leon to whip up the same menu he served them—quiche with homemade sausages, American crab with Mississippi pecans and mustard sauce, striped bass, corn sticks with black bean soup, prime ribs with baked potato, sour cream and chives, Mississippi pecan pie with whipped cream, and an assortment of cheeses and cognac. But if you give him a few days' notice, we're sure he'll consider it. Now the only question is, can you finish it?

Leon claims that in almost 30 years in the business, he's never seen a regular luncheon customer come to the Coach House for dinner. At noon you'll find Wall Street brokers as well as socially oriented matrons who are donating their time to charity in the Village. At dinner you'll run into everyone from Tennessee Williams (you know what a sucker he is for cornpone) to George Stavropoulos, from Pauline Trigère to Ingrid Bergman. Obviously dinner is the time to drop in! And if you happen to be there on those rare nights when both Julia Child and James Beard have dropped by to swap recipes, you'll know that the rumors about Leon's taste are justified!

A seat in what was once the hayloft will afford you a view of the entire goings on, but a seat on the main floor will put you in closer proximity to that gorgeous dessert table. Looking at that legendary chocolate mousse cake, the fresh pecan pie with whipped cream and the dark apple tart, not to mention the Continental parfait aux marrons, it will be all you can do to finish three courses before digging into the sweets. But resist them at least until you finish some iceberg lettuce chopped up with cucumbers and cheese, and until you clean off that Blue Willow plate full of rack of lamb, pepper steak, or Seafood Mediterrannée (two tiny lobster tails, three shrimp, three clams and a marinara style sauce perfumed with pernod).

Always be sure to ask what's particularly good when you stop in; Leon is as adventurous in his food as he is on his California wine list. You might find that he's prepared whole fresh bass, or that he's found fresh oysters to stuff into his alderman's carpetbag steak (just $36 for two).

By the way, you might think you've won Leon's favor on that day when he seats you without a reservation... but you won't really be sure until Christmas Day. If one of his famous plum puddings is waiting on your doorstep, you'll know for certain you've not only found a wonderful chef—you've found a friend for life!

La Côte Basque   5 E. 55TH ST.   10022
                     688-6525

We all come to New York with one special goal. There are those of us who wouldn't dream of leaving without seeing the Statue of Liberty. Some insist on going to all the first-run Broadway shows. And then there are those who refuse to set foot on that plane going home until they've been seen at least twice in the *Women's Wear Daily* "Eye." If you're one of the latter and time is running short, don't despair... the simplest expedient is lunch at La Côte Basque. If there isn't a *WWD* photographer or two ensconced nearby with an alert eye trained on the front door of La Côte Basque, it can only mean that the Duchess of Windsor is lunching at La Grenouille!

La Côte Basque has a marvelous heritage; it was the site of Henri Soule's famous Pavillon. Today Madame Henrietta Spalter and her gracious son Albert operate their charmingly understated La Côte Basque on the premises which housed his wonderful four-star restaurant.

Naturally there are those who claim it doesn't compare to its predecessor—Pavillon is a hard act to follow—but Van Cliburn and Imelda Marcos seem to disagree. Not only did she come for lunch, she stayed to plan a private party that involved screening off the entire front room for her guests. While Mrs. Marcos opted for a menu of cold striped bass with cucumbers, filet of beef with an assortment of vegetables, Bibb lettuce and endive salad, and a lemon soufflé, you could settle for the $24.75 prix-fixe dinner quite happily.

The only thing you *shouldn't* settle for is the wrong table. La Côte Basque is known for playing favorites, so make it quite clear when you make your reservation that the first banquette on the left or one of the cozy little lunch tables in the bar is for you. One of our friends of note insists that she'd trade her standing table at Elaine's for Jackie O's spot at La Côte Basque, but *we* think that if you approach Madame Spalter correctly, you can keep both. Tell her how much you love her Bernard Lamotte murals of Biarritz and the Basque country. Let her know that you appreciate that mulberry and gray carpeting, and the red and green Basque motif. Compliment her on her lovely wooden bar. Before you know it, you may have the left front booth for every meal of the day!

The menu changes every day, so you'll want to maintain good relations with La Côte Basque's maître d's in order to get accurate recommendations. At that left front banquette, cultivate Gerard's favor; in the back room, it's Ronnie. Tell them you want a light lunch, and they'll probably recommend that you start with a cold hors d'oeuvres plate, a sampling of champignons, cold cabbage, tuna with egg, and oysters in season. There's also that wonderful pâté Côte Basque which is worth putting on an extra pound to enjoy. Follow it with sautéed *mignonnette de boeuf à la moelle* or any kind of omelet your heart desires. *Délices de sole bonne femme* is wonderful if you feel like a light fish subtly sauced. Follow that with crepes Côte Basque and you'll have to add $4.00 to that $15.25 luncheon check; but it's well worth it!

Dinner is a dressy event at La Côte Basque. We used to see women in pant suits turned away at the door—Madame was one of the last holdouts in New York. But today she's altered her rules and that latest St. Laurent pant suit is welcome. Still, patrons lean toward putting their best foot forward when they plan a long, leisurely dinner at La Côte Basque. Our favorite entree is roast duck with cherries, so we always try to start out with a less-than-filling hors d'oeuvre: vichyssoise, *madrilene en gélee,* or *melon et jambon.* We also have a favorite little side dish which we'll be glad to pass along, a purée of mushrooms which seems to be perfect with almost anything. If duck isn't what you had in mind for this evening, why not try one of the other Côte Basque specialties: steak au poivre with peppercorns (add $7.00 to that $24.75 prix fixe), or lamb Edward VII. And of course each day brings its own plat du jour; chicken in light champagne sauce, *escalope de veau,* or sole grilled with *sauce moutarde* would be typical.

While the cheeses are nice, they're hardly worth giving up dessert for (what is?). That spectacular dessert table holds chocolate mousse, strawberry tarts, *coupe aux marrons* and strawberries and liqueur with spun sugar. For truly special occasions, insist on raspberry soufflé. Of course, Arthur Rubinstein always gets a cake for dessert, but then maybe that's because he seems to celebrate most of his birthdays there. Take it from the master; when Madame Spalter sets out to plan a meal, it's a symphony of flavors the likes of which you'll find in precious few other New York restaurants!

Le Coup de Fusil   160 E. 64TH ST.   10021
751-9110

In French it means a shock, or something completely unexpected. But whatever can the shock be? It couldn't possibly be the check. From the moment you realize that Count Guy de Brantes is functioning as a greeter and passing out red roses at the door you know you'll have to expect a heavy bill. (He's taking time out from being Diane von Furstenberg's financial adviser to find you a table for two.) Nor can it be the fact that the minceur cuisine is mouth-watering. Why shouldn't it be—Comtesse de Brantes lifted her chef right out of Régine's New York kitchen.

Maybe the surprise comes when a Secret Service man thrusts his walkie-talkie in front of you as you come through the front door. There seem to be dozens of them every time Prince Faisal and oil minister Sheik Abdul Yamani of Saudi Arabia drop by with their usual spectacular entourage. Even Bernard Lanvin and Jean-Paul Belmondo take a moment out from their mousseline of snapper to take a peek at that.

Or perhaps the shock is that Carol Lynley bothered to go to her yoga class, a tap-dancing class, then home to change into her omnipresent thrift-shop wardrobe before coming in for dinner. You'd think she'd have the good sense to make Coup de Fusil her first stop when she stepped off the plane!

Well, at least the *food* never seems to be a surprise... it's uniformly good. You might order a salad of fresh green beans, cooked to be a bit crunchy and then decorated with foie gras. Or quail roasted with fresh fall fruits (apples and grapes) and then sauced with red wine, port, and cream. Or perhaps you'll want their wonderful cream of mussel soup. Since the menu is reprinted every week, there's always something new to greet you on your return. Everything is a la carte, so lunch may run about $30 for two, and dinner about $60 for two.

As for the atmosphere, despite the exalted names, it remains cozily elegant. The tiny restaurant is bistro style, with dark-red walls and banquettes, Lalique lighting fixtures in old silver, etched glass partitions, old French Christofle silver, and attractive pink-clothed tables. The seating is more informal in the front part of the restaurant than the back but both halves seem equally popular with Marisa Berenson Randell, Jean-Pierre Aumont and Estée Lauder. Just take a quick look, decide on your own preference, and talk to manager Patrick Marachel about it.

And by the way, if that apple tart has you hooked, take heart. You can always sign up for one of the cooking classes that Marina de Brantes gives with partner Ludovic Autet. Can you think of a better way to beat the price of eating in New York?

Le Cygne 53 E. 54TH ST. 10022
759-5941

Some people don't *need* to be seen. Some just don't *want* to be seen. Imagine the problems they have keeping their calorie count high while they keep their profiles low! The lucky ones find Le Cygne.

Gerald and Michele are always standing ready to welcome you into their quiet fifteen-table French restaurant. You can hide behind just tons of fresh flowers for an intimate tête-à-tête, or wrap yourself up in a quiet atmosphere while closing your next oil deal. But you'd better make your reservation early or you'll run the risk of missing your chance to do either; space is at a premium at Le Cygne.

Le Cygne is a combination of red carpet, white tablecloths, and 18th-century Parisian florals that can't help but give you a warm and comfortable feeling. As if that weren't enough, the duck is magnificent, and we never pass up the sweetbreads when they're on the menu. Start with *escargots de Bourgogne*, even if they will take you a touch above the $22.25 prix fixe. After all, with a decent wine your dinner for two will probably end up costing $80 anyway, so why not splurge?

Le Cygne's raspberry soufflé is so good that many New Yorkers will only come when it's in season, at which point they then proceed to crowd in as many as four dinners a week. That's more than just devotion, that's the kind of food that earned four stars from the *Times!*

Daly's Dandelion   1029 THIRD AVE.   10021
                                        838-0780

It's illegal to call Daly's Dandelion a saloon, so we won't. We will tell you that there are eight bartenders (Tommy and Jimmy have been there the longest) and thirteen bar stools; that the crowd at the bar is usually three deep; that the place is reputed to make the best Irish coffee in town. But *some* people do come to Skitch Henderson's uptown establishment to eat, so Daly's Dandelion is legally a restaurant.

Aren't there some days when you tire of chateaubriand and nothing sounds better than a cheeseburger? Barbara Walters and Walter Cronkite have both had those nothing-but-a-big-juicy-burger-will-do days, and they've stopped in at Daly's (Skitch says he hasn't changed the portions of his burgers in the last ten years). When Burt Bacharach gets the burger urge, he heads for the VIP Room in back, where John Lindsay is frequently found. Al Pacino has been known to drop into the VIP Room after a shooting and stay there till 3 A.M.

Skip the VIP Room if you'd rather mix with the regular Daly crowd. Prime seating is in the sidewalk café area—fist-fights have broken out over tables there, so prepare to protect your territory. Once you're seated, part of the fun of the place is seeing all the college kids just hanging out. Call it a slice of life over a slice of cheesecake. (We might add that theirs is delicious, but don't forget to try the homemade cobblers, too.) Inside, the decor, complete with peeling brown plaster, is strictly original. And how quaint to see the white-capped chefs preparing the burgers and salads right before your eyes.

For a more sedate crowd, try Daly's Daffodil in the Sutton Place area. Skitch and his partner George opened this one to appeal to the Upper East Side set, an older crowd that still likes cheeseburgers. It's still just as relaxed as the Dandelion. If you stop in at either spot on a Friday, try the clam chowder.

David K's	1115 THIRD AVE.	10021
Chung Kuo Yuan	371-9090	

With all the trying years we've spent learning to use chopsticks with the aplomb of a Chinese diplomat, now David Keh's come along to confuse the issue; after all, who wants to confine themselves to simple sticks of wood when the finest sterling and crystal are decorating the table?

David's been working in New York's Chinese restaurants for years, and this one represents the culmination of a dream for him... a restaurant worthy of competing with the finest purveyors of Italian and French haute cuisine.

The decor is exquisite—beige print carpets, scads of fresh flowers, brown and beige linen, rich silver serving pieces and Rosenthal crystal. And as for the service, tuxedo-clad waiters make sure it's equal to any in the city.

The food is authentic (a request for chop suey or chow mein will produce nothing more than inscrutable looks) and delicious. We always start with Hsiao Leng P'an (assorted cold hors d'oeuvres) and make a point of including some of our special favorites in the menu. Try the Chiao Yen Ch'ang Yu (Pomfort fish with chef's special sauce), the Pei Ching K'ao Ya (barbecued duck, Peking style), and the Su Ts'ai Liang Mein (cold green noodles with sesame sauce). And if you have thoughts of developing an even more elaborate menu, why not consult Chinese cuisine expert Danny Kaye... now that he's devoted some time to planning the dinner for David Keh's Chinese New Year's dinner, he's sure to know the menu by heart.

One of our favorite ways to spend a warm spring evening with a group of friends is on David's enclosed garden patio in the back of the restaurant. But do remember before you invite *too* many friends that you'll probably be paying $20 apiece for dinner and then adding on something extra for wine. Just think, a Chinese restaurant that takes your fortune at the same time they're giving you one!

Elaine's 1703 SECOND AVE. 10028
831-9566

We've heard people complain about Elaine's... the ones who can't get in, that is! They go so far as to claim it's not really a restaurant; it's a private club. What none of them ever bother to point out is that there's such a ridiculously simple way to become a member of that club. Why, all you have to do is write a best-selling novel. What could be easier than that? Then Elaine and maître d' Elio will welcome you with open arms!

Fourteen years ago Elaine was a waitress in a restaurant that was a literary hangout. Today she's moved both the food and the intellectuals uptown to her place on Second Avenue. They're there every night between eight and two... people like Irwin Shaw, Sidney Lumet, Peter Moss, Ben Gazzara, Woody Allen, Chevy Chase, Herb Sargent... eating squid salad and *osso buco*, trading thoughts over *tortolloni primavera*.

Naturally, all these free thinkers are more concerned with ideas than decor, so Elaine has been able to get by with a rather haphazard earthiness. The group is so closely knit you might just imagine yourself in her living room rather than in her restaurant.

If you've got the clout to arrange it, you'll want one of the first seven tables as you enter the room—the prime spots. For a spot in the back room (a great place to sample dessert and cappucino), you can slip in by being just a minor celebrity. But do be careful, whoever you are—you're pushing your luck if you come without a reservation and without one of Elaine's regulars by your side!

The Empire Diner 210 TENTH AVE. 10036
243-2736; 243-9870

People arrive by truck, taxi, limousine and foot. Twenty-four hours a day you'll find them crowding into Carl Laanes and Richard Ruskay's spruced-up genuine 1940s diner. And really, love, before you insist that even a spruced-up version of a diner sounds less than attractive to you, take into consideration that Carl's redecorating included adding everything from mirrors to black-glass tabletops (a sure guarantee that their daily bill for Windex is at least as large as their tab for French bread) to a piano player.

The diner isn't far from Soho and Greenwich Village, so the clientele is both individual and unusual. And since it's open 24 hours a day, it's just the perfect place to stop by for a homemade pastry after taking in the late show at Reno Sweeney's... though Saturday and Sunday brunch is a treat, too. The $5 breakfast is enough to boggle the imagination—fresh orange juice, hot cereal, eggs any style with sausage, bacon, or ham, new potatoes gently fried in their skins, a basket of warm Italian bread, corn muffins with butter, and real, hearty coffee. And by the way, not only does it leave you full enough to skip lunch, since that $5 includes tax you can splurge and buy a pack of gum on the way out.

The $8.50 dinner's a New York favorite, too. A different menu is written on the wall each night... treats like zucchini and watercress soup, leg of lamb served with two vegetables and salad, and a dessert (the chocolate silk pie shouldn't be missed); or pea soup followed by lamb with cracked wheat and asparagus, green peppers, and for dessert, homemade Boston cream pie.

Though almost every seat in this chromed, mirrored, and black-patent-leather-upholstered bit of nostalgia is good, our favorite is the one at the end of the bar which faces the whole diner and affords you a view of both the patrons and the behind the counter operation. It's close enough to the piano player so that you can get the full impact of those jazz improvisations without losing your bird's-eye view of bowls of chili and assorted omelets being tossed around by the Diner's chefs (former jugglers, we surmise).

While the Empire Diner might be a bit below your budget, you really must admit that it's nice to find some place that's open 24 hours a day. After all, even a big spender has to find one or two spots where he never has to worry about arriving late!

The Four Seasons   99 E. 52ND ST.   10022
754-9494

Yes, Virginia, there *is* a Four Seasons. And yes, it *is* everything everyone ever told you it is. It is perfect! If you are the least bit surprised to find that coming from us, it's only because you haven't experienced Tom Marguittai and Paul Kovi's masterpiece in the Seagram Building. One visit and you'll agree that it's one of the most beautiful restaurants in New York (request a seat by the pool when you call Allen for reservations). One meal and you'll know why even lunch for two can ring up an $80 check (we'd pay any price for the planked steak tartare—unequivocally the world's best).

At least 500 people could be served in five dining rooms—two public and three private—plus the bar and cocktail lounge, yet the atmosphere is still intimate. The bar is unusually large, so even when it's exceptionally busy you needn't worry about bumping elbows with the world's wealthiest private people. There's room enough for all of you to have a leisurely drink and still enjoy Picasso's treatment of a stage curtain which first appeared at the Théâtre de l'Opéra in Paris in 1920. The abstract sculpture by Richard Lippold over the bar is actually brass rods dipped in gold, and yes, those tapestries are Mirós. These works will become old friends after a few visits to the Four Seasons; you can look forward to seeing them whenever you return (unless, of course, some of the pieces are on loan to museums, as frequently happens).

In keeping with its famous name, the rest of the restaurant changes its appearance as the seasons change. When the vernal equinox decrees it, beige upholstery replaces the black on every Mies van der Rohe chair in the house, to see us cheerfully through spring and summer. At the same time fresh azaleas and birch trees announce that spring has indeed sprung. By the time Tom and Paul bring out the philodendrons, the meals will be getting as light as the evenings—not only does the interior of the restaurant change with the calendar, so does the menu. A summer without the sabayon and fresh strawberries is like winter without a new fur—unbearable.

Whatever the season, you can depend on dinner par excellence once Oreste guides you to your table. Though you won't want to make any hasty decisions about your meal, do plan to spend at least 15 minutes perusing the wine list. With 30,000 bottles waiting in the basement's two wine cellars, we're certain you'll find something perfect to accompany your meal. We chose Pouilly-Fumé de *Ladouepte* last time and it was magnificent. If you chance to be celebrating something triumphal ask for Moet & Chandon Dom Perignon 1966—but be prepared for your reward to double your bill. Surely your success deserves it, and no price is too high to pay for this champagne.

We relish the game pâté with pistachio nuts as an appetizer. If you prefer a hot dish, shrimp shoyu is a zesty beginning. Though we toyed with thoughts of medallions of veal with mushrooms and onions, and charcoal-broiled lamb chops, we opted for red snapper in vermouth accompanied by raw mushrooms with Malabar dressing. We know the spinach soufflé is marvelous, but oh so filling. When we come here we *must* leave room for dessert. You can believe Barbra Streisand when she tells you that the Chocolate Velvet is wonderful. It's so rich that you'd swear it was 90 percent chocolate, 10 percent gold.

While you're in town you may need to throw a private party. We assure you there's no finer place. Even if it's just a simple little birthday party, you'll join the ranks of such celebrated folks as Norman Mailer, who turned fifty at the Four Seasons. Jackie's birthday dinner party for JFK was an intimate affair, but think of the fun the Secret Service had tasting the food beforehand. The chef shuddered when one asked for more salt. Previewing a film in one of the private dining rooms is fairly common. All the rooms are complete with concealed projection rooms as well as open- or closed-circuit television equipment. Irwin Allen took advantage of the facilities to preview *The Towering Inferno* but not one person thought to request baked Alaska for dessert.

The Four Seasons may just become your favorite restaurant in the world. You won't be alone; it has been ranked among the best by numerous authorities. But in the final analysis, you are the authority. We already know what you'll think—is *love* really the proper word to use about a restaurant?

Gino's   780 LEXINGTON AVE.   10022
838-9827

So, you thought your shopping trip at Bloomingdale's was complete as soon as you got that package out of the gift-wrap department. Wrong again! Finishing a Saturday shopping spree at Bloomie's without having lunch at Gino's is a Manhattan mortal sin!

Not that Gino's is as slick as Bloomie's; no one calls black linoleum floors, red walls with zebras, plastic flowering wall planters, and overaged waiters slick. It's just that it's the chic-est place in town for Saturday lunch.

To say that it's crowded, it's noisy, and it's full of men would be the understatement of the year. Bodies are jammed from the bar to the kitchen. Naturally there are no reservations; why should Gino's make it easy for you? Just fight your way in and look for Mr. Torres. He's owned Gino's for years, so he's the logical one to ask for one of those tiny white-clothed tables.

Except a hearty lunch. Broiled fish is served with boiled potatoes. *Osso buco* on Mondays. Veal parmigiana always. The waiters have been there so long that they're an institution. They make friends quickly and are never shy about telling you if you look as if you could use a little more to eat.

A hearty lunch or dinner with a modest wine will run you $20. The minuscule price tag hasn't discouraged New York sophisticates from dropping in, though, so don't be embarrassed to do so yourself.

La Goulue   28 E. 70TH ST.   10021
988-8169

It's absolutely terrible! First Jean pours you into those New Man jeans over at his boutique, De Noyer. Then, when it's all you can do to sit down, he takes you over to his restaurant to make sure that you won't be able to fit into that new purchase in the future! It's a wonder he isn't losing friends! But judging from the gaggle of models, art dealers and advertising executives waiting for those precious tables, he isn't.

After spending the morning gallery-hopping in the neighborhood, anything less than La Goulue might be a shock to your artistic sense. Not only is it the prime lunchtime gathering place for local art merchants, it's also beautiful. Every one of the authentic French antiques and art nouveau treasures was gathered by Jean in France, making this the closest thing to a Parisian bistro that you'll find stateside. The tiny little front room contains a diminutive zinc bar, some banquettes, one small table, and some huge palms to make negotiating your way through the crowds even more interesting. These are the prime seats for ensuring that you'll see every face which passes through the front door. In the inner room, crystal sconces and beveled mirrors reflect etched crystal room dividers, lace curtains, and comfortable brown leather banquettes. With its dark wood paneling, it still manages to be a warm, masculine room despite the crystal and mirrors.

La Goulue was in and out so many times in its first years that even Lee Radziwill was confused. But today it's firmly entrenched as a B.P. hangout. Just ask Michael York. You'll find Pascal at one of the front room banquettes, nibbling Jean's *coquilles St.-Jacques* or *terrine de canard* while he studies the crowd which will, in all likelihood, be having dinner at his place before the week is out. Chalk up the rushing and bumping to La Goulue's French bistro flavor, then insist that Jacques give you the second table on the right in the inner room. Simply everyone will notice you having your celery remoulade with vinaigrette and mayonnaise, and your *coq de veau aux morilles* in cream sauce if you secure *that* choice seat.

Though dinner for two will run around $50, you won't be required to add an exhorbitant wine to the bill. Most of Jean's selections are in the $10–$15 range, and he even has a few carafe wines for those days when you're fresh out of the Knoedler Gallery, the proud owner of a new canvas, and insist on budgeting for a few hours to make up for your extravagance.

Dinner quiets down a bit, and the crystal sconces lighting that rich, dark wood make it a lovely place to enjoy a leisurely basscalu, sea bass in butter with a wonderfully light sauce. Since it's not too filling, you can follow it with Jean's orange Napoleon: sections of orange marinated in a mandarin sauce. After all, you haven't had time to get attached to those New Man jeans yet, have you?

The Grand Café 28 E. 63RD ST. 10021
355-2121

If Busby Berkeley were still alive, he'd plan a musical at the Grand Café. You half-expect Fred Astaire and Ginger Rogers to come out dancing, but you'll probably have to be satisfied with just sitting near enough to Alan Jay Lerner to hear him hum. Art deco can be commonplace, but at the Grand Café, it's magnificent. It's the most visually exciting restaurant we've seen since Warner LeRoy's Tavern on the Green. Ladies can't help feeling beautiful wrapped in the pink walls and the gentle glint of the chandeliers. Every bit of brass is hand-polished daily to maintain its gleam. The sconces on the walls are about the only treasures left from the old Le Passy restaurant which Café owners Allen and Donna Stillman stripped to the bare bones.

Bill Riggs has done foyer murals of unlikely ladies in twenties dress that are repeated in a thematic etched-glass treatment in the dining room. Once the lights go on, the room is a twinkling mélange of glass and brass. With all this sparkle and folderol, those waiters in blue ticking aprons come as an interesting contrast.

Ask Ray to seat you in the front room's left banquettes, or better yet at that table in the back corner that gives you a good view of everyone who enters. Then, having arranged yourself in the most visible of all possible seats, turn your attention to the menu.

It's a wonderfully practical idea—Allen and Donna offer each of their entrees prepared in two very different fashions. Some of us will feel like ordering the all-American treatment; some of us will want to lean toward French haute cuisine. Thus you have your choice of grilled half young chicken or *poularde aux herbes:* roast chicken stuffed with thyme, rosemary, and bay leaves; or broiled boneless sirloin, butterflied and prepared in red wine and shallots. How very clever of them, and even better when you start your meal with wonderful fresh asparagus and walnut dressing or the chef's coulibiac of salmon *en croûte.* As if you're not already bursting the seams of that drapey little Chloé number you wore for the occasion, the Grand Café offers a "grande finale" of assorted fresh fruit, cheeses, and homemade candies and cookies served on a suitably art deco epergne. And once you've resigned yourself to being overweight, you might as well add on an order of their *coupe clo-clo;* chestnuts in vanilla sauce and maraschino liqueur served over vanilla ice cream.

A Grand Café ritual is the wine sampler. Before you order, your waiter will bring you a tiny tray with samples of the six French wines which the house recommends. There's never any trusting to the taste of others. Simply take a sip and decide for yourself. Of course if what you decide is that no $7.50 wine is good enough for *you,* you'll have to resort to the supplementary list of *les plus grandes* grapes. And no ... they're not offering free samples of that $45 Dom Perignon!

Lunch for two at the Grand Café will probably run about $25; dinner closer to $45. But it's well worth it, even for the decor alone. As John Canaday of *The New York Times* declared when he first saw it, he'd have to give this restaurant four stars even if it served sawdust.

La Grenouille	3 E. 52ND ST. 10022
	752-1495

New York's French restaurants *do* have a pecking order, though whether you peck *first* at La Caravelle, La Côte Basque, Lutèce, or La Grenouille is purely a function of personal preference and how early you made your reservations. If you live your life by the stars, you'll choose La Caravelle, since *The New York Times* gave it four. If you think that money is minted just to be spent (what else?) you'll opt for La Côte Basque and its prix-fixe $15.75 lunch. Purists will turn to Lutèce, where André Soltner, the foremost saucier in New York, reigns supreme. But those of you who have lunch strictly for social reasons wouldn't dream of going anywhere but to *WWD*'s own frogpond, La Grenouille! Everyone who is, was, or is-soon-to-be "beautiful" has lunched at La Grenouille. Gisele Masson, who watches over the famous restaurant, says she was thrilled to serve the Duke and Duchess of Windsor. Her artist son, Charles, was even more elated when Salvador Dali chose to be surreal in their midst. Mr. and Mrs. Gregory Peck choose La Grenouille when they're in from the West Coast, and Mick and Bianca Jagger love the Grand Marnier soufflé. If you haven't noticed them sampling it quite so often since Régine brought *la cuisine minceur* (less cream, lower calories) to town it can only mean that even Mick has reached the age at which he has to remember calories. Time *does* fly by, doesn't it!

Gisele leaves her lovely ladies and gorgeous gentlemen in the capable hands of Jon, the maître d'. We will never understand how he remembers everyone's name—they don't give a memory course at Alliance Française, do they? Nevertheless, we have yet to see him fail.

If you're a special customer, you can rest assured that Jon will steer you away from Grenouille's own Siberia in the back. If you *do* find yourself walking in that direction, rebel and ask for the Front Room and Captain Marcel. In fact, insist on it when you make your reservation.

If you're a *very* special customer, Marcel will make sure you enjoy one of the dishes that isn't on the menu. Dijon pigeon diablo, perhaps, or grilled squab in piquant sauce. But first have him bring you hors d'oeuvres from the trolley. They're really quite fantastic, particularly if you ask for a selection of five or six different kinds and get some of Chef Henri's special pâté.

At lunch Halston might be sitting right across from you, so you'll probably want to watch your diet and eat something light. If a slice of beef seems just too bleak, try a Happy Rockefeller favorite; the Scotch salmon. When it's cold outside you'll prefer a heartwarming bowl of lobster bisque.

The decor is as special as the food. We're almost positive that

Calvin Klein gets some of his spring color ideas when he sees the flowers at lunch showing up under that brighter-than-usual French restaurant lighting. Even when it's snowing it looks like May inside—credit Gisele and her artistic sense, not to mention the daily trips to the flower market. The hours spent arranging Grenouille's bouquets are well worth it; what would we do without a breath of spring in the dead of winter?

For dinner you must splurge. Beluga caviar is so common; why not try the *terrine de foie gras* or smoked salmon—Henri has some special touches that make each a rare treat. Sentimentalists will want to try *les Grenouilles provençales,* frog legs that are well worth being namesakes. All Henri's sauces are rich classics —the chicken in wine with herbs and the duckling aren't exceptions. And like Mick and Bianca, you'll adore a soufflé with Grand Marnier or fresh raspberries. Dear me, if you forgot to order one early and haven't time to wait that extra half-hour, try one of the pastries prepared by Gisele's younger son, Philippe.

How wonderful! All this splendor is available for a prix fixe of $23.75 per person in the evening. Add on an immediate $25 for the Beluga caviar, and $3.75 per person for that soufflé. Don't forget a wonderful Bordeaux or Burgundy. Then expect to have a check for at least $80 for two. If you're more conservative at lunch and settle for a simple $8 Pouilly-Fuissé, you might get by for $20 apiece.

Healthworks	148 E. 57TH ST. 10022
	838-8370

Have you started to feel that the big city is out to get you? That the chefs of Lutèce, Madrigal and La Côte Basque have formed a pact to pursue you to the ends of the earth bearing raspberry soufflés, or at least to keep after you until you're too tubby to consider anything at Henri Bendel? Is it getting ever more difficult to reach down and zip those Ferragamo boots in the morning? Well then, it's time for Bruce Zenkel to come to the rescue with his luscious salads, soups and yogurt creations.

Don't worry—we're not going to drag you into one of those artsy-craftsy California coastline combinations of class-B pottery, plants, and poorly crafted oak furniture. Healthworks is to salads what John Kloss is to clothes (in fact, John designed those sleek jumpsuits your young waitresses are streaking around in). The entire facility reflects a serious concern for contemporary design: Pirelli floors, Milanese plastic tableware, giant outdoors super-graphics, and sleek polished furniture of natural wood.

Personally, we've learned to like the hubbub, although the noise level can be somewhat discouraging if you've the stubborn idea of carrying on a conversation with your luncheon partner. But then if the whole thing gets to be more than you can handle, Healthworks *does* offer you the option of bagging one of their creations in a photodecorated takeout container and sneaking away to munch in the privacy of your suite at the Pierre.

Healthworks features five generously portioned salads daily, which are chosen from the rotating specials produced by "Salad Designer" Cari Wyman. We particularly enjoy turkey Bombay (diced turkey, celery and scallions with peach slices and crunchy roasted peanuts topped with Madras curry dressing), and *salade niçoise* (tuna filets, feta cheese, Greek olives, capers, crisp green beans and whatever other vegetables happen to be fresh that day, with a dilled vinaigrette dressing).

But give serious consideration to the Popeye (spinach), Tuscany (cabbage with minced turkey, ham, and scallions), Atlantis (shrimp, avocado, watercress, oranges, tomatoes and dill) or such good old standbys as the Waldorf and the chef's salad.

You can team the salads with the day's soup if you feel up to a higher caloric intake, and you can even go hog-wild with a portion of frozen yogurt.

As to the best seats in the house, the emphasis is more on the *healthiest* seats in the house. Following the example of such people-pleasers as TWA and Pan Am, Healthworks divides patrons into smoking and nonsmoking sections. So while some might enjoy the view of the crowd you enjoy from the back corner of the room, if you intend to keep puffing while you pick at your fresh vegetables, you'll just have to make plans to pack up those Dunhills and move to the front of the restaurant.

Lutèce   249 E. 50TH ST.   10022
 752-2225

When Jackie and Lee come to lunch, André leaves his kitchen to personally shoo the *WWD* reporters away from the door. When everyone in the city already knows you're the best, getting more publicity is only asking for trouble. Leaving New York without a meal at Lutèce is tantamount to departing Paris without having sipped champagne at Maxim's... simply not done, my dear, simply not done.

One test of status is being able to book a table at Lutèce in the first place. But a better test is seeing whether André will pop out as you pass by his kitchen and give you a big hello and a key to the specials of the day. Expect him to recommend the Dover sole... if it hasn't been flown in fresh he just won't serve it. He might put in a good word for the *ris de veau financière:* sweetbreads prepared with olives, mushrooms, and ham in a rich dark sauce. Then of course those seasonal floral menus mention his famous *mignon de boeuf en croûte Lutèce,* an individual filet with goose-liver pâté and mushrooms baked in a pastry shell; not much to look at until it's topped with its truffle sauce, but from that moment on, it's a delight! Then for dessert, *soufflé glace aux framboises,* a frozen raspberry soufflé you won't soon forget. Now aren't you glad you only had fresh salmon for an hors d'oeuvre?

Lutèce may be one of the most expensive, but it isn't the most pretentious restaurant in the world. The curtains in the small straw-chaired bar are of green and white gingham, the floor is brick, and the entire effect is that of having entered a modest French bistro. Once inside, there isn't a bad seat in the house. Downstairs the room is one long garden with two rows of tables and wicker chairs à la sidewalk café. With skylighting and heaters everywhere, it can't help but have a light, comfortable feel. The upstairs room is a bit more elegant, and also a bit more difficult to negotiate. Don't attempt that tiny winding staircase if you've been sipping André's '55 Lafite Rothschild. It's bad enough you're going to have to pay $175 a bottle without adding on a bill from the orthopedic surgeon to boot! If you plan to stumble, stick to the house Beaujolais at $10 and apply the extra $165 toward major medical. Once you're upstairs you'll want to ask for the room near the front. That way even if you can't check *WWD* to see who ate at Lutèce, you'll have a good enough view of the street to be your own society columnist.

Lunch is usually an event which finds U.N. ambassadors and delegates sitting next to artists, businessmen cheek-by-jowl with the ladies who lunch. If you're planning on abstaining from dinner, ask André to give you his venison pâté followed by lobster flambé pernod. But if eating dinner is included in your plans for the evening, stick to quiche lorraine and *potage germiny* as a lighter choice.

Even a light lunch is prix fixe $15; and with modest wines you can count on relieving yourself of $80 for a modest dinner for two—but then those bills *were* getting a bit heavy in your pocket, weren't they?

Madame Romaine 32 E. 61ST ST.   10021
de Lyon   758-2422

Problems, problems, problems. It's so difficult to make it through a meal without caviar, but some days you're simply too full to cope with a three-course lunch. What's a person to do?

Madame Romaine is the answer—ask for her $11.50 omelet and you'll not only get your caviar, you'll get a healthy combination of ham, bacon, mushrooms, truffles, and sour cream underneath. Now *that's* what we call an omelet!

If that doesn't happen to appeal to you, the kind madame offers another 600 varieties of omelets to choose from; let's hear no more of those "there just isn't a thing I like on the menu" complaints. Besides, the dear woman whips every single one of them up with her own little hands. You wouldn't want to insult her, would you?

She does those sweet little menus by hand, too. The ones that tell you all about her omelets, breads, salads and desserts. If you don't understand every one, ask Yvonne to explain. She's the enthusiastic lady who just seated you.

It's a tiny place, with room for only 65 people at any one time. But of the 65, you'll often recognize eight or ten. The last time we stopped in Paul Simon was at a nearby table, while Anne and Dustin Hoffman were waiting to get in (no, they don't even take reservations for the Marathon Man). Paul Newman and Joanne Woodward stop in when they're in town... you should, too!

Le Madrigal 216 E. 53RD ST. 10022
355-0322

Le Madrigal's long, narrow quarters are decorated with light, bright French murals and omnipresent flowers. Generally the clientele leans more toward quiet class than toward ostentation. There's a token sit-down bar at the entrance and what passes for a garden in the midst of Manhattan in the back—the perfect place for an eight o'clock dinner on those nights when you don't feel like being seen by every person passing by those coveted front banquettes.

There are two things we look forward to with particular delight when we anticipate a visit to Le Madrigal. The first is the treat of seeing what awaits us on the extraordinary cold buffet at the entrance. Don't worry about missing it—there's simply no way to enter the restaurant without passing it. On a typical night it will be decked with such delicacies as tomato salad, beef salad, carrots, hearts of palm, ratatouille, celery root, fresh asparagus, salami, garlic sausage, shrimp, *salade niçoise,* cold striped bass with cucumbers, hot pâte *en croûte,* hot sausage *en croûte,* cold fillet of beef with fresh stringbeans, Bayonne ham and pâtés of goose, duck and wild game. The second surprise awaits us within Raymond's resplendent silver serving cart. Who knows what wonderful roast he's hiding in there!

Usually a meal at Le Madrigal will be accompanied by simple things: boiled potatoes or vegetables, perhaps, so you can feel free to splurge a bit beforehand with hors d'oeuvres of crabmeat and chives soaked in Pernod and then covered with Russian dressing and herbs. If that sounds a bit rich, try the *truite fumée* served with sour cream and horseradish.

Every day has its own specials. You might choose between roast veal and beef stew, or perhaps *rognons de veau* poached and served with plain boiled potatoes, or deep-fried strips of sole with tartar sauce. Or you might ask Raymond for one of the dishes that has made Le Madrigal famous: striped bass *flambé* Madrigal is a wonderful combination of Pernod, white wine and vegetables which will take about 45 minutes to prepare (fill that time by sipping a bit of white wine and sampling the caviar). *Pojarski Perigourdine* is their well-known veal, chicken, and ham steak smothered with truffle sauce. And of course there's always that good old standby, *entrecôte à l'auvergnat;* steak with red wine sauce and mushrooms. Have you left room for chocolate mousse or strawberries with melba sauce kirsh and cream or *oeufs à la neige?* Let's hope so!

Lunch is a lighter meal—after all, you do still have to make a few stops on Fifth Avenue—crêpe with minced chicken perhaps, accompanied by salad, or their wonderful veal with morilles. It's even lighter on the pocketbook, usually around a $30 check for two as compared to the $50 you can expect to pay for dinner (of *course* that doesn't include the wine—you know better than that!). But then who could object to the prices when one quick look at the editorial pages of *The New York Times* will tell you that's little enough to pay for the pleasure of finding one small spot of civilization in today's world!

Maxwell's Plum   1181 FIRST AVE. (AT 64TH ST.)   10021
                       628-2100

Plum crazy, that's what it is... the way people line up to get into Maxwell's! So many crowd in on Friday nights that the doors have to be barred shut. It's not enough to settle for getting a good table in the back room, you have to worry about being on the PPX list just to make things tolerable! Make sure that maître d' Van adds you to that select list of fifty customers who receive Preferred Personal Extras, or at the very least see that he adds you to the list of 450 who receive Personal Extras. Once he gets to know you better we're sure he'll add that coveted "Preferred" star next to your name.

Missing Maxwell's on your first trip to New York City would be tantamount to missing the Statue of Liberty or the view from the World Trade Center—almost a sacrilege. During the week the truly chic will be found getting PPX treatment in the back dining room, while the BBQ's (singles from Brooklyn, Bronx, and Queens) scuff their Guccis against the front room bar, and order Dewars and water from Jesse the bartender.

Maxwell's Plum was the inspiration of Warner LeRoy, whose Hollywood origins (son of Mervyn, nephew of Jack Warner) are all too obvious in both the decor and his demeanor. You'll recognize him by his costume, be it Moroccan, Western or just flowered velvet, and his wife Kay, who sticks by his side. Theirs was just one more of those Maxwell's Plum romances—a stewardess who met the young entrepreneur of her dreams. The only difference was that she managed to come up with one of the few young entrepreneurs in the city who could guarantee her getting a table there if she felt like having dinner. Very clever, Kay!

Find a time when the place isn't too crowded (and be sure to let us know if you do) and you'll be able to appreciate the art nouveau treasures and pseudo-antiques (circa 1969, the year the restaurant was born) that adorn every inch. Warner designed the back room's stained glass ceiling, as big as a tennis court and illuminated by 1,200 bulbs, as well as the bright copper ceiling studded with figurines and flora which brightens the café. You'll recognize this informal dining area by the hanging plants and bright green menus. But continue back to the dining room (check for the blue menus just to be sure) and ask for one of the four tables overlooking the brass-railed bar. Young waiters in black pants and tie and red aprons hustle in and out serving lunches of Russian caviar, melon and prosciutto, black bean soup, or curried chicken salad with dates and pineapple. Half the patrons order that good old Maxwell's luncheon standby, the cheeseburger. The other half wait for Friday, when lamb stew is the *plat du jour*.

During the week, the waiters get an hour or two to take a breather between lunch and dinner, but on the weekends it's so busy that the two meals run together without a break. Café dinners are similar to what you'll find on that red luncheon menu: roast marinated spareribs, bouillabaisse or cassoulet Toulousain followed by a banana split or a slice of Maxwell's scrumptious butterscotch pie. The 60,000-bottle cellar will certainly have something to suit your taste—how about a $175 bottle of Cheval Blanc '47 to keep that foot-long hot dog company?

Now, about the back room, where 6'6" Van Ribbet maneuvers his guests with the skill of a chess master. But then he has to, doesn't he... it would be embarrassing if the Shah of Iran's sister had to wait for a table! Regulars avoid Friday and Saturday nights. Even Van can't take the clamor on weekends; he turns his job over to a captain.

He will probably recommend that you start with the avocado vinaigrette. Then he'll tout you on the sirloin steak chunks sautéed with sour cream and spices, or the striped bass braised with fresh fennel and shallots in white wine sauce. And don't try to get away without downing at least one slice of Maxwell's Black Forest cake or their *tarte tatin mit schlag*. Don't worry, it's not as bad as it sounds. Schlag is just one more way of saying whipped cream. Add a nice bottle of wine and you'll have spent about $40 for two. Though at Maxwell's you can have a super casual dinner for $25 for two or lunch from about $15.

It's hard to figure out how Maxwell's might manage to serve Carly Simon and James Taylor, John Denver, Mr. and Mrs. Jacob Javits, and Debbie Reynolds all in one night—until they confide that they normally serve 1,400 meals in a single evening. Then you know the answer. Everyone in the world comes to Maxwell's at least once in their life!

Moon's   155 E. 80TH ST.   10021
                650-1096

Feel like running over to a friend's apartment for dinner? Moon's might be just the place. Nestled in the tiny garden apartment of a brownstone and just big enough to seat 30, and complete with its own backyard barbecue grill for preparing lamb, steak, or fish, it's the ideal little spot. Now all you need to do is make friends with Marvin Safir; as all of those vacationers who used to frequent his Bumbleshoot's in Southampton can vouch, he's not too tough to get to know.

Another good friend to make at Moon's is Marie Marquez. As *chef de cuisine,* she can give you an accurate kitchen-side account of which dishes are good on any particular night. The menu is never printed, but is just described by Safir, as it varies according to his day's selections. It usually includes such house favorites as a succulent leg of lamb Provence, grilled over charcoal with herbs and served fresh and flavorsome, or the carpetbagger steak for two, a double or triple shell steak stuffed with oysters seasoned with shallots, herbs and butter, the whole grilled and sliced at table by Moon. A typical day might feature fresh Florida stone crab with mustard sauce, or Bob White quails served with wild rice and followed with endive and Arugula salad. But whatever our choice, we always start our meal with Moon's variation on the escargots theme—plump mussels bathed in garlic butter, then broiled until sizzling. Everything is a la carte—so dinner for two might run about $50.

Moon's decor has the same ethnic country flavor as Marie's cooking. The tiny dining room has the feeling of a cozy French country inn, with an open fireplace, cheerful salmon-tinted walls and polished brass sconces. As for the art, it's less French than back-yard Americana—really, how often are you going to find "Moon over Miami" sheet music hanging in the place of honor in Provence? Oh, well ... Marie manages to ignore it as she turns out yet another frightfully rich chocolate mousse, and once you've tasted her desserts, you'll agree ... who are we to quibble?

The restaurant is closed Sundays, but it's open every other night from 6 to 11.

Mr. and Mrs. Foster's Place 242 E. 81ST ST. 10028
535-1234

As if it isn't enough that she *looks* like your mother, she nags you to death too! But as you might have suspected, the fact that she keeps people coming back despite her demands that they order their entrees when they make their reservations, that they take her advice on how to dress, and that they listen to her warnings about tardiness, can only mean that the food's superlative. It is!

The sign which reads "Mr. and Mrs. Foster's" is such an artsy-craftsy red-on-white combination, it looks as if Mrs. Pearl Foster might just have climbed right on up there and painted it herself. Pearl runs the show alone now in the grand Foster tradition. She's the chef and specializes in American cooking, which by *her* definition includes any sort of dish she happens to fix. Don't bother to quibble about the ancestry of beef Wellington or chicken Polynesian. If Pearl says they're American, just nod your head in agreement and enjoy.

You'll generally be able to recognize Pearl by the black dress, white apron and diaphanous pink silk scarf. Not that she'll be cooking during the dinner hours, but she will be running around making sure that every customer is happy with his or her order. This is one of those restaurants in which you can become friendly with the owner quickly, particularly since she's at your elbow watching every bite.

Pearl's more concerned with cleanliness and nutrition than atmosphere, so don't be surprised to see the icing on your chocolate cheesecake has been smeared on with a spoon. It's that homemade look she's trying for.

The decor isn't much to look at either, but let's talk about the real reason for coming: it is the food! As a rule, Mrs. Foster will start you with a choice of four soups. You might be offered Virginia peanut soup, shrimp consommé, cold apple soup, hot lemon soup, or a corn and shrimp chowder. Typical entrees include Spanish shrimp broiled with dill butter, baked stuffed rainbow trout topped with macadamia nuts, flaming bourbon beef and oyster pot, or her famous crustacean plate with a pound-and-a-half lobster plus a generous helping of shrimp and crab.

Since you've just barely taken the edge off your appetite, she'll be sure to offer dessert. Choose between southern pecan pie, southern yam pie or frosty lime pie.

Mrs. Foster generally takes two seatings: on Saturdays at 6 and 9, and weekdays at 6:30 and 9. (The restaurant is closed on Sundays and Mondays.) The later time tends to draw a more interesting crowd, but whichever you choose, don't be late. Mrs.

Foster and good cooking wait for no man. A steam table has never darkened her door, and if you don't intend to arrive on time, she'd just as soon you didn't either.

A six-course dinner will probably cost $15 to $20 per person, with the addition of a wine from her California list. By the way, from the end of June through the middle of August, Mrs. Foster takes her annual vacation. If you develop a craving for pecan pie during the summer season, you're just going to have to go elsewhere!

Nicola's	146 E. 34TH ST. 10016
	249-9850

It's a literary agent's dream—one trip to Nicola's and he can corner half the authors he's been dreaming of adding to his list. Lots of them stop in, and they each leave behind a memento... a signed copy of a book jacket. Nick loves the idea so much that he frames them and hangs them smack in the middle of his wood-paneled walls. Nora Ephron's *Crazy Salad* is tucked side by side with Doris Day's autobiography; Dan Jenkins' *Semi-Tough* sits next to *Serpico*. Even Peter Maas' *King of the Gypsies* has found a spot to settle at Nicola's.

Authors aren't the only ones fighting to get into Nicola's; the demand is so heavy that reservations are a must, and even then a wait can be expected. Luckily it's only crowded from eight in the evening till four in the morning... show up at 5 A.M. and you're a cinch to get a table.

Since Nick does the seating and takes the orders, you might try getting your table faster by slipping him a copy of your latest book jacket *before* you eat. As for those of you who have yet to write a book (are there any of you left out there?), the wait could be a bit longer. Or perhaps if you told him that you've just returned from his family's hotels in Italy and can't bear to go one more day without a Spagnoli meal, it will do the trick.

There are seventeen tiny tables at Nicola's, five of them in the Orient Express Room. If you're seated there, it's a sure sign that you're traveling second class. Do insist on front-room seating. During the week you might find yourself side by side with

Michael Cody (see... we promised you that you'd have a chance to be written up in the *WWD* Eye column!) or Mario Puzo, but on Saturday night the chances are that you'll find yourself sitting next to a tourist instead. As for Sunday, that's family day at Nicola's—early, relaxed, casual and just full of the right people.

No matter which night we stop in, we like to start our dinner with squid salad or fresh roasted peppers with anchovies. After such a light start, we hardly feel guilty ordering *fruitti di mare,* that wonderful linguini dish with shrimp, lobster, scallops and clams. Now that you're off your diet, you might as well have a broiled veal chop and ratatouille, too. And you wouldn't want to hurt Nick's feelings by saying "no" to his homemade apple tart ... would you?

When you can get all that and still walk out with a dinner check of only about $25 for two, it tempts you to come back with your friends, doesn't it! Be forewarned, Nick only cooks for parties of twenty if they're his *very good* friends. But don't be disappointed—maybe if you bring him *two* book jackets he'll change his mind!

Oh-Ho-So   395 WEST BROADWAY   10012
966-6110

Mary Anne Lam watched her parents run their Chinese restaurant for just enough years to realize that it was the sort of thing she'd simply hate to do herself. After all, as she told them, they always smelled like fried rice! Now that she's running a Chinese restaurant herself, she only has one comment... at least, she points out, hers is *chicken* fried rice! And if that's not class, we just don't know what is!

Besides, Mary Anne spends as much time going from table to table chatting with Calvin Klein, Carol Horn, Cathy Hardwick, or any one of a number of young fashion and film figures as she does serving eggroll. She served lunch to Cher the day she stopped at Tiffany's to get the ring that marked her marriage to Greg Allman, and catered a party for 150 after the Coty awards. Every dinner sees artists from SoHo trading spareribs with models or art dealers, and chauffeurs cooling their heels in the street outside while their well-heeled employers savor Mary Anne's crazy drunk chicken with peanuts, mushrooms and liquor.

Oh-Ho-So is far from the typical Chinese restaurant. She and her husband, artist Kwong Lam, started with an old garage, gutted it, stripped it down to the bare brick walls, then painted heating pipes and steel struts a vivid sky-blue. The place is three stories high, giving you a wonderfully spacious feeling. And though there is a small upstairs seating area which affords you a wonderful view of everything which goes on in the restaurant, you should be forewarned that it can get hot at the top.

A typical night sees dozens of people sharing coconut chicken and conversation at one of the massive claw-footed oak tables, each distinctive, and each collected by Mary Anne and Kwong personally. The two-story-high bamboo plants which shoot up by the carp tank had to be brought back into the city on the top of their Toyota, but the cheesecake and pecan pie which they serve for dessert (who cares if they're not Chinese, Mary Anne happens to like them!) are a bit easier to come by.

Not all the food at Oh-Ho-So is so typically un-Chinese. Some of the favorite dishes include the hotpot filet steak: good-sized strips of steak marinated and served sizzling in a pottery bowl at your table. Swimming along with it in that hotpot are tiny little baby corn ears and scallions, a delicous combination. Try it with spinach and crabmeat as an accompaniment, or with deep-fried squab with lemon.

The menu, which is ceremoniously presented printed on a paper plate, is changed every two weeks. It might include anything from oyster soup to wine crabs Cantonese (crabmeat with honey sauce), from stuffed hot and sweet peppers with garlic sauce to an appetizer tray with crab, oysters, mussels, clams, and spareribs, from steamed fresh carp to the king's lobster salad at a mere $25 per serving (but then you didn't really expect two whole live lobsters steamed with prawns to come cheap, did you?).

This is a wonderful place to visit when you feel like wearing nothing more formal than a pair of jeans and a sweater, but as you might have guessed after listening to a list of Mary Anne's specials, a pair of *tight* jeans is not recommended! After 10 P.M. is a prime time to come for celebrity watching; they seem to want to avoid the early crowds. And, by the way, if you've been wanting to know how that SoHo landmark Spring Street got its name, one visit to the constantly running water in Oh-Ho-So ladies' room will supply the answer.

One If By Land—   17 BARROW ST.   10014
Two If By Sea   255-8649

It used to be Aaron Burr's carriage house. But despite the reputation of its former owner, the chef at One If By Land—Two If By Sea will never betray you.

Armand Justin was an economist with the Treasury Department, and his brother-in-law was with the J. Walter Thompson Advertising Agency when they decided to buy this historical landmark and convert it into a restaurant. The result is a lovely combination of magnificent brick walls, fireplaces, and a rather eclectic collection of simple black chairs or beige ostrich banquettes, candlelit tables and wall sconces, primitive early American rural paintings, mirrors, and contemporary art. When the pianist isn't playing show tunes, the jukebox is featuring Blood, Sweat and Tears. All in all, its the perfect jumping-off point for a night in Greenwich Village. And since their generous bar is a warm and welcome fireside spot that seats over 20, it also makes for a cozy spot to finish a snowy evening. Though the help is dressed formally, and a good portion of the customers come in oozing uptown chic, jeans, too, are welcome and look quite at home. The upstairs balcony is quiet and affords a wonderful view of the whole proceedings, but on cold wet nights we love sitting among the couches and fireplaces on the first floor. And in the warmth of summer the light and airy outdoors dining area is a must.

The food is good, but not gourmet. You might start with chilled melon slices with a lime-honey dressing, or snails Rapa Nue. There's also a lovely cold vichyssoise or a tasty clam chowder and a delicious bacon, mushroom and spinach salad.

The service is exquisite. Busboys whisk crumbs from the table while the maître d' adopts you as foster children for the duration of your stay. He might recommend shrimp in beer batter with an orange honey mustard sauce for an entree, nine or ten overwhelmingly large crustaceans dripping in sweet, mustard sauce. Or he could bring you the crisp duckling with bing cherries. For a lighter evening meal, try the scallops cooked in white wine and served with carrots and zucchini . . . with the desserts that are about to follow, that light touch will be welcome!

A decision between the chocolate layer cake, a praline cheesecake, a cheesecake made with amaretto, and a marvelous Black Forest cake is not an easy one to face when you're already weakened by a generous dinner. So make your task easier by opting for *our* favorite, that praline cheesecake.

One If By Land is a warm and comfortable restaurant made even more so by the consistent presence of welcoming hosts, Armand and Mario. Rex Harrison and Earl Wilson like to hold birthday parties there. But don't *you* wait for a celebration. One If By Land—Two If By Sea is open seven days a week.

Orsini's 41 W. 56TH ST. 10019
757-1698

As you do the Luncheon Circuit, your first stop may be La Grenouille if you are a recent disciple of *Women's Wear Daily,* but if you are a true believer and have followed the Beautiful People, Cat Pack and Fun People from the days when they were merely "jet set," you'll go to Orsini's without hesitation. To be seen at the Big O, or better yet, to have your picture taken there, is still positive proof that you have arrived. You'd best be dressed for the occasion. We suggest you choose an American designer for your initial Orsini appearance. There are so many Seventh Avenue faces at lunch that you're bound to pick something by one of them. Bill Blass certainly wouldn't comment if he saw you in one of his designs, but he'd definitely remember you. We know Françoise de la Renta would be touched to see you've chosen Oscar's little black dress.

The tall, dark and handsome man (aren't they all at Orsini's?) you see talking to Françoise is either Oscar (but you'd know him at a glance) or Armando Orsini. Armando and his brother Elio started the restaurant almost 25 years ago when it was merely a coffeehouse. It was ten years ago when the brothers added the second floor and that little coffeehouse became the 12-to-3 home for the chic.

Lunch is served only in the second-floor dining room. When you've known Nino for a while, he'll seat you at one of the banquettes along the wall or at a sought-after round table. Act nonchalant if you're seated next to Adolfo. But for dinner ask Isodoro to seat you at a table near the bar on the main floor—the downstairs is far more romantic.

Not everyone comes here for the food. They think that all there is to the Big O is chic, chic, chic. Those fools. They overlook the *mozzarella in carrozza* as an appetizer; they pass up the *trenette al pesto* with the delicious flavor only the freshest basil can give. They haven't delighted to scampi with Orsini's special sauce. Chef Renaldo Morandi wouldn't think of using anything but *plume de veau* in his veal piccata. And we wouldn't think of ordering it anywhere else; Renaldo has spoiled us. We're even more spoiled when it comes to fish—we only order fish that Elio caught that morning and rushed back. The striped bass is heavenly. Do you suppose it could have anything to do with his bait?

The fettuccine Alfredo merits special mention. Renaldo prepares it exactly the way we loved it in Rome with never too much cream. Though we've tried, we can't get the recipe for carbonara sauce; it's truly one of those family secrets that has been pleasing customers for 25 years.

Orsini's is still serving supper when most restaurants have closed. Though the real scene is at lunch and dinner, many fashionable people do stop in after the theater.

The Oyster Bar GRAND CENTRAL TERMINAL
E. 42ND. ST.   10017

As long as you don't *have* to, there's something almost invigorating about fighting the hurried masses at Grand Central Station. Particularly when you know there's a place like the Oyster Bar to recuperate once the initial rush is over.

The first problem you'll have with the Oyster Bar is finding it; the best solution is to simply give up, swallow your pride, and ask the local news vendor. Once he's steered you correctly down to the second level, you'll find the refurbished Oyster Bar, a cavernous combination of redwood paneling, brown upholstery and marble pillars, where mink coats mingle with wrinkled work shirts. The casual, congenial clatter can get to be a bit much at times; if you want a quiet lunch, turn to Stanley in the salon room. If you'd rather be elbow-to-elbow with the masses, stand right up at the oyster bar and choose from nine different varieties.

Fresh fish has been the major draw at this underground institution for over 60 years—when the Fulton Fish Market's closed, so is the Oyster Bar, which means you'll have to limit your visits to weekdays. Dinner's a bit quieter, but lunch is much more fun. You'll find Andrew Haskell, president of Time-Life publications, choosing between bluepoints at 38 cents apiece, malpeques at 80 cents, and Bay Laan from Maine at 85 cents each. Ramsey Clark has been known to favor the oyster stew, which is a New York classic. And as for you, you can pick your own Maine lobster from the tank as you walk in and then order it plain or stuffed. The price for this varies from day to day, depending upon the extent of the lobster catch and the going wholesale rate . . . negotiate before you eat!

Menus are printed daily, with prices omitted from those items which haven't been available fresh that morning. You might be choosing from a whole Florida pompano at $6.10 or fresh perch with hot biscuits and french fries at just $5.35. Don't fret about the reasonable prices, you can always up the ante by ordering one of the 152 California white wines which are featured on the back of the menu. Or go for broke and order the bouillabaisse at $6.50 . . . it's the next best thing to the South of France! As for the cold buffet, our favorite is the scallops and mussels in mustard vinaigrette served in half an avocado.

If you're planning to hold a private party at the bar while you're in town, you might want to duplicate the menu that was prepared to honor five of France's premier chefs: Malpeque belon: Wellfleet oysters served with a Mondavi Fumé Blanc; bay scallops and mussels in mustard vinaigrette and Heitz Pinot Blanc; Philadelphia snapper soup; Maine lobster from Spruce

Harbor with Michelob beer, followed by Chateau St. Jean Johannisberg Riesling 1974; and then for dessert there was...

P. J. Clarke's
915 THIRD AVE. 10022
RESERVATIONS: 759-1650; FRONT: 355-8857

And to think they're stuck in such an unpicturesque neighborhood! That low red-brick building nestled among the midtown skyscrapers on 55th and Third is P. J. Clarke's. It was built in 1890, and despite the encroachment of 100-story wonders, owner Danny Lavezzo and his many devotees have managed to fight progress and preserve their hangout.

It's open 365 days a year—but unless you're one of Frankie's buddies, be sure to make a lunch or dinner reservation, or you may have to wait. Not that we wish to imply that he favors his steady friends, but we *did* hear of one couple from Kansas that's been standing at P. J. Clarke's bar for so long that the price of the hamburgers has gone up three times. What's worse, the bar's so busy (averaging bodies four deep on weeknights), it's rumored they haven't even seen each other for two days!

Today the place with its glass-enclosed bar and large warm restaurant is a landmark, a habit for most of the New York bachelor set, and a home away from home for ad execs and businessmen, as well as the next best thing to being at the game on football nights. Don't be surprised if the man next to you is Bill Rudin, Jeff Sheretsky, or Willis Reed.

P. J.'s chalks its menu up on blackboards and consistently tries to include everything from truly divine hamburgers with cheese and bacon to relatively rarefied chicken breast and vichyssoise. If you've worked up a big appetite, order their smothered steak and down it with a selection from their extensive list of imported beers—Danish Tuborg, Yugoslavian Pilsner—P. J.'s has suds from every country! While the veal sauté marsala is as good as most you'll find, the homemade apple and walnut pie is obviously head and shoulders above almost every other slice in the city!

Sunday brunch is so busy that business doesn't slow down from 11:30 A.M. until late afternoon. But you don't really mind spending an hour loafing in blue jeans by the front room jukebox if a bowl of P. J.'s chili will be waiting for you at the end of your vigil . . . do you?

The Palace	420 E. 59TH ST. 10022
	355-5150

You have donated your Renoir to the Metropolitan with the request that you remain anonymous. You've lent your villa in Majorca to Caroline Kennedy for a disco party. Valery Giscard d'Estaing has sent a note to remind you that you left your skis at his chalet in Courchevel. You are ready for dinner at the Palace.

It won't bother you that the prix fixe is $65 per person, but we know you'd prefer owner Frank Valenza to simply raise it to $75 and forget the mandatory 23 percent gratuity. It does make such a messy bill. If you order his best wine he will have to add $300; wine is not included in the prix fixe. All in all it is a small price to pay for a nice dinner and wine. What's money for, if you can't enjoy yourself?

At the Palace, money is for effect. Perhaps the eight-course meal could cost less, but how would Frank and his wife Bibbi ever get any return on their half-million-dollar investment? They set out to create the most elegant restaurant in the city, and they did, right down to the $10 crystal cocktail glasses. The 50 guests who can be seated by maître d' Guy come to feel pampered and most could care less that the Maryland soft-shell crabs are oozing with caviar butter or that you can actually hear the rolls crack as you break them. They like the atmosphere.

It would be difficult not to be entertained by Claude, the captain. He does encourage you to speak French and will help with any words you might have forgotten. He may not explain that *perles noires de la Volga* is the same Russian caviar you get at other fine restaurants, but he will tell you that the quenelle of sole is absolutely fresh and garnished with pistachios and white raisins.

You will be served eight full courses. Your wineglass will never be less than half full, nor will any plate remain on your table when you've taken your last bite. The service, as you might expect, is flawless.

With Claude's help and our dear waiter's patience, we chose our meal from the right side of the menu—*l'escriteau*—but next time we will exercise the privilege of calling in advance for the *sur commande* choices on the left (Chef Claude Baills tells us his bouillabaisse has yet to meet its match). *Pour commencer,* choose Russian caviar with gravlaks: Scotch salmon cured in dill marinade. Next the lobster bisque flaming with cognac; the cream of mussel soup with saffron and bay scallops is pure heaven. Then the soft-shelled crabs swimming in caviar butter or the scallops *provençale.* Cleanse your palate with lemon ice floating in cassis as you contemplate the entrees to come . . . the veal, the lamb, the capon. Delight in the salad, so refreshing in its lightness, followed by *les fromages, les fruits* and toasted Bremner wafers. Nearly three hours after you entered the Palace, you will still be feasting on desserts . . . mousses chocolate and strawberry, apple tarts sprinkled with Calvados, petits fours, more pastries. Even as you sip your coffee, you will be offered miniature ice cream balls dipped in chocolate. The brandies and cognac will come later, at your leisure.

Bibbi spent a quarter of a million dollars dressing the Palace. Each new setting of sterling is gleaming. The Irish linen tablecloths look lovely, even with the crumbs from those flaky dinner rolls. Frank explains that the sterling silver trolley which goes into the kitchen is worth $15,000. We love the flowered carpets, the red carnations at every table, the crystal cocktail stirrers. But what can we expect from a place called the Palace that is so quietly tucked into the Sovereign apartment house near Sutton Place?

The unlisted phone number is 355-5152. A Dior would be fine for her, a Cardin suit for him.

The Palm
837 SECOND AVE. 10017
682-9515

To sum it up, it's real! Even the sawdust on the floor is the genuine article. The waiters are really fast and noisy. The clientele is really a cross section of Americana. The food is really good!

The Palm was started three generations ago by a Ganzi and a Bozzi. Today it's run by Walter Ganzi, Jr. and Bruce Bozzi, neither of whom would consider changing the customs their father and grandfather set before them. Cousin Larry runs the Palm Too across the street. Walter and Bruce brought him in when the overflow from their original restaurant became so great that they decided to have more seating across the street. That's fine for Larry, but it's not so good for you. Accepting a table in the Palm Too will deprive you of half the charm of the restaurant (the other half being the unsurpassed steaks and lobsters). You'll miss the Steve Canyon characters Milton Caniff used to paint on the walls to pay for his dinner before his hero made him rich and famous. You'll miss meeting Marino, the only waiter in the world known to have beaten football's own Sam Huff at arm wrestling (if Marino recommends something to you, don't argue!). You'll miss the clatter of the downstairs and the quiet of the upstairs. The only thing you won't miss is the prices.

Dinner for two at The Palm will cost you about $50. It may even cost you $100. That's not hard to understand when you start adding a $25.00 double steak to a $25.00 lobster to a $2 chopped tomato and onion salad and a $2.50 order of creamed spinach. Throw in $2.50's worth of cottage fries and a $2.50 slice of New York cheesecake (what else!) and the whole thing becomes clear. Be grateful we're telling you these things—no one's going to give you a menu or prices. You'll have to listen to your waiter to find out what's available, and really, you wouldn't want to embarrass him by asking him how much things cost, would you?

Some people say that these are the best steaks and fries in the country; Jack the doorman, for one. But then he's been here for 20 years, so he's bound to have developed some loyalty. Those people lined up waiting for a table don't have any reason to be loyal, though, and if they're willing to wait an hour to pick up a $100 check in a no-reservation restaurant, it *must* be good. It's at times like these you're glad you know Walter and Bruce! You may be the only recent arrival who gets an immediate table.

Mac Miller, the president of the American Cartoon Association, is the one who does those wonderful caricatures that cover the walls and ceiling. He's already immortalized your neighbor—Peter Falk—at the table across the way. Smile nicely, drop in often, and before you know it, he may be painting you, too!

Parioli	1466 FIRST AVE.	10021
Romanissimo	288-2391	

He remembers to give Babe Paley small portions, to feed her husband William cream sauce instead of tomato, and to keep meat away from Lillian Hellman's plate. The personality of the owner, declares Rubrio Rossi, is 40 percent of the success of a restaurant; and in the case of Parioli Romanissimo, the owner's personality is slanted toward pleasing his guests. You won't find better Italian food than at Parioli Romanissimo (four stars, my dear), or nicer people, either!

And to think that the Rossis were considering opening a boutique, instead! Game lovers (no, not baccarat) rejoice that they didn't, particularly during the winter when partridge and quail arrive accompanied by rich, red Brunello di Montalcino from Tuscany. Rubrio insists it's the only wine in Italy which can be aged as long as 100 years, but really, why wait?

Let Rubrio know you're coming—the restaurant is tiny, seating only about 50, so diners without reservations run the risk of a wait. And though it's noisy, it's worth listening to. If you're not overhearing Ruth Gordon and Garson Kanin raving about the chocolate cake, you'll be eavesdropping on Stephen Smith while he savors his carpaccio. And of course if you get a table toward the front of the raised, grillworked dais you'll have a splendid view of Mike Nichols, David Rockefeller, and Senator Javits when they rush in for a pasta fix.

The room is semiformal... a warm combination of red brick, kerosene lamps, and old art nouveau windows. You'll want to complement it by dressing for the occasion. Don't be shy about wearing an Oscar de la Renta. He's in so often with Françoise that they're all but commonplace at Parioli Romanissimo.

Once in, soothe your nerves with a negroni, a 100 percent

Italian combination of campari, vermouth, and gin. If you're terrifically hungry, follow it with *tortellini alla parma,* topped with nutmeg, cream sauce, and truffles in season, or with *antipasto Parioli,* stuffed mushrooms, baked shrimp, mussels, and clams. If you'd prefer to leave wearing the same size eight de la Renta in which you entered, order the endive and arugala salad instead. For your entree you'll want to try the beef *a la romana* with capers, mushrooms, artichokes, and a light red Grignolino. Accompany it with asparagus sautéed in butter and cheese. Then celebrate finishing all that food by ordering espresso and a slim glass of Sambuca with its own fresh coffee bean.

Real Parioli lovers come often. They always remember to ask for the venison even though it's not on the menu, and to ask for the back banquettes if they feel like a bit of peace and quiet, even if they're *not* quite so chic!

Patsy's 236 W. 56TH ST. 10019
247-3491

Although his sons Sal and Joe operate his 35-year-old Italian restaurant these days, Papa Patsy says he still gets his say-so in the kitchen. Some people think the light olive oil is the secret to his *linguine marechiare,* but we know better—it's Patsy.

Try to get a table upstairs if you can. You'll find the same bright lights and plastic flowers that you find downstairs, but the walls are a cheery pink and the noise level is lower. You may feel a bit tacky surrounded by those red velvet picture frames and the lighted sconces, but once you taste the scrumptious scallopine and the zesty ziti, you'll forget about the atmosphere. Everyone else has!

You won't go wrong ordering anything here. You particularly won't go wrong ordering the shrimp and baked clams or stuffed eggplant and mushrooms to start. Dinner for two might run $25, but if you're just in the mood for an inexpensive Italian fling, some *linguine marechiare* with hot peppers, clams, garlic, and tomatoes plus a glass of the house wine for each of you will only bring your total to $12. And if you have a sweet tooth do try the rum cake—it's only $1.30. Hot towels after dinner are a nice touch, and *they're* on the house!

A number of celebrities frequent Patsy's, and each new star gets his picture added to the family album on the walls. Frank Sinatra was a steady customer for a while. Mama Concetta insists that his pictures stay up, in hopes that he'll come back soon.

Pearl's Chinese Restaurant	38 W. 48TH ST. 10036 586-1060

During her forty years in business, the empress of New York's Chinese cuisine has built a list of devotees that's longer than most of those Oriental scrolls you saw preserved in the Metropolitan. You remember, that museum you went to after your last visit to Tiffanys? So when you aren't in the mood for French food, and a hamburger just won't do, depend upon Pearl. And don't worry about what you're going to have . . . just worry about how you're going to get *in!* Especially on Sunday night; with her years of standing reservations, it's as good as a club by the tail end of the weekend.

Once you get in, Pearl will order for you anyway. Just tell the little lady how much spice you can handle and leave the rest to her. But if she hasn't brought out that special Peking duck and lemon chicken before you see the fortune cookies coming, *do* request a bit of each.

You won't find petrified fire-breathing dragons or packs of Foo dogs on the walls at *this* Oriental hideaway. Pearl's is decorated in the best of taste. But then would a shareholder like Geraldine Stutz of Bendel's or Donald Brooks have it any other way? Of course not. Brown carpet creeps up the walls to set off white enameled Stendig chairs. You'll find 26 tables, every one of them packed, so be sure to make a reservation before you go.

Among Pearl's two luncheon seatings and three dinner seatings you'll find a mixed array of television personalities, executives and designers. Its cool, clean decor makes it a relaxing respite for lunch—just ask Gene Shalit or Jim Hartz, who make it a weekly habit—and its chic evening crowd attracts regular patronage from director Sidney Lumet and his wife Gail.

So enjoy your dinner, and your fortune cookie, too. What did it say? Oh, yes... "He who brings six after making a reservation for four eats on the sidewalk." Keep it in mind—and if you really want to enjoy good luck, *do* call ahead!

Pietro's   201 E. 45TH ST.   10017
                                    682-9760

Luckily the food's marvelous, because the atmosphere is less than elegant; even if Leo saves you that very special table by the window, the best you'll see is a second-story view of some rather tired streets. Here it's the people that make the atmosphere: garment industry heads, entertainment types—even David Susskind reports that he loves it.

Nat Donini is both owner and chef. Though his kitchen is probably the tiniest little thing you've ever seen, he manages to cook everything to order. And yes, that *does* include those things you feel like ordering even though you *don't* see them on the menu. As aromas escape and you look around the room you'll discover that your biggest problem at Pietro's is indecision—anyone who can sit there without coveting at least six of the entrees that go by is inhuman.

The general atmosphere is casual, but if you insist on wearing a jacket, ask for a table downstairs. Those who don't feel up to that degree of formality opt for the upstairs room, where jackets are not required. As for reservations, if you're without one you may have to look elsewhere for your Veal Milanese. Pietro's is very small, very busy, and possesses only four bar stools, so they don't really cater to a crowd of reservationless diners hovering around waiting for a table.

The dinner menu never changes, but lunch is different every day. Despite all this variety, we have our special favorites. We wouldn't dream of starting off without a half-order of scampi—it really is delicious. Their steaks are among the best in the city, though we can't help but think that the chicken broiled with garlic is even better—so perfect with broccoli Hollandaise on the side! As for dessert, Pietro regulars know that even with zabaglione, spumoni and tortoni available, it's the melon that's a real winner. Or maybe it's that Pietro regulars know that after antipasto and lobster *fra diavolo* with linguine and lobster sauce, the melon is the only thing they'll have room for!

La Petite Ferme   973 LEXINGTON AVE.   10021

                                                   249-3272

Part of the charm of Greenwich Village was a minuscule restaurant called La Petite Ferme. Its Village ambiance beckoned even the uptowners like Oscar de la Renta and Jackie Onassis, the downtowners like Gloria Steinem, and the out-of-towners like St. Laurent and Valentino. Now it's moved uptown.

If it's fully booked (as usual), you'll find yourself bumping elbows with the person next to you. If you suffer the least bit from claustrophobia, forgo Charles Chevillot's restaurant. We hope that you'll overcome the phobia, however, as it *would* be a shame to miss Monsieur Chevillot's billi-bi, a mussel soup with a dab of cream, parsley, onions and stock. You'll find daily treasures listed on the blackboard menu—anything from steak *au poivre* served with delicious shredded zucchini, to filet of sole; from individual plates of shredded carrots, sardines, prosciutto and melon in a basket, to spinach and mushroom salad; from poached bass cooked with shallots and vinegar butter, to cauliflower with purée of potatoes or turnips. Any could be accompanied by a Pouilly-Fuissé or a Chateau Margaux. And all should be followed by La Petite Ferme's famous dessert, *clafoutis,* an apple tart with crepe base simply floating in liqueur.

La Petite Ferme is a mélange of fresh fruit and fresh flowers hanging in brass pots, and copper pots filled with bottles of wine. The dishes are blue and white, and there are oversized cotton napkins. Bread is served on a wooden slab or in rush baskets with a tremendous tub of butter, and by the time you reach dessert, you feel so pastoral that you expect the cows to come home. When you return to reality, expect the tab for two to run about $35.

While Charles is usually there, he is developing a tendency lately to run down to South America and check on his newest restaurant. If he happens to be south of the border when you arrive, ask for our favorite waiter, Pierre. Mention our names and he'll make sure your meal is perfect!

Quo Vadis   26 E. 63RD ST.   10021
                  838-0590

Just to prove how popular it is, Bruno Caravaggi brags that he and partner Gino Robusti have 5,000 on their Christmas card list, all of them charge customers. And while it might be some comfort to know you can charge your meal when you get the bill for their famous Saturday night Beef Wellington, good credit alone won't help you get one of those coveted tables in the bar. You're competing with a few thousand for the honor!

From the start, you know you can expect an Old World elegance and comfort; it's an opulent place, complete with velvet-covered walls in light gold, ceilings painted in fresco, and red velvet banquettes. No wonder Jerry Lewis prefers to eat his steak Diane with caviar in the relative simplicity of that darkened bar! Andy Warhol, Bill Blass, and the princesses (both Lee and Jackie) share that predilection with him, though the main dining room does find a few fans like Mrs. Irving Berlin and Mrs. Richard Rodgers during lunch. With so many familiar faces in residence, we're not even sure if it's important that Gino and Bruno are there to greet you at every meal!

Still, to give them their due, they're part of the tradition. They've been on this ground since they opened the Brussels Restaurant there after the 1939 World Fair. And they're there to this day; maybe it's because they've never had a lonely moment!

The last time we stopped in for dinner we ate cold trout with horseradish sauce while Diana Vreeland sampled her cream of pea soup with noodles at the next table. Our breaded sea bass with mustard sauce was delicious ... but then her rack of lamb looked wonderful, too. Both came with a delicious ratatouille, which you may or may not find on the menu when you stop in as a new one is printed each day on the Quo Vadis printing press.

But what matter—as Bruno points out, the menu is only a suggestion; they're really happy to fix anything you want, particularly if you call a day or two in advance. And of course they're wonderful at helping to plan those special dinner parties—little combinations of *filet of sole Polignac*, beef Wellington with *pommes soufflés*, zucchini, two soufflés for dessert, two wines during dinner and a champagne, all for an amazing $40 per person. Will wonders never cease!

The average price for lunch for two at Quo Vadis would be about $25 (add your own idea of what a wine should cost), for dinner $50. As for the average post-theater crowd, it might contain anyone from Anna Moffo Sarnoff to Beverly Sills, and that's far from average, isn't it!

Rajah's   1204 SECOND AVE.   10021
            355-8100

Le Glacier   1022A MADISON AVE.   10021
               249-2975

As if you didn't already have enough on your mind, we've just found two new ways to fatten you up! Now, now ... don't thank us yet. Wait until you've tasted them to express your gratitude. And if you really like them, be sure to drop us a note. We'll respond posthaste with the address of your local Weight Watchers headquarters. See how thoughtful we are!

The first sinful pleasure is Rajah's. It's such a small street-level ice cream parlor that you might have missed it if you didn't have us to help you along. Rajah's has just four seats in the entire shop. But then you'll probably be so busy running back and forth sampling their cinnamon apple, honeydew, saffron, rose, and pumpkin ice creams that a chair will be the furthest thing from your mind.

Not only does Rajah's make ice cream cones in these rather exotic flavors, they'll prepare their fabulous Indian desserts garnished and decorated for your next dinner party.

You say that saffron on a sugar cone doesn't really tempt you? How about some fresh blueberry frozen yogurt, instead? You'll have to fight your way through the slightly fanatical clientele, but if you do manage to reach Ron Canizares' wooden counter there will be a worthwhile prize waiting for you on the other side.

Le Glacier, Ron's own frozen yogurt parlor, does amazing things with familiar strawberry, raspberry, and vanilla. As if their homemade version of frozen yogurt weren't enough, they're also prepared to heap on fresh fruit, sesame seeds, nuts, freshly grated chocolate, or butternut with a touch of rum. If you're not willing to trust us when we tell you it's better than good, why not ask the lady who's bought nine quarts in two weeks. There she is now . . . that chubby lady in the corner!

To satisfy unmovable frozen yogurt bigots, Le Glacier also serves a wonderful selection of natural ice creams: butterscotch, mocha fudge, walnut, strawberry swirl, blueberry, cantaloupe, peach, coconut, apricot brandy, double chocolate fudge, mango . . . oh, we really shouldn't go on! Why torture you if you haven't planned a trip to New York in the near future.

But if you *have* planned a trip to New York, bear in mind that Le Glacier is open seven days a week. See . . . there's simply no escaping it!

| **Russian** | 150 W. 57TH ST. 10019 |
| **Tea Room** | 265-0947 |

Your table will be waiting for you at Sardi's after the theater, but you really could use a quick snack before. What a bother . . . six-ish is really a bit early to expect them to be serving cold Scotch salmon at Le Madrigal. Luckily Mrs. Stuart Faith Gordon is ready to come to the rescue, just as she has for years and years. You'll find her at the Russian Tea Room, waiting among her blinis and Stroganoff, her dilled meatballs and Sirniki.

The Russian Tea Room is a welcomingly colorful clutter with red booths, pink tablecloths, green walls covered with paintings, and generous bouquets throughout. The name was accurate once, when Mrs. Gordon and her first husband, Sidney, served glasses of tea and cookies. But since then she's broadened her horizons to include complete meals both Russian and American.

You can order table d'hôte or à la carte, but with so many interesting imported dishes to choose from, it seems a shame not to retain your freedom to order dish by dish. Don't finish a meal without their baklava, a thin-layered pastry with ground nuts and honey. You'll love the *kholodetz:* jellied calves feet with horseradish sauce. And of course the blinis with black caviar are an all-time favorite.

Ask Annette to give you a banquette at the side of the room; then settle down to enjoy the sight of Rudolf Nureyev or Virginia Graham, Joan Fontaine or an entire selection of the musicians from Carnegie Hall. Even if you're *not* hungry, it's a wonderful way to sneak a peek at those sold-out Broadway shows!

Sardi's   234 W. 44TH ST.   10036
                               221-8440

Tony Perkins is sitting in one of the "good" banquettes to the left, Jack Gilford is chatting with Ray at the bar, and Tammy Grimes is heading for the Belasco Room upstairs. Ho-hum . . . just one more night like every other night at Sardi's. If you don't see at least a *dozen* of the celebrities caricatured on Sardi's walls show up in person, it means there's been a strike at Actors Equity, because its *the* place for supper after theater; not only for the onlookers, but for the performers, too.

Of course, if you're really part of the in crowd, you'll be upstairs in the Belasco Room waiting for the reviews to come in. Many a tear has been shed there. Even a piece of Sardi's famous *boccone dolce* can't soften the blow when the 11:00 P.M. news tells a producer his new play isn't going to make it. If you wangle an invitation to this upstairs haven, do try to be quick on your feet. Its all one can do just to stay out of the way while the producers, actors, and publicity people pace nervously by those opening-night TV sets. But it's worth the risk—one good word from Richard Eder and the champagne flows!

If by some freak of circumstance you *haven't* wangled an invitation to the Belasco Room, you're going to have to make sure you get a good table. One possible way is to study those caricatures on the wall—arrive with one of those famous faces, and Mr. Sardi and George will make sure you're not left sitting in the back. Besides, if you arrive with someone who's familiar with Sardi's, they'll even help you find your way through the menu.

If they're a good friend they'll recommend that you start with the smoked trout with horseradish, a fresh spinach, zucchini, and bacon salad, and that wonderful homemade cannelloni. If they're an even *better* friend they'll watch out for your waistline and tell you to just have the hot shrimp a la Sardi or the avocado stuffed with lump crabmeat instead.

Lunch at Sardi's is fine (with the exception of Wednesday afternoon when the matinee crowd arrives from out of town), and after-theater supper is a wonderful time for deviled beef bones with mustard sauce or eggs Benedict. And just any time is the perfect time for deal-making. But if you don't happen to have a hot play or a need for Broadway angels, comfort yourself with an extra helping of the frozen cake with zabaglione sauce, and watch the action.

| **Sea Fare** | 25 W. 56TH ST. 10019 |
| **of the Aegean** | 581-0540 |

Here's a wonderful way to see impressionist paintings while you nibble on Greek olives and feta cheese. And while owner Chris Bastis tells us that he gets many requests from various international museums to lend them some of his art, *we've* always been more prone to ask him to loan us his recipe for Aegean *flogiara* (just the perfect dessert to serve the next time you have a Greek shipping magnate to dinner!).

While you're at it, you might convince him to give you his recipe for shrimp Santorini style; jumbo Mexican shrimp baked with Greek feta cheese and grilled with tomato and Santorini sauce. Or if you don't like shrimp, there is a marvelous steamed Monock striped bass, also in casserole, with mixed ground herbs and sherry.

Sea Fare of the Aegean has a cozy and intimate atmosphere in which to enjoy a great variety of fish and shellfish. There are specialities which range from bouillabaisse to Maine lobster, from curries to creoles. Of course, selecting between them becomes ever more difficult when you're distracted by a menu decorated with reproductions of the marvelous art hanging in the restaurant itself—you know how hard it is to concentrate on broiled spring chicken or baked apples when what you really have on your mind is whether Chris's Vlaminck painting would be right for that bare corner in your living room.

As for the seating, though, the decision is simple. Banquette No. 6 on the street floor (Sea Fare has three stories) is really the only place to be seen. Of course, you must resign yourself to moving on to No. 4 or 5 if Frank Sinatra or Carol Burnett happens to be in—it's their favorite spot. And at lunch, don't count on getting that nice round second banquette on the left without having Leo Jaffe, chairman of the board of Columbia Pictures, put up a fight. But Chris is so pleasant, most of the time you'll find it a simple matter to sit wherever you please.

Naturally *we* wouldn't dream of eating before 8:30 or 9:00, P.M., but Costos, our favorite maître d', tells us people have been known to be seated and ordering at Sea Fare as early as 4:30 in the afternoon. Really... have you ever heard of such a thing? Maybe they're just determined to get their order of fresh strawberries or Aegean peaches with rum sauce in before the supply is exhausted.

Sea Fare's decor was inspired by the Palace of Knossos, a combination of columns and vivid reds from the Minoan period on the island of Crete. And after all, isn't it nice to know that even if that shipping magnate doesn't fall head over heels in love with you when he's plied with *flogiara,* you can still be a Grecian princess for a day for just the price of a bottle of Retsina Cambas and an Aegean salad?

Serendipity   225 E. 60TH ST.   10022
                 838-3531

According to Webster, "serendipity" means the art of finding the unusual or the pleasantly unexpected by chance or sagacity. According to Stephen Bruce and Calvin Holt, it's all that plus a taste for desserts and espresso. And had Webster had the opportunity to sample Mrs. Milton's lovely fudge pie or Aunt Bubba's sand tarts, he'd surely accept the newer definition.

Serendipity is a whimsical blend of marble-topped ice cream tables, hanging Tiffany lamps, a two-ton clock from 1918, ceiling fans, and out-of-work actors and artists disguised as waiters. You're as likely to find a loaf of bread shaped like a valentine heart there as you are to locate an implausibly large banana split topped with that rarity, real whipped cream—because the owners have established a refreshingly different boutique of collectibles while establishing their modestly priced restaurant.

Serendipity is now located on East 60th Street, one of the most unusual shopping streets in the city, for every store located there seems to have managed to maintain its individuality in the face of Manhattan's daily changes. Serendipity is no exception. When you walk down the three steps leading in, you'll suddenly be standing amidst hanging T-shirts, enormous tapestries, dishes, books, improbable dolls, all sorts of posters, handmade soaps, and anything else that Stephen and Calvin have stumbled across and designated as special enough to wear a "for sale" sign in their store. It would be worth a trip just to browse through their crafts and their own house newspaper (when you're not around 60th Street you can always pick one up at the Museum of Modern Art). But there's better news in store for you—Serendipity has all those things you've loved indulging in since you were a kid: ice cream sundaes, banana splits, mochachinno, and foot-long hot dogs with chili and onions. More grown-up tastes will appreciate the jellied chicken consommé and curried chicken amandine. If salads are your thing, there's a shrimp-stuffed avocado for just $4.75, or you might order an omelet of green chilis and cheese with sour cream for $4. And of course there are always the good old American treats like hamburgers with barbecue sauce and chicken salad sandwiches with watercress ($3.50).

But on to the *pièce de résistance;* half of New York shows up at Serendipity just for the desserts. Choose from pecan pie with or without chocolate, lemon icebox pie, dark double-chocolate mousse, and the fruit and cheese plate. But don't have any of them without an accompanying Tiffany (piping hot espresso with honey and whipped cream) or a frothy cappuccino with a topsy-turvy whipped cream peak. There are all types of teas, too—jasmine, Ceylon, Uruguay.

All in all, attitude is the name of the game at Serendipity. The entire Bloomingdale's crowd knows that it can come here on Saturday afternoon to move their pulse rate down after a hectic morning of fighting for Ralph Lauren tennis clothes. Even Sue Mengers, the famous Hollywood agent, feels free to sit in relative privacy. Bette Davis wasn't so lucky. She was a regular who finally had to stop coming in because her waiter was so enamored of her he kept insisting on picking up her check.

The Sherry-Netherland Grill   781 FIFTH AVE. (AT 59TH ST.)   10022
                                    355-2800

The Sherry-Netherland Grill is, and always has been, a clubby, warm, low-ceilinged room in masculine greens and blacks. There's a nice long bar with brightly polished brass trim, just long enough to serve as a resting spot for drinks for everyone from the fashion, show-business and cosmetics industries.

Look for a lunch table at the Grill and you'll find yourself competing with Bill Cosby and Dick Cavett. Try to elbow your way into the bar at 6:00 P.M. and you'll be in a contest with the entire city. The Grill *does* take reservations for tables at the cocktail hour, but if you're five minutes late, you've forfeited yours. And don't count on getting the one by the door anyway—it always goes to the owner of the Philadelphia Eagles.

The Grill is owned today by a triumvirate—Eddie Clauss, Tony Cece and George Bagazi. Now you may have heard—heaven knows we did—that the Sherry-Netherland Grill was falling into a state of disrepute. Those rumors were put to rest as soon as Eddie, Tony, and George entered the scene. Their first step was to bring back fresh caviar so that the place would be every bit as good as it was when Prince Obolensky ran it, and starting at that vaunted point, you can just imagine the rest.

Beyond arranging for suitable piano solos for entertainment, the three partners are taking care to ensure that every dish the Grill serves is of the highest quality. Every day will reveal a new *plat du jour*, and with two head chefs planning for a seating of 40 customers, each will get special attention.

Is that Michael Cody sitting in the corner with June Weir taking notes for the "Eye" column of *Women's Wear Daily?* Maybe they're noting the fact that Danny Kaye just came in for lunch, or that Luba was here in between designs. Eva Gabor has her special table, as does Estée Lauder. And George Burns spends so much time there that Eddie even had to make arrangements to bring the pianist in on Sundays to keep him entertained.

Business lunch... end-of-the-day drinks... or late-night piano. It's hard to choose a favorite hour for the Sherry-Netherland Grill.

Shezan   8 W. 58TH ST.   10019
371-1414

Sorry you didn't get invited to at least *one* tiger hunt before they became nonexistent? Always had a yen to be an Indian sultan? Provinces are getting considerably harder to come by these days, but you *can* still enjoy at least one night of Indian splendor through the simple device of taking a trip to Shezan.

We haven't had such exquisite Indian food since we left London; but then we haven't been at a Shezan since the last time we were in London. The New York version of this British restaurant offers the same cuisine that made it a four-star selection on the Continent. And while gray-carpeted walls and a reflective aluminum ceiling may seem less than authentic, the Indo-Pakistani-Bangladesh artifacts will serve to remind you of the exotic offerings to come.

First ask for one of those plush suede banquettes you'll find in the larger dining room; then make yourself at home with the menu, which is the same for lunch and dinner. Our favorites are the dishes prepared in Shezan's tandooris, those huge clay pots which serve as India's roasting ovens (yes, of course they're self-cleaning!). Since this sort of cooking is so hard to find in New York, we always make it a point to have at least one tandoori dish at the table. Usually it's a skewer of tender lamb, chicken, or beef, fragrantly marinated and just perfect with those dry spicy cakes of deep-fried lamb and lentils they call *shammi kebab luckhnawi.* Shezan's version of *harahi kebab khyberi* is sensational, too—a sumptuous portion of diced chicken grilled with spices, chopped tomato, and green peppers.

Curry fans can choose a vegetable version which is only mildly peppery and redolent with coriander; gingery *bhuna gosht* (lamb) curry; or *chingiro jhol,* a shrimp curry throbbing with hot peppers. But with any of the three, be sure to order *raita,* the seasoned blended yogurt that will prevent your mouth from becoming as spicy as your entree. No meal at Shezan is complete without a *meetha* (dessert). Our favorite is the *halwa Mumtaz Mahal,* a sweetly potent concoction of fresh fruits and almond-flavored milk with shreds of saffron. We've heard that some people enjoy it because the pudding is so extravagantly light. As for us, the attraction comes on top of the dessert—but then you know how we are, edible silver leaf *always* gives us such sweet memories of Tiffany's!

| **SoHo Charcuterie** | 195 SPRING ST. | 10012 |
| **and Restaurant** | 226-3545 | |

It used to be an Italian restaurant. It also used to be dreary. Not now... not since Francine Scherer and Madeline Poley decided that catering for the Museum of Modern Art out of their apartment kitchens was not enough to keep them busy. Voilá: the Soho Charcuterie and Restaurant.

This trendy addition to Soho is a minimally decorated white-on-white restaurant offering the traditional French charcuterie, chock full of a sampling of pâtés, strawberry cream cheese, tuna curry and German style liverwurst with sliced onion.

Half the designers on Seventh Avenue send their assistants out to fetch little lunches consisting of vegetarian heroes (Brie, avocado, tomato, green pepper and vinaigrette on French bread); the other half comes in personally to nibble on *croque madame* (with chicken or ham) or a wonderful little brioche stuffed with lobster salad. You might spot Oscar de la Renta sipping almond syrup and soda water (those in the know call it *orzata*), while John Anthony sits across that virginal room fighting the desire to order a slice of Miss Grimble's famous cheesecake. It's popular with Wall Street types, too.

Dinner is a slightly more elaborate affair (enough so to attract Diana Vreeland and Charlotte Ford), with a wonderful medley of late-night faces jamming in during the 11 P.M. to midnight period. You'll suddenly find yourself subjected to impossible choices offered by Mss. Scherer and Poley: will it be fresh sole delicately sautéed with pine nuts after being marinated in dark beer and anisette ($9.75), or rare breast of duck garnished with pears and figs, topped with pâté and served on a generous mound of wild rice ($19)? Or would you be even happier with the chicken breast stuffed with *pâté verte* and served with spinach and mornay sauce ($8.50)? You can start with a rabbit pâté or a smoked salmon mousse with caviar; you can proceed to a wonderful soup of leeks, potatoes, and apples; and then you can accompany that entree with an order of freshly braised endive. And of course you'll want to sample the orange mousse served in the merest shell of fresh orange.

This probably isn't any time to mention brunch to you; but be brave for a moment and listen. Not only can the Charcuterie grace your Sunday mornings with a selection of omelets, eggs, quiches, smoked fish platters and salads, but they'll also let you choose among three wonderful "banquets" New York style (no, darling, that's not the one where they jostle you and shout a little on the way to the table!) Irish style, or French style. The New Yorker will receive a platter of smoked fishes, creamed herring, a wedge of Jarlsberg, a variety of cream cheeses, and a basket of bagels. The French connoisseur will enjoy his choice of quiches, salad, and a pannier of croissants and brioches with sweet butter and homemade preserves. And the Irish will receive fried or scrambled eggs with a platter of Irish bacon and blood sausage, home-fried potatoes, toast, and Irish soda bread with sweet butter and orange marmalade.

By this time you must be convinced; you'll want to know that Madalyn is the one to call for reservations. And by the way, when you call her, ask her if the Charcuterie has gotten its wine license yet. After all, one should know ahead of time if it's bring-your-own vintage Bordeaux.

Tavern on the Green	CENTRAL PARK WEST AT 67TH ST. 10023
	873-3200

Don't have your limousine deliver you to owner Warner LeRoy's pastoral front door—it would be far more fitting to commission a carriage at the Plaza and ride through Central Park to the Tavern on the Green. All that pomp and circumstance is just what Warner LeRoy's latest enterprise deserves. If you'd prefer to ride your own horse in for Sunday brunch, rest assured that Warner has provided one in help to guard the horses and one in help to guard the bicycles while their respective owners dine on cold salmon, lamb stew, and turkey in aspic. It's hard to believe that it used to be a sheepfold when you're picking through the caviar, isn't it!

You might have heard that it cost Warner $3,000,000 to refurbish the historic Tavern, but did you know the city still owns it (and gets $60,000 in rent)? Oh, well, Warner had a dream, and no municipal ordinances could deter him. Once he realized his previous dream, Maxwell's Plum, he set his sights on something bigger, more spectacular and more in keeping with his razzle-dazzle Hollywood image. He found the last 9,000 feet of wormy chestnut in the whole country and paneled the Elm Room with the wood. He tracked down the company that made the street lamps on the Champs-Élysées to order lights for the entrance to the Tavern. He assembled sixty cooks, and six full-time polishers who do nothing but clean the antique Baccarat and Waterford chandeliers. As Andy Warhol gasped while standing next to us in the buffet line at the opening party, "Look at those chandeliers, look at those chandeliers. I just love it here. I want to come back and get a chicken sandwich on potato bread. It's only two-fifty."

The restaurant's practical charms aren't lost on a host of New Yorkers who glory in dining amid cherub-bedecked ceilings, glittering period glass, floral-printed tablecloths and light white chairs. The airy feel of floor-to-ceiling windows is continued in an outdoor dining area that lets you be a part of the park.

Dazzling deer romp in the rafters, while fresh flowers bloom all around. The Tavern is a combination of fun and whimsically wonderful workmanship.

When the Tavern opened, 600 guests turned out to see what Warner could do to top Maxwells. Eugene McCarthy stood next to Mollie Parnis; Richard Rodgers got food tips from James Beard; and all were impressed with the mountainous ice cream sundae that was double anything Guinness ever heard of (7,250 pounds of ice cream, 150 pounds of chocolate topping, 50 pounds of nuts and strawberries, and 25 pounds of cherries). Naturally they all loved the idea that this Central Park pavilion wasn't priced just for the rich—hamburgers are about $2.85, rack of lamb for two is around $24.50, and for $18.50 the Beluga caviar comes complete with buckwheat blinis.

Warner's Tavern is so much fun just as it is, we can't imagine why he's bothering to plan Halloween festivals, Easter egg hunts, fireworks, and Christmas revels. Perhaps it's that nagging thought at the back of his mind which keeps telling him that it takes over 1,000 people to fill the place for each sitting. When Warner asks, "Guess who's coming for dinner?", the only logical answer is, "Half of New York City!"

The 21 Club   21 W. 52ND ST.   10019
                  582-7200

It's not that they're really snobs—it's just that they have a tendency to banish people from the premises if their behavior isn't quite up to par. Legally, 21 is a public restaurant; there are no written rules for what makes people acceptable. Of course, money, name, social position and fame are helpful, but even the social register is no longer a safeguard from being dropped from 21's ranks. It's tough to get by four screeners (Chuck, Monte, Michael and Tom—count them), but it *does* help if you don't break the house rules.

If you arrive with too much liquor under your belt, you might as well have stayed home. Lack of a necktie will keep you out too, though Sammy Davis, Jr. solved that by taking one of Chuck's and knotting it around his head. Of course there *are* exceptions to any rule; Marc Chagall is allowed in the dining room in a plaid shirt and slacks, so long as he gives his order to Pete Kriendler in the form of a sketch. And Rudolf Nureyev has been known to slip in without a jacket; 21 has never made a habit of refusing entrance to anyone who might dress up the place or enhance its glamor or prestige!

The original club was a speakeasy—no one was allowed through the front door who wasn't known to the house personally. After all these years, that hasn't changed a bit! 21 is so discreet that ladies of note can dine with their lovers upstairs while their husbands drink blissfully (and ignorantly) downstairs. The Kriendlers, Berns and Tannens wouldn't dream of telling. The only thing that's different is that your chances of being recognized are getting better now that more of the family is working there. Just ask for Pete, Jerry, Jack, Charlie, Mac, Bob or Sheldon.

Naturally, all this discretion doesn't come cheap. In fact, it's rumored that the men's room attendant (who functions behind an unmarked door... if you can't find it, you simply don't belong) makes $50,000 a year. One regular claims that he could eat in any other restaurant for what the men's room of 21 costs him. 21 has been described as a melange of an English pub, a provincial hotel lobby and an old-fashioned New York residence, but we see it as pure Americana. There are clubby wood-paneled walls, leather chairs, sofas, television sets and a roaring fire. Masculine Remington paintings and bronzes are scattered about. Some of the fine silver and china was gathered from the estate sales and auction rooms of Europe; King Alphonso's gold-trimmed wine glasses proved to be just the thing for the Duke and Duchess of Windsor.

Over the magnificent sixty-foot mahogany bar hangs a ceilingful of memorabilia... miniature airplanes, footballs, baseballs, 7-Up trucks, a Greyhound bus and a statue of Casey Stengel. They're all symbols of the 21 regulars. But even *they* don't get a bar stool—21 simply doesn't have them. If you feel like sitting, you'll have to ask for a table.

When you do, make sure it's the right one. Most of the celebrated professional folk, as well as the posh younger crowd (like Chris Cerf, who stops in regularly to check his private cellar of Chambertin Clos de Beze), congregate in the first section of the noisy, gregarious bar, better known as the kitchen room. Here there are special tables permanently reserved for special people. While Jackie O retires to the relative quiet of the upstairs, her sister Lee can be found amid the barroom's clatter. The sections are geographically labeled by the original townhouse addresses—21, 19 and 17. Siberia is the Easterly section, 17, where Alan King insists on being seated because, "I want everybody who sees me sitting there to know I am enjoying real security."

Conservative patrons like the Shah of Iran and the Kissingers like it upstairs where it is more spacious and certainly more subdued. Numero Uno tables upstairs begin with Number 115 at the top of the stairs and work their way through the front door, the most obvious and viewable being the most coveted. Here the staff seats and serves regulars like Ginger Rogers, former Mayor Robert Wagner and David Susskind. As is the case downstairs, the cold shoulder is felt in the Easterly section, as well as in the three rooms on the North side of the restaurant where the "Saturday people"—tourists who have flown in for the weekend—are supposedly stashed away. Of course there *is* always a way to get the upper hand in this house. Just call Sheldon Tannen and book one of the private rooms for a party. Then *you* can arrange the seating!

Once seated, order a 21 specialty. The little window on the right side of your menu will tell you about the daily specials: if you're adventuresome you might try baby pheasant grilled with currant jelly, or Scandinavian snow grouse. For the faint of heart, the 21 burger has always been a luncheon standby—ground sirloin with a little nutmeg, some Worcestershire sauce and a bit of bread crumb and celery. Some of our other luncheon favorites include the omelet 21 (which is made with chicken hash, some mornay sauce and Parmesan cheese) and Jack and Charlie's special sandwich (smoked turkey, ham, and a slice of pâté on two slices of rye toast). And for the lightest lunch of all try the Sunset Salad with Lorenzo dressing (cabbage, lettuce, ham and chicken mixed with a dressing of chili sauce, watercress and French dressing).

Dinner can be more formal. It's marvelous to start off with a dry martini, then have mushrooms *à la daume* prepared with minced onions, strips of ham and brown sauce, served over artichoke bottoms. If that sounds like a bit much, the cold salmon with pressed cucumbers and green sauce is simply delicious. Then on to *escalopes de veau Charleroi,* veal with mushrooms, onions, heavy whipping cream and Parmesan cheese, some madeira wine and brown sauce, served with long-grain rice. With that try the famous palm soufflé and 21 potato puffs. Fish lovers request 21's Long Island bay scallops, or their marvelous bay crab. And of course no one leaves without sampling the *chocolat pots de creme.* As for the wine, trust to your somelier. He might suggest Number 926, a Chateau Las Combes 1957 at $27.50, or a Clos Vongcat 1966 at $26. But fear not; if those don't pique your palate, there are dozens more to choose from.

Are you asking about reservations? Well, darling, 21 is *always* jammed. It's impossible to pass through that front door at any hour of the day or night without becoming involved with at least one commotion of people hand shaking and cheek kissing. But then what can you expect from a restaurant with 10,000 charge accounts and a mailing list more than twice that size? Need we say more—call ahead!

Uncle Tai's   1059 THIRD AVE.   10021
Hunan Yuan   838-0850

Isn't New York wonderful! Not only can you visit the Museum of Modern Art, you can also drop in on half the provinces in China. The latest one on the list is Hunan, a Chinese province whose food, like that of Szechuan, is characteristically very hot to the palate. If you loved Szechuan, you'll think that Hunan is *really* hot stuff!

Uncle Tai (no, it's not that the waiters are his nephews—in China, "Uncle" is a term of respect) both owns the restaurant and cooks for it. While the atmosphere is more blue floral wallpaper and ferns than Oriental lacquer, the food has attracted such fans as Chinese food connoisseurs Danny Kaye, Shirley MacLaine and Robert Redford.

They find his hacked chicken mouth-watering—literally! It's the best of the cold hors d'oeuvres, and though it doesn't sound as if this method of preparation shows much respect for a chicken, the sauce more than makes up for the humiliation of being hacked. For a delicious hot appetizer, order the diced boneless squab packages at $4.75.

After that, make a quick stop for the hot and sour fish broth, which is quite tasty and just a bit spicy, though not too much to handle. It will get you prepared for some of those authentic entrees.

Don't miss the sliced duck with young ginger root and water chestnuts. It's delicious served on a platter with asparagus spears as a garnish. Or how about Uncle Tai's shrimp cooked with sherry or Chinese wine, chicken broth and ginger. They're the giant shrimp you've always admired as you've passed by Chinese fish markets, and they're every bit as delicious as you've always suspected they might be.

Uncle Tai also fixes a phenomenal chrysanthemum hotpot for just $22 (enough for two to four): a large tureen of boiling consommé with four kinds of sliced meat and four varieties of vegetables which you cook to taste by dipping into the boiling stock, then into a bowl of beaten egg just before eating. Really delicious and lots of fun to eat, provided you've brought a bib to cover that new Dior. This isn't the neatest dish to eat!

To finish your dinner, don't miss the sesame apple, a caramelized apple dipped into cold water, or of course the standard Chinese after-dinner lichi and loquats.

As if Chinese isn't tough enough to translate already, Uncle Tai further complicates things by decorating his menu with a series of circles and stars. Allow us to translate: if a dish has a star next to it, this is the first time it's been served in New York; a circle indicates that it is hot and spicy, but can be altered to taste. And, of course, at the bottom of the menu they point out that they will eliminate monosodium glutamate from your order if you so request.

The people of Human are a hearty group who have developed a rather unique and spicy cuisine which helps them keep warm during the long, cold months. And we can't imagine a better way to stay cozy on a freezing Manhattan day—unless fate has provided you with a full-length sable!

Le Veau d'Or   129 E. 60TH ST.   10022
838-8133

What a wonderful place if you're young and have solid nerves, a bit of patience, and a taste for unpretentious hearty country dishes and stews in generous casseroles. You'll love this pleasantly comfortable bistro with its old photos, its symbolic portrait of a sleepy young cow resting on her lace pillow, its red-and-white checked tablecloths and black-and-white tile floors. The traffic is so regular that it's as good as a club. A word of warning, though. The noisy clatter of waiters (no, darling, there are no captains here) dealing with customers who've just spent an hour waiting for their table at the tiny midship bar often accompanies every bite.

Howard Cosell tells us the veal stew is as exciting as any Ali bout. Since Dustin Hoffman lives in the neighborhood, he's able to drop in often enough to assure being there when the *civet de lapin* is on the menu. As for us, we like to start with *céleri remoulade* at lunch, then follow it with quiche lorraine, Gerard's concession to those droves of Bloomingdale's ladies who are taking a shopping break. Every time you glance up he seems to be kissing one or another of them hello and suggesting something new from his "bourgeois kitchen."

Dinner's a touch more subdued. The regulars sample *coquilles Veau d'Or, cassoulet* or *canard rôti aux Cerises.* They're smart enough to call ahead and have a soufflé Grand Marnier waiting for them at the end of their meal. But if you haven't had their brand of foresight, you'll be happy to know that the fruit tarts are excellent, too.

Gerard likes to label Chef Roland's cooking as strictly unpretentious, but we think calling it "bourgeois" is a bit unfair. The mere fact that Prince Egon Von Furstenberg is sitting at that choice "table rose-garden" to the left at the front of the restaurant takes it out of the realm of just country cooking. How can you possibly make light of *escargots de Bourgogne* which has the endorsement of a prince?

| **Windows on the World** | 1 WORLD TRADE CENTER 10048
938-1111 |

Getting a bit bored with that view from your penthouse atop the Hilton? Is a craving for new vistas setting in? Luckily we have just the solution: Windows on the World, relatively new and such a marvelously touristy attraction that even King Kong insisted on dropping in during his last visit to New York. Or was he just trampling on their roof? In any event, if he insisted on seeing it, you probably should, too. But beware, travelers with vertigo... Windows on the World flies 107 stories above ground. Truly, it's like being suspended in air—you have the island of Manhattan at your feet.

Be sure to tell your driver to drop you off at the West Street entrance. It will save you a lengthy tramp through the World Trade Center lobby. Then up you go (assuming you're not wearing a leisure suit, that's a no-no!) to the top of the Trade Center. Jackets are required for men.

At lunch Windows on the World is a private lunchclub, complete with showers, a library, sauna, masseur and resident hairdresser. Members are free to buy and store their own wine in the Wine Cellar in the Sky. And if they're in a rush and can't finish the whole bottle, cellarmaster Alan Lewis will be happy to cork it up for them and save it for as long as a week. The savings on wine alone is enough to justify the club's initiation fee, so if you simply can't wait until dark to see the Brooklyn Bridge from 107 stories up, reach into the pocket of your Pierre Cardin and extract $420. Then try to make friends with the other members quickly—if you bring along a guest for lunch, it's an extra $10.

After 3:00 P.M. Windows is open to the public. A good first stop is the Hors d'Oeuverie, where appetizers are served all night. When you don't feel like staying for dinner it's a wonderful stop for a drink, a plate of hot hors d'oeuvres or cold smorgasbord, and an awesome view. If you become so enchanted by the Empire

State Building to the north and the skyscrapers of midtown that you lose track of time and stay longer than you've planned, you'll delight to the fact that there's dancing at night, too.

If you're staying for dinner, ask Joe Baum for a table. It's difficult to say which are better; it really all depends on what you'd like to see. How about a spot from which you can keep an eye on Harry Winston's? It shouldn't be too tough to find; the room is terraced so that every table has a magnificent view, more than a few of them toward Fifth Avenue.

Though this large pastel room seats 350, it's been divided into intimate groupings of just a few tables each, so you never feel part of a crowd. There's lots of brass, and fabric-covered walls, and if you like the feel of cool, custard-colored vinyl against your back, you'll simply love the decor.

Entrees start around $7 and work their way up to $13. You can order a complete dinner consisting of deviled crab, sorrel soup, compote of squab with country currants, southern rice, salad, blancmange with brandied apricots and nuts, and coffee at just $16.

Well, if you don't feel like ordering a complete dinner, you might consider starting with cheese profitero hot, which makes a simply marvelous snack. If you'd rather resign yourself to ordering something cold, try the iced curried fruits or the minted sweet tea iced soup.

Entrees range from such selections as striped bass in lettuce leaves to red snapper steamed with vegetables and sauce moussoline ($7.95) or rack of lamb James Beard, which is $12.50 per person. You might supplement this with french-fried zucchini or baby eggplant grilled with soy and ginger. Or better yet, you might just forget the vegetables and save yourself for dessert. If we had to choose from all of them, our vote would be for the mocha mousse praline or the custardy lemon tarts with paper-thin slices of lemon. But then again, there's the frozen soufflé crusted with bitter Italian macaroons and amaretto.

The idea of making a reservation two or more weeks in advance is a bit tough to handle. But the mirrored ceilings and the view make dinner there an experience worth having more than once.

Out of Town

La Cremaillère NORTH ST., BANKSVILLE, N.Y.
(914) 234-3306

Even restaurateurs need a day in the country once in a while, so Fred Decre and Robert Meyzen started La Cremaillère. Rejoice; as a result, you can now leave the City without leaving behind the food and attention they've been spoiling you with at Caravelle. All it requires is an hour's driving to Banksville, which in itself is a pleasure, as you'll be traveling along foliage-rich roads in the spring and through drifts of golden leaves in autumn. At the end of your journey you'll find the reincarnated golf course clubhouse which is now La Cremaillère.

It's a homey, wood-paneled place, made more authentically French by Fred's porcelain collection and the hand-painted canvas walls depicting the provinces of France. Be careful of studying the area which depicts the Burgundy region . . . it might inspire you to order their Clos Oegeoth 1865. Its $600 price tag leads some to study the Bordeaux mural instead; for less discriminating tastes there are 17,999 other bottles to choose from in the wine cellar.

Speaking of the wine cellar, it's the perfect place to host a dinner for six or eight. Request this small private dining room well in advance, it's quite popular. We suspect this might be because it's used as often for tête-à-têtes as it is for parties! We can't think of a more romantic spot for getting together than La Cremaillère, but it does get awkward when you keep running into old friends like George C. Scott or Anthony Quinn every time you rendezvous there.

The menu is as spectacular as the wine cellar. Those in the know are aware that though venison and rabbit stews are specialties of the chef, they're not mentioned on the menu. Order them anyway, and start your meal with a sample of Cremaillère's wonderful escargots. If venison happens to be scarce the week you stop in, substitute the lamb curry or the *sole anglais au vermouth.* They're enough to make you glad that deer got away! You'll find that *ratatouille niçoise* is a good accompaniment for any of these delectable dishes. There now, ladies, wasn't that a surprise? You never suspected you'd be begging your husband to drive for an hour just to take you to a golf club, did you!

CLUBS

Le Club 416 E. 55TH ST. 10022
  355-5520

No doubt you remember the building. It's the one you used to drop in on when Avedon was using it for his studio... he *did* ask to photograph you, didn't he? Today it's the 17th-century French antique haven that's known as Le Club. It might be a bit harder to get past the front door than it was during Avedon's day—after all, manager Patrick *does* have a waiting list that's infinite. And as if that weren't problem enough, he *does* have to keep choosing between domestic and international millionaires, between playboys and celebrities. Since it's the most popular club in New York, you just can't be too careful about who's doing the hustle with whom!

Still, *you* shouldn't have any trouble getting in. The club is owned by its 1,000 members and you're sure to know an ample number of them. Try starting with the board of governors for a quick okay. A phone call to the Maharajah of Jaipur might do it, or a telegram to Rex Harrison. Or you might try the Cassinis —Oleg or Igor—depending upon who happens to be in town that week. Or if you're in Los Angeles, try asking Ray Stark.

Once you're in, your *real* problems begin... worrying about getting that perfect table. The one right by the edge of the dance floor that Al Pacino had last night. He *always* gets special attention.

Dinner is served from 8:00 P.M. on, but no one under the age of 80 would dream of showing up earlier than 11:00. Around midnight, the rush of elegant internationals really begins. It's at that point you have to be quite careful not to be relegated to a table in the back of the room. Even Le Club's fresh caviar, vichyssoise and *steak au poivre* can't make up for that kind of embarrassment. Better to head upstairs to the backgammon room and chat with Robert Sarnoff, Douglas Fairbanks, Jr. and the Duke of Bedford, instead.

The best spot to be seen enjoying your veal Marsala is by the marble fireplace, so perfect for kir and conversation. Don't worry a bit about topping it off with one of their heavenly desserts—you'll work it off on the dance floor in just no time at all. You might be dancing next to Henry Ford, or even Bob Evans if he's gotten over his objections to their suit-and-tie requirement.

Despite the fact that Le Club has a rule limiting each member to two guests, it gets so crowded after theater that it's difficult to do more than a step on that tiny dance floor without getting at least one elbow to the back. Don't worry—if it gets too rough out there you can always call on Patrick to give you some help. After all, he *did* spend a few years as a probation officer for delinquent boys. There are very few problems which Patrick can't handle! And he's so tall and handsome you might just want to come up with one for the simple pleasure of having him get you out of it.

Doubles   783 FIFTH AVE.   10022
               751-9595

Doubles was the first club in a good long time to challenge El Morocco and Le Club. Obviously it didn't top them, but it did build a name for itself as *another* private club in New York.

Giorgio Massini, its manager, can take credit for the excellent service. Giorgio has El Morocco, the St. Regis and the Carlyle to his managing credits and continually admits that since Doubles is not number one (or even number two), they do try harder.

Membership at Doubles is more difficult to obtain than the competing clubs'. New members need letters of reference from five members and they must be well known to at least five members of the board. If interested, do get to know five of the following: Porter Ijams, president; William Blair Meyer, Donald W. Scholle, Gloria Muller, T. Suffern Tailer, William Bancroft, Pat Buckley, or Jane Dudley. If you move in the international circle we're sure Renaldo Herrera of Caracas and Emilio Pucci of Florence will be happy to recommend you once they remember where you met. After you've been approved, it's merely a question of the $2,000 initiation fee. Even before the club opened its doors, there were 1,300 members. Not bad for the Avis of private clubs.

The best time to be seen at Doubles is at lunch. Every day there's a different buffet. You'll find a variety of hot dishes as well as cold salads—all displayed beautifully. The guests, like the lunches, are diversified. You'll find anyone from Lee Radziwill to Mrs. Doris Stein. They're coming here from both coasts—from the East you'll find Nancy Ittelson, and from the West Mrs. Fran Stark.

Elmer's 307 E. 54TH ST. 10022
 752-2960

Elmer's is merely a smaller, less pretentious version of its daddy El Morocco. Elmer's atmosphere is a bit more relaxed; it looks more like an old-fashioned wine cellar than a street in Casablanca.

With its brick walls, gingham tablecloths and marvelous cheeseburgers, it's perfect for lunch. We also love the omelets, and when it's available, the striped bass at $6.75 is a lo-cal treat.

Elmer's wine cellar atmosphere isn't just for looks. The wine list is superb. We especially liked the St. Emilion Chateau Simard 1970, which was $15.50 per bottle, and in the white wine family, the Chablis Premier Cru Mont de Milieu at $13.50 was marvelous. In the champagne category we recommend the Piper Heidsieck Florens Louis 1966, $38 per bottle.

Look for the same high quality of food and service of El Morocco. No need for men to wear ties, especially in the backgammon room.

| El Morocco | 307 E. 54TH ST. 10022 |
| | 752-2960 |

Régine may attract the hot press names and Le Club may be filled with international millionaires, but El Morocco consistently draws class. Old money and new seem quite at home there. Huntington Hartford, Mrs. Stanley C. Hope and Mark Goodson might all be in speaking distance one night—it doesn't seem to matter how old the money is at El Mo's. Tradition and good taste are still the passwords at this private, nonprofit establishment. Save your Philippe Salvet for Régine; Dior and Givenchy will be more apropos. Men will need suit and tie before Angelo will seat them for dinner.

Dinner is still the highlight at El Morocco. It's one of the few clubs left where you can have *anything* you want for supper. If you aren't tempted by the menu (though we can't imagine passing up the veal chop El Morocco or the arrugola salad when it's in season) ask the chef to prepare whatever you'd like and if it's possible, you'll have it. We usually start with fresh caviar at $15 per ounce, enjoying every dram of it, and finish with the soufflé glace.

When you become a regular at El Mo's, Angelo will add you to his 45-year list of special members. This maître d' has seated everyone from the late Aristotle Onassis and Jacqueline to Paulette Goddard and Joan Fontaine, as well as Renaldo Herrera, the Venezuelan millionaire, and Joseph Norban, who owns the land underneath El Mo's, and John Meyer, the Olympic Airlines man. Favorite tables are on the zebra-striped banquettes, but don't worry, there's no Siberia section anymore (in the old days the front section over the dance floor was taboo seating, and a table there was enough to warrant skipping dinner and spending the entire evening on the dance floor). So anywhere you sit is perfectly all right.

Today the orchestra section has been replaced by a tapedeck and what was once a romantic dance floor is now a discotheque. How lively depends on the crowd each night; some evenings the Charles S. Munson (at 83 he's the oldest man on the club's board of governors) set brings back the romance of dancing cheek to cheek.

Whether it's disco or good old-fashioned music, fantasy always pervades the dance floor. Ellen Lehman McCluskey kept the Desert Song atmosphere when she decorated El Mo's a few years ago. Those white palm trees sprouting out of blue walls, the Moorish grilles, the zebra banquettes—it isn't Casablanca, but it works. And those famous twinkling stars in the ceiling keep the fantasy flowing. "It seems like every night is New Year's Eve," says Eileen McKenna, the lady who has been there every night for 25 years passing out cigars and cigarettes.

For special parties you'll have to contract Geoffrey M. T. Jones, the club's secretary. You may want to lease the Champagne Room for your next affair, but it holds only about 100, so it will have to be a gathering of only your most intimate friends. Confer with Geoffrey on all the details; he'll make sure that your party reflects the El Morocco tradition of elegance.

And one last point to remember: if you bring guests for dinner, be selective; the people who come to John Perona's El Morocco are among the chic-est in the world.

Régine's 502 PARK AVE. 10022
826-0990

It happened in Paris. It happened in Monte Carlo and again in Rio. Then *finally* in New York. Régine came to town. She brought every bit of glitter, gold and glamour that have made her discos famous, and she brightened up Park Avenue. Pauline Trigère thinks it's like "being in another world" and Howard Oxenberg finds the place "amusing." Elizabeth Taylor likes all the mirrors; they give her that fairest-of-them-all feeling again.

Personally, we find Régine's everything a good club should be. It's lively, the food is marvelous, and the music is right. Members pay $600 a year if they live in New York, but out-of-towners get the best bargain at $400. There's a $10 cover charge for non-members. New York cards are good in all the other Régine spots, but Parisians who've tried to use theirs in New York ended up paying the cover. Manager Pepe Vanini screens all the applications; call him for yours.

Dinner, à la Michel Guérard, is always light and delicious. You must try the scrambled eggs and caviar, Régine's favorite. Or you might commence with asparagus tucked in a pastry and delightfully smothered with asparagus purée, followed by *le gigot de poulet à la vapeur de cresson* (chicken leg stuffed with sweetbreads in a watercress sauce) and finish with crepes with praline sauce and apricot liqueur. *C'est magnifique, oui?* And thanks to Monsieur Guérard, who developed *la cuisine minceur* (that fabulous low calorie French cooking), there's no need to worry about eating every last morsel. Even when the food is gone, the table is still appetizing—those huge geranium-patterned dishes from Villery & Boch are a treat unto themselves. Chef-suggested dinners range from $29 to $35 per person, not including wine.

When you're not eating dinner, you'll be dancing on a plexiglass floor around a hearth of neon lights, bumping into the likes of Marisa Berenson Randell and Margaux Hemingway (aren't you glad the food's not fattening?), or George and Eleanor McGovern, who've been seen dancing cheek to cheek at Régine's. And when Ethel Kennedy and Paul Getty, Jr. show up on the same dance floor as Diana Vreeland, Danny Kaye, and Andy Warhol, you know Régine handled the guest list—she's famous for her party mixes.

The disco queen spends one week in six in New York, and even chose to spend Bastille Day here to celebrate the club's opening. Her guests included 300 of the hottest press names around, and when they weren't ooh-la-laing Régine's aubergine palace, or marveling at the fact that everyone *really did* wear red, white or blue, they were simply enjoying the cancan.

IV. EATING IN
Adventures in Food Shopping

WE REALIZE it's difficult to believe, but there's bound to come a day when you're sick of poached salmon at Caravelle and couldn't care less about being seen in your new Missoni. You say the last time that occurred was a day when you were in withdrawal from a trip to the Golden Door? Well, be patient, it may happen again. Let's just hope it doesn't happen on the cook's day off!

If it does, don't panic. New York has fresh food available right around every corner. It's just a matter of searching, and you're sure to find the most fabulous delicacies in the world hidden away between dress shops and drugstores. Everything from homemade pickles at the Country Host to macadamia nuts at Maison Glass; from fresh live carp at Wing Woh Lung on Mott Street (a good block for anything Chinese), to 24 hours' worth of fresh vegetables at Three Guys From Brooklyn or the Medallion Fruit Market (never can tell when you're going to get a craving for fresh strawberries!). Even meats get that special New York touch at Meatique, where you can shop for prepackaged beef Wellington that will pop into the oven and impress all but the most jaded guests. And even *they'll* take notice if you've stopped to pick up goodies at Balducci's on Sixth Avenue.

These are just a few of the magical shops beyond the ones we describe here—there are hundreds more out there just waiting for your discovery. See—you're starting to calm down already, and we haven't even *begun* to tell you about the caterers! Push your scale into the corner, and let's start shopping!

BAKERIES

Betsy's Place	144 E. 74TH ST. (2ND FLOOR) 10021
	734-1855

Betsy's not publicity shy . . . but she is hard to find. In fact, there was a time when she was doing business strictly through the mail, which becomes a bit difficult when you're dealing with a bakery.

Betsy's specialty is a wonderful confection of a fruitcake (known to those familiar with the world of New York bakeries as "Betsy's Loaf"), a darkly rich confection consisting of honey-sweet dates, cherries, large crisp walnut meats, orange rind, and vanilla. Perfect with a dab of sour cream or cream cheese. Wonderful for breakfast or a light lunch—and even better for a post-dinner snack when soaked with brandy for a day or two.

Betsy has added other delights to her repertoire (ginger bread and carrot loaves to name just two), as well as an address. You can now find her second-floor bakery at the corner of East 74th and Lexington. She's well worth walking up for.

Bonté	1316 THIRD AVE. 10028
	535-2360

There is a regular stream of New Yorkers who wouldn't dream of starting a day in Fun City without that early-morning stop at Bonté's for a *pain au chocolat* (croissant dough wrapped around chocolate). Both Tricia Nixon and Luci Johnson trusted him to produce the wedding cakes that sent them on their way to living happily ever after; the least *you* can do is give him credit for baking the eye-opening sort of pastry that will help you muddle through till lunch at La Caravelle.

At Maurice Bonté's charming shop, complete with red-and-white-checkered walls, you'll be able to see awards from royalty, as well as some of the chic-est French pastry lovers in New York. Why not? He produces an incredible variety of goodies in immaculate (and tasty) style.

The man in the immaculate white cloche is Maurice. Don't think he doesn't care just because he's not stopping to chat. Getting up at 5 A.M. every day makes anyone short of the irrepressibly cheerful a touch antisocial. Besides, by interrupting him you might be depriving yourself of one of his famous bread-loaf-shaped brioches (perfect when toasted for canapés or foie gras).

Other Bonté specialties include the Succulent: a high and handsome golden triangular cake made of alternating layers of crisp meringue, golden genoise cake, and Grand Marnier buttercream, sharpened with the flavor of bitter Seville orange rind. Equally delicious (and a bit less rich) is the Gateau Breton: double layers of buttery *pâté sucrée* with a thin filling of fresh apples, a wonderful choice when heated and sprinkled with vanilla confectioner's sugar, and marvelous "schnecken."

He also has the best cream puffs... napoleons... chocolate and mocha eclairs... puff pastry barquettes filled with custard cream and topped with perfect fresh raspberries or strawberries ... eggshell-thin cups of dark, bittersweet chocolate heaped with fluted puffs of rich and airy lemon or chocolate mousse... pastry tartlettes of plums, peaches, or tiny sour cherries nestled in rum-spiked *crème patisserie*... and, well, we think you have the idea!

Le Cheesecake	150 E. 70TH ST.	10021
Elegant	861-8740	

We wouldn't dream of leaving our how-to-get-fat-quick theme without telling you about Le Cheesecake Elegant. After all, this is America. Everyone should have freedom of choice in deciding how they personally would prefer to become plump.

Le Cheesecake Elegant is really just the tiny retail outlet of a New Jersey bakery called the Cheesecake Pantry. It's a shop that supplies a number of fine restaurants in New York City. But knowing how you hate that drive to New Jersey, we thought we'd let you know how to get the same scrumptious product without the extra miles (you know how impatient the chauffeur becomes when he has to spend Saturdays in New Jersey) and driving time.

Stop in and be prepared to queue up (particularly at lunchtime, when everyone in the city seems to go on a sweets binge) to buy their mini cheesecakes, simply swimming in a little crown of cherries, pineapple, or other seasonal fruits... then go forth munching.

But we must tell you about their cheesecake. It's rich and creamy, and made with the highest-quality cream cheese, fresh eggs, pure vanilla extract, and surrounded by a butter cookie crust.

Their fudge brownies are nothing to complain about either— they're rich and chocolatey, and are frosted with chocolate cream cheese icing. Thank heavens they're available in both 7- and 14-ounce tins.

There is also a marvelous pecan pie which is a blend of Vermont maple syrup, brown sugar, melted butter, heavy cream, and pure vanilla extract, topped with pecan halves. It's baked in a cream-cheese pastry crust, and if you *really* want to be naughty (and don't we all), serve it warm with softened vanilla ice cream.

Creative Cakes	400 E. 74TH ST. 10021
	794-9811

If Betty Crocker had heard that it is possible to get $200 for a cake, she might never have begun selling the mix! Only an ex-advertising and public relations girl would have the mind to realize how simple it can be to turn a little flour into a lot of dough; and of course Stephanie Crookston *did* have the advantage of being bequeathed her grandmother's famous chocolate cake recipe. Betty Crocker had to learn hers on her own!

Since she opened her cupcake-sized shop in the early 1970s she's made over 600 personalized cakes, all but 15 of them chocolate. Unless you can prove you're allergic (a note from your doctor might help) you're going to eat the family chocolate cake recipe. Not that you should consider that a form of torture—it's among the best in the world.

Marvin Hamlisch celebrated his birthday with a pink piano. Otto Preminger ate a camera. Arthur Ashe's surprise was a buttercream tennis racquet. Charlie Rich, Joan Crawford, Chita Rivera, and Margaux Hemingway have eaten their own portraits without a moment's hesitation.

While Stephanie's creations range from $25 to $200 (the most lavish being a five-tiered wedding cake of such proportion that it was designed by an architect), the average price for a 15- to 25-person dessert is around $40. Production is limited—under 40 cakes a week—so be sure to make a reservation for yours about two weeks in advance.

Now what will it be . . . a Rolls-Royce with buttercream upholstery . . . a two-layer replica of the Hope Diamond?

Dumas Patisserie 1330 LEXINGTON AVE. 10028
369-3900

116 E. 60TH ST. 10022
688-0905

Madame and Monsieur Dumas started their Lexington Avenue bakery almost 30 years ago. Now they have two shops, and there are ten bakers and helpers in the back of the Lexington Avenue shop who turn out the most marvelous baked goods, quiche Lorraines, croissants, and brioches to be tasted west of the Champs-Élyseés.

Have you ever had a croissant filled with almond paste? We refuse to have you hold us responsible once you do—they're addicting. True that at 75 cents each, it's a habit that's more easily afforded than some (it's just buying an entire new wardrobe that gets to be a bit expensive). Madame Dumas also has some marvelous frozen hors d' oeuvres, pastry filled with cheddar cheese, mushrooms, and sausage at $2.50 a dozen. Her quiche of traditional Gruyere cheese and ham is unsurpassed.

Sacré bleu! The woman is full of surprises. Now she's bringing out the Tourte Maisons: thin slices of ham with Mornay sauce and imported Parmesan cheese.

The *pièce de résistance* is the Dumas Les Buches Mousse, a cake roll in chocolate or toasted almond which is rich enough to be sold by the pound. They also will sell you chocolate mousse which is normally made to serve 4 to 6, or 8 to 10, but can be made for up to 75 people.

We needn't go on much longer. You can already see that this is a definite must on your list of palate pleasers in New York, but we should at least mention the ice creams. Dumas stocks both Haagen Dazs and a wonderful ice cream called Sedutto which is especially irresistible in cassis sherbet. And so you shouldn't go entirely hungry before dessert, they allow you to pick between French *foie gras* and fresh caviar for appetizers, as well as a selection of cheeses.

As you can see, the Dumases have quite a few accomplishments to their credit, but few please them more than the accolade they won when *New York* magazine selected them as the first-place winner in the citywide competition for the best croissant in Manhattan. With so many bakeries in New York, that's no small praise!

Leonard Baking Co., Inc.	1412 THIRD AVE. 10021 734-2300

While we're on our sinful kick, we might as well make mention of another bakery in New York which has marvelous mousse, cakes, and pastries. It's a rather simple street-level shop with most of the baking done right on the premises, but despite that innocent exterior, you know you're in trouble the moment you enter and are engulfed with the aroma.

Mortimer Philips started over fifteen years ago with a very tiny shop at 95th and Second Avenue, where he contented himself with producing countless dozens of his famous Leonard's creamcheese cake. Half New York still swears by it; the other half has heard about his new strawberry mousse and that wonderful apricot bundt that he makes with spongecake, apricot and cake crumbs.

But back to the creamcheese cakes—having perfected one area of potential overweight, Mortimer stumbled on to some new recipes which allowed him to expand to his present quarters on Third Avenue. Granted, they don't look as if they were decorated by Angelo Donghia, but they do have a sort of middle-American Formica charm all their own. And one mustn't judge a mousse cake by its display case!

You *can* judge it by the quality of the clientele who gobble it up: Mrs. Anne Gimbel might be seen emerging with one of Leonard's famous mocha mousse cakes, while Mrs. Jack Rudin nibbles on the anything cake, a winsome combination of pure butter, chopped pecans, and meringue with pieces of chocolate sandwiched in at just the right spots. With a recipe like that, even Angelo would be willing to forgive Leonard!

Miss Grimble's Bakery   1042 MADISON AVE.   10021
535-0380
305 COLUMBUS AVE.   10024
362-5531

She's a fraud—an absolute fake! And so wicked! Admit it . . . any woman who would adopt a name that positively reeks of lavender sachets, neat white gloves, and therapeutic Red Cross shoes—just so that she can bring out the devil in you—deserves to be exposed.

Our first accusation is that Miss Grimble does not exist, beyond the rather flighty figment of the imagination of one Sylvia Hirsch, who arrived in New York from Dallas in 1965 to help her husband open a barbecue restaurant. True, he asked her to come up with the perfect dessert—but 'fess up, Sylvia, did he really insist that you go on to undermine every New Yorker's willpower? Not that we mean to imply that your cheesecakes are rich, my dear, but people *have* been known to rush off for a book on the low-carbohydrate diet after just one.

So there she sits, wearing that pseudonym which would lead you to believe that you're dealing with either the headmistress of a very fine but conservative finishing school or the proprietor of a tiny Upper East Side needlepoint shop where the matrons of Manhattan gather to sip tea and pick at each other's petit point. And what does she actually do? She entices you!

First she tries a plain old 8-inch cheesecake. Looks innocent enough. Couldn't possibly hurt to have just a tiny sliver, could it? Oh... you shouldn't have done that! Now she has you hooked. If you liked the classic vanilla, you'll want to mainline the chocolate marble. As for the hazelnut—she must have cooked that one up on a day when she was feeling particularly sadistic toward sweet-fiends. And to make certain that no one escapes, she also does cheesecakes in lemon, orange, rum, raspberry marble, apricot, strawberry, and coconut.

We know people (we're embarrassed to reveal their names—they shall remain anonymous) who have gone through twenty varieties in order to come up with their favorite, and though vanilla seems to be the mother of them all, it's the chocolate for us. The cakes come in 7- and 10-inch sizes, with 12-inch available on order.

If you think it's being unnecessarily cruel to yourself to have an entire cake sitting at home tempting you every time you walk to the refrigerator, you'll be happy to know that you can get just a piece at any one of a number of New York restaurants (the Sign of the Dove, Sand's on Second Avenue, the Harmonie Club, etc.). We're sure that with a little research you'll find one nearby, so that you'll never have to go through cheesecake withdrawal.

Oh, really, Miss Grimble... have you no heart? Now they tell us you've come up with a chocolate sachertorte and a sweet potato pie which threatens to bring as much attention to the good old South as Rhett Butler. As if that's not bad enough, there's that quiche Lorraine with asparagus and onion, and the most perfect holiday applesauce spice cake with rum frosting. And like that fragile but perfect pecan pie, they all freeze, thus enabling Phyllis Newman and Mrs. Vladimir Horowitz to gorge themselves without leaving the sanctuary of their own homes.

It used to be easier to avoid this particular source of temptation—Miss Grimble used to carry on her devious doings from within a rather small Columbus Avenue shop nestled among laundromats and *The New York Times* home delivery depot. Of course, some who noted the sign "Cheesecake—Retail—Wholesale" and smelled the beckoning fragrance were still trapped. But you *did* have to go out of your way to fall into her web in those days. Today there's no escaping. Miss Grimble's clutches have extended to Madison Avenue, offering a reward to boutiquiers who manage to get as far as 79th Street. A word of advice: sample the clay-potted *pot-de-crème after* you do your try-on!

Okay, Miss Grimble—enough is enough! Why are you deviously grinning from among your clean white cheesecake boxes? What are you cooking up next?

Or is it just that you know that since you deliver twice daily (10:00 A.M. and 3:00 P.M.), we're all going to be hooked forever!

William Greenberg, Jr.
1100 MADISON AVE.   10028
744-0304

1377 THIRD AVE.   10021
876-2255

17 E. 8TH ST.   10005
674-6657

William Greenberg is a touch publicity-shy. Perhaps it's because he knows that if the world found out about his wonderful brownies, throngs would be beating at his door. And for a retiring man, that would be most unpleasant. But in keeping with our policy of revealing some of our favorite things (share and share alike we always say), we simply had to tell you about Mr. Greenberg's brownies. Not only are these unbelievably and deliciously rich, they're surrounded by many, many marvelous things which range from bread and croissants to dinner rolls, cakes, and cookies. Well, we're taking the risk, and we hope that Mr. Greenberg won't be *too* angry with us if we recommend that you look for his red-and-white shops and stop in to try those brownies, and of course, anything else there that might catch your eye.

Sorry, Mr. Greenberg. You know how hard it is for us to keep a secret!

GOURMET FOOD STORES

Cheese Unlimited 1529 SECOND AVE. 10021
861-1306

Despite what some say about Cheese of the World, we still swear by Cheese Unlimited. The only people we've found who *don't* like it are the ones who find it too difficult to make a decision among the 650 types of cheese available. But we have a simple solution to that problem: just ask Saul or Gus, "What's good today?"

They might recommend the goat's cheese with green olives at $4.98 a pound that Arthur Godfrey took home with him after his last visit. Or Lena Horne's favorite, St-André, a rich creamy French cheese for breakfast (plain) or dessert (with herbs). Or you might find yourself going home with Fontina from Italy —Katharine Hepburn did.

The store is a mélange of colorful oranges and yellows, brown-striped paper, and heaps of sourdough and pumpernickel breads. In the corner you'll find fondue pots or a racklette oven to melt cheese by ultraviolet rays for the mere pittance of $160. (How's that for a grilled-cheese sandwich?) The walls are covered with plaques instructing you on the proper methods of serving the various types of cheese at Cheese Unlimited. Every accessory you'll need to do it is there, too, from cheese spreaders to 50 different varieties of crackers, to pâté as an accent.

Brie seems to be the most popular cheese (no surprise!), and comes in 6-pound wheels at $22. We also came across a cheese called St. Otto during our last visit which was 95 percent fat-free—naturally, it smelled simply ghastly, so we took some Frisian instead. Not easy to keep slim, is it! Seasoned with bits of clove, Frisian was ideal with the figs we just picked up at Plumbridge Confections. Our last selection was a Spanish cheese called Manchego made with sheep's milk, but if you're less adventurous you'll be safe with something a bit more common, like farmer cheese or Feta.

E.A.T.   1064 MADISON AVE.   10028
         879-4017

Can a nice boy from Zabar's deli find happiness in a new Porsche and penthouse? Face it—who couldn't! Not that Eli Zabar has much time to enjoy such things now that he's opened E.A.T. at Henri Bendel's, too.

He's up by 6:30 A.M. daily to do the cooking before he starts such chores as checking the stock of jams that just arrived from a little old lady in England (all waiting to be popped into your Bendel's shopping bag). Then he rushes back to the main Madison Avenue shop to cook some more. That's how he's ready with a perfect breast of veal stuffed with fresh herbs when your husband calls to say three friends are flying in from St. Tropez and expect an early dinner.

Thank heavens for Eli at times like that!

Come to think of it, thank heavens for Eli any day of the week. Who else would fly all the way to France just to make sure that you can buy a slice of the legendary Swiss Vacherin cheese in New York? Evidently no one, since E.A.T. is the only source in America. But we're not at all surprised. From the very start, Eli has insisted on stocking limited quantities of the very best.

You can find that wonderful Gaspé salmon, and fabulous French pâtés of game, goose, or wild rabbit at $12 a pound. They carry loose herbal teas which are home-grown and dried in the cellars of their Shaker friends in the Sabbathday Lake community in Maine, as well as Jackson's teas from Piccadilly. Choose from rose hips, spearmint, peppermint, or camomile at $6. Don't plan ahead when you go to E.A.T.—you may walk in and find that Eli has just whipped up marinated artichokes and breast of chicken stuffed with cheese and herbs. Or it might be salmon *en croûte*. Or a big green bouquet of fresh asparagus. Just don't go there hungry!

While we do argue with Eli's perchant for pairing the Baccarat crystal with plastic plates, we won't quarrel with the look of fresh begonias and scrubbed wooden tables as the setting for apple tarts and croissants. The scenery, of course, is partially the influence of Eli's wife, Abbie. It's her graphic design background which accounts for the striking E.A.T. bags and shop decor.

And though her passion for food might not be quite so deep as Eli's, she *will* admit that it was responsible for her finding the love of her life—they met at Zabar's, the place Eli's father and uncles founded.

It didn't take long for Abbie to realize that any man who cared enough to send a taxi out to New Jersey every morning so that New Yorkers could have fresh eggs and butter couldn't be all bad. One trip to E.A.T. and you'll agree!

Fraser Morris	872 MADISON AVE. 10021
	988-6700

Pity the poor hostess who leaves for her holiday ski trip to Sun Valley without knowing that Fraser Morris will ship their famous smoked Scotch salmon—or any other of their delectable goodies—to any corner of the world. Woe to the lady who expects a crowd to come off the ski slope and be satisfied with less than country-style baked ham, Iranian caviar, and a tureen of French *pâté de foie gras*. Serving less could well be the cause of an apres-ski rebellion!

You say you don't know what Fraser Morris is? Where have you been all these years? Fraser Morris is simply the only place where Candice Bergen would dream of stopping if she developed a craving for Beluga caviar (about $95 for 14 ounces) while strolling down Madison Avenue. Happily she needn't make it any further than 71st Street before restocking the pantry.

It's the place where Woody Allen searches myopically among the frozen crablegs and quiche for that perfect snack. It's the store where Kirk Douglas finds his country ham and smoked whole turkey. And as far as we're concerned, it's *the* store to visit for chocolate lace, a finely wrought wonder that can be yours at just $5.95 for the 14-ounce package. If that doesn't appeal to you, how about the Lindt chocolates from Switzerland, or the Perugina from Italy. For those less daring, we're happy to report that the low-calorie candies are available in 28-ounce containers at $4.95 each.

Every time we hear the words Fraser Morris, though, we have visions of the finest Scotch salmon swimming in our heads—after all, that *is* the reason Leonard Morris started the shop. He imports it, slices it paper-thin, then reconstructs it on a platter that can be shipped to you anywhere, or, better yet, devoured right on the premises. The genuine Scotch salmon runs $19.95 a pound, which we realize sounds expensive, but it's worth every morsel. If you had bad luck in the options market this week you might compromise on the Nova Scotia at $12.95.

The shop has delicacies, fruits, and thousands of specials culled from around the world. If it seems a trifle confusing to choose among 481 cheeses, ask for help from Mr. Freirchs. With his twelve assistants, he'll be able to plan that perfect tray for your next party, or a gift basket impressive enough to wow the Shah of Iran. If you so request, he'll even include a wonderful bottle of burgundy from the Fraser Morris wine and liquor shop across the street.

There, now. Don't you feel more relaxed about going on that next ski trip?

Simon Pure	49 E. 57TH ST. 10022
Better Diet Shop	832-3238

Anne Bancroft, Mel Brooks, Van Johnson, Clare Luce, Robert Redford, Red Buttons and Tony Perkins have something in common—when they get that yen for clean living, they take a brisk walk to Simon Pure. Not that it's such a long walk—Sam Simon is located on East 57th, within easy reach of most high-living addicts.

Not only does Sam supply upper-crust Manhattan with organic produce, low-calorie foods, honeys, dried fruit and nuts, nutritional books, and health foods, he also takes the time to supply them with an explanation of what each vitamin and food he recommends is doing for the body. He's always available in the shop for a personal chat; you'll learn to rely on him and his daughter Melanie for all your health-food advice.

By the way, a portion of Simon Pure is devoted to wonderful gourmet eating—being a student of human nature, as well as of nutrition, Sam is willing to recognize that even the best of intentions can go astray!

Zabar's   2245 BROADWAY   10024
787-2000

We hear that shopping for the kitchen is one of the things most people enjoy doing, and one of the best places for it is Zabar's. So we called Saul and Stony Zabar and their partner Murray Klein, and asked them what their store was all about. At first we felt a touch odd shopping for kitchen utensils and groceries (no matter how fancy), but once Murray let us know that he'd catered a party for Cartier's, we began to feel right at home.

Murray walked us past the breads, meats, fish, and produce all the way back to the cheeses, coffees, loose teas, and Zabar's own special pastry tray complete with divine rich and gooey Russian coffee cake.

Hanging from every inch of the ceiling is everything from kitchen bowls to egg beaters, salamis to net bags of apples, cheese boards to teas, salt grinders to ... well, we're not quite sure what that last thing is.

As you walk in, to the right there's an assortment of 60 breads that run from Moishe pumpernickel to bagels. Past that is a variety of 40 knives, while on the left is the meat and the deli which honored us during our visit with a Hungarian sausage festival (anyone for a Polish Kielbasa?).

On the ceiling are various teapots that range from $3.98 to $50, while on the open counters are fresh fruits and 40 different types of beer. If you've had a craving for pistachio nuts this week, you can positively steal five pounds for $39.95. And if your weakness is for things a bit sweeter, you'll be happy to know that Zabar's is importing Bassetts, a wonderful ice cream from Philadelphia (to New Yorkers, that's importing!).

If you go there on a Saturday night or a Sunday morning, watch out for the crowd of brunch shoppers stocking up on meats, fish, fresh chopped liver, and salads at the glass counters on the left, and on cheeses of every sort imaginable in the back. For a unique taste experience, try some farmer cheese with nuts and raisins or with berries at your next New York brunch. Friday nights you can buy herring, gefilte fish, or fresh smoked salmon (lox) as late as midnight, though the rest of the week you'll have to make your decision between their inexhaustible selection of coffees by 10 P.M. By the way, New Yorkers in the know say Zabar's stocks real (and rare) Jamaica Blue Mountain coffee.

Well, Zabar's has convinced us. We might just be able to handle grocery shopping after all. It's just when we look at that 15-quart stockpot ($149) that we begin to run scared! Not scared enough to stop eating, of course; just scared enough to call a caterer!

CANDY, NUTS, CONFECTIONS

| **Colonial** | 782 LEXINGTON AVE. 10022 |
| **Nut Shoppe** | 838-6056 |

Ever had a dream in which you're turned loose in an old-fashioned candy store with a large bag and fifteen minutes to fill it? Well, we're about to make it come true. Better yet, if Joe Namath happens to be making one of his regular visits to the Colonial Nut Shoppe, he might be willing to help you make the run down the aisle shoving nuts, chocolates, Lafayette mixes, gumdrops and peppermint lentils by the dozens into your bag.

Harris Zaharia and his wife opened their tiny Lexington Avenue shop in 1960, and almost immediately began weighing out imported fresh raspberry candies for Lauren Bacall, chocolate sponge candies for Angela Lansbury, coffee beans for Mel Torme, and bridge mix for Roddy McDowall.

The shop is a potpourri of good things. Beyond candies, they carry a selection of shelled nuts. Also look there for dried fruits, crystallized violets and oranges, Danish licorice cuts, and Verkade cookies. They also have homemade Greek baklava with a generous helping of pistachio nuts which Mr. Zaharia is willing to ship anywhere.

To say the least, this is a very good excuse to leave the chauffeur behind and take a walk down Lexington after your next shopping trip to Bloomingdale's!

Godiva Chocolates   701 FIFTH AVE.   10022
593-2845

Difficult to believe that the original Lady Godiva made her reputation by taking things off when this Godiva so obviously makes theirs by putting things on. Frankly, by the time you finish admiring a typically decorated Godiva box, you're not particularly concerned any more about whether they've bothered to put anything in there. True, it would be somewhat of a disappointment to find that there wasn't even one of your favorite cognac cremes or hazelnut pralines. But being handed one of those exquisite fruit- and feather-covered boxes is quite a thrill in itself.

Packaging is of immense importance at Godiva. You might find your half-pound of chocolate nestled in a Limoges egg for $40. If that bores you, ask for the $500 French crystal bowl filled with chocolate ... the bowl, by the way, holds about $8.50 worth of chocolate, which ups the bill to $508.50 (not too important after the initial $500, is it!). Run-of-the-mill gift boxes start at $14 a pound—and as paltry as this sounds, we know of at least two men who managed to send out $5,000 worth last Christmas.

Of course, if that $500 French crystal isn't quite up to your standards, you might have your driver run in that Ming Dynasty vase you've had kicking around for ever so long and fill it right up with Grand Marnier-flavored chocolate. Godiva will mail anywhere in the country if you're feeling generous.

To the little blue-coated ladies in Godiva's antiseptic French blue store, nothing is unusual. They've packed valentine heart boxes with real diamond rings. They've made chocolate centerpieces for sweet freaks. They've sold hazelnut crunch "golf balls" by the dozen. But we're sure *you'll* come up with something that will keep them talking ... won't you?

Kron Chocolatier   764 MADISON AVE.   10021
472-1234

Thomas Kron started making chocolates for his father in Hungary in 1956. Today he makes them for the stars. If he's known as the King of the Chocolate World, it's only because you have to pay a king's ransom to wrest a pound of chocolate from his hands. At least he reigns over his chocolate empire with a great sense of humor and a smidge of semisweet on his lips. Anyone who's willing to carve the word LOVE in chocolate and then ship it out in a wooden crate can't be taking things all too seriously!

There's a machine in the back of Tom's shop from which a river of chocolate flows like the muddy Mississippi. But Tom's special Mississippi is turned into handmade goodies that are regularly mailed all over the world by fans who just can't wait to share their epicurean discovery with friends.

It's almost satisfying enough just to watch Tom dipping plump strawberries or raspberries into chocolate...it can take you into raptures to watch him inserting the orange slices into bittersweet chocolate, but aren't you glad you can do more than just watch?

While you're deciding what to choose you can stand by and watch while Tom interrupts this breathtaking process to help producer Ray Stark select a pound of chocolates for playwright Neil Simon, or assists Leonard Bernstein in satisfying his infamous truffle hangup.

Don't worry. They won't buy out the store. Tom and his wife Diane were saving the chocolate alphabet for you. At just $4 per letter you could send a short note to a friend and come back with change. Solid bricks of chocolate—white, milk or semi-sweet—sell at $8 for 16 ounces. The almond log of pure ground nuts covered in semisweet chocolate is $5 for 12 ounces. He also has pure cocoa powder complete with its own perfect recipe—8 ounces for $3.50.

To those of you who don't have the good fortune to be staying in New York for long, we're unhappy to report that Tom's chocolate-covered fresh strawberries, oranges and cream truffles are not available for mail orders. Now here's the good news: all others can be packaged and travel well by mail: first-class, of course! Or, naturally, you could drop by his Beverly Hills store.

Plumbridge	33 E. 61ST ST. 10021
Confections	371-0608
and Gifts	

Really, it's ever so proper. Settled for three generations in a town house on East 61st Street, it can't help but be known as "confections to the carriage trade." Douglas Patrio will be there to help you Monday to Saturday, or by special appointment if you happen to have a crying need for spiced pecans.

You might find Joanna Carson at Plumbridge picking among figs in antique china porcelain bowls, or Babe Paley selecting dessert fruits and apricots in natural wood spice boxes. French mocha nuts made from the family recipe are found in Indonesian stack baskets, calico tins are filled with coffee beans, and prunes reside in papier-maché boxes.

The Kirk Douglases are but two of the customers who pay from $7 to $1,000 for their dates, depending on whether they're wrapped in cellophane or stuffed into fine antique bowls. But if you find that you're having such trouble elbowing past Lynn Revson that you don't think you'll ever get to the mocha java, ask for the seasonal catalog. Not so much fun, but it *will* let you bring the Plumbridge experience home with you.

CATERERS

Colette	1136 THIRD AVE. 10021
French Pastry	988-2605

Any old pastry cook can slap together a passable croissant or brioche. There isn't a baker in town who can't produce a plum tart or fudgy chocolate cake. Colette is no exception. Her *pain de genes* can stand up to the best of them. So far it sounds rather run-of-the-mill, doesn't it? Just a few perfect French pastries and unflawed cakes? That's because you haven't found out about Colette's secret.

If you're really nice to her, she'll ghost-cook your next dinner party, and no one need be the wiser. Good grief—Colette won't tell.

So feel free to call her to have a *blanquette de veau* sent up to be popped into your oven just as if you'd produced it yourself (you'll be about $8 poorer per person, but well worth it). If that doesn't appeal to you, ask for the *poulet à la crème* for $5 per portion. Also on order are pastries filled with ham, seafood, or mushrooms, and a mousse of chicken, as well as one of ham or seafood. And if you want to serve something that your guests might actually believe you made yourself, settle for Colette's quiche Lorraine of heavy cream with ham, spinach or onions.

The store is closed Sundays and Mondays, but feel free to plan a dinner party courtesy of Colette any other day of the week!

Glorious Food 230 E. 48TH ST. 10017
421-1082

They're yours for the asking in Manhattan all winter, but even better, when you want your party on the Hamptons catered in style, Christopher and Sean at Glorious Food will follow you out there—you can reach them during the summer through Country Living in Southampton.

Christopher was involved in music before he fell in love with catering; Michael worked in television. So you can bet that any party they put together for you will be well orchestrated. You can also bet that the first waiter who tries to carry out one of their hors d'oeuvres on a silver tray covered with a doily is likely to have his hands slapped—they just can't stand the sight of doilies. That's why they'll probably come over to visit you well before they start cooking, just to see what nifty little pieces of antique silver or china are available for serving. Let's hope they find something they like—if they have to run out and buy a tureen or two, this dinner might end up costing you $3,000, and that's six days' budget!

A more accurate figure (assuming your serving pieces pass muster) would be around $20 to $30 per guest, with a minimum of 16 guests. If that doesn't leave you enough leeway to fit in all the friends you were planning to have to a sit-down dinner, feel free to invite 500 or 600. Christopher and Sean can cope, just so long as *you* can handle the bill for the waiters at $40 apiece.

The boys are the darlings of New York society. They'd rather stay home than come over just to fix something as run of the mill as *boeuf bourguignonne* or beef Wellington, so you can count on having the unusual when they join forces with your stove.

It must have been the bee-pollen bread (made of scallions, parsley, watercress, garlic, potato flakes, tapioca and, of course, bee pollen) that convinced Halston they were the only ones just right for dinner parties at his town house.

It's rumored that Diana Vreeland first fell in love with their artichoke beluga (fresh artichoke hearts, beluga caviar, poached egg, homemade mayonnaise, and the tiniest truffle), then continued the affair through a dinner for 550 in the Costume Wing of the Metropolitan Museum. See, we told you Chris and Sean were good with crowds!

Our favorite dinner, when we invite a crowd of 20 or so, starts at 8:00 P.M. with baskets of fruits and raw vegetables served with a fine wine. (You know, that country-elegant style that Christopher and Sean prefer—blue jeans welcome, providing they're by St. Laurent of course.) Next we'll sit down and nibble on that artichoke beluga, and follow it with a simple roast of veal with Chinese snow peas. After all, you will want to save room for the chartreuse soufflé that's been planned for dessert!

Now you know why Geraldine Stutz and the Auchin-closses are willing to follow Christopher and Sean to Southampton—and we wouldn't be surprised if you considered tagging along behind them, too!

Manganaro's 488 NINTH AVE. 10018
563-5331

Four generations of people like us have been calling Manganaro's for their six-foot sandwich. It's perfect when you've asked some friends up to your hotel for drinks and a snack. You'll find six kinds of meat, mixed vegetables, peppers and two kinds of cheese nestled on a bed of lettuce sandwiched between two gigantic slices of French bread, all for $49, delivered, complete with a knife to cut it. If you think your crowd will still be hungry, order some homemade pasta, too. Their riceballs are a specialty. And when your friends start asking where you got the masterpiece, do refer them to the Manganaros; after all, we want them to go on for at least another generation...

David McCorkle/ 216 CENTER ST. 10013
Frank Davis 925-5074

A touch of the unexpected—that's what we love to find. And if having your wedding breakfast delivered to you by a tall, red-headed young actor via bicycle isn't unexpected, we just don't know what is! The menu for that breakfast? Well, it was typical of David McCorkle's yen for elegant simplicity and the best fresh ingredients. Start with a crystal glass of freshly squeezed orange juice, move on to his own hot-out-of-the-oven croissants served with cappucino, then follow it with scrambled eggs with *crème fraiche* and herbs from his garden, topped with fresh caviar in hollowed eggshells. Now your only problem is keeping the groom equally happy with every breakfast you serve him in the years to come. Oh, well, since David's so reasonable you might consider having him make your kitchen his first stop every morning!

David used to be an actor (still is once in a while) who discovered that a taste for fine food couldn't be indulged on an irregular salary. So he cast himself as a caterer and has been playing to rave reviews ever since. His crew is drawn from his friends—a group of artists, actors, musicians, potters, and writers—who supplement their income by coming along with David and his partner Frank Davis. It's not unusual to have your party graced by waitresses clad in full-length ballet skirts or brightened with a bit of a tune from a singing part-time waiter or two. It brings a special sort of energy to parties, which makes everything just a little bit more fun!

A typical McCorkle/Davis menu might include country crudities served in natural wicker baskets, cold cucumber soup, Russian kulebiaka (whole poached salmon wrapped in a rich pastry), broccoli sauteed in Danish butter and garnished with eggyolk mimosa, and homemade cantaloupe sherbet. The feel is unpretentious, and yet elegantly stylish.

David's served on a bus, cooked in the park, and planned meals for from two to two-hundred. No doubt he'll be able to fulfill your requests with equal aplomb.

V. RAGS FOR THE RICH

OF COURSE you've heard that Seventh Avenue is in New York; you just never realized that the whole *world* is there. Don't doubt us; it is! Whether you're looking for Italian silks and leathers, French gabardines, or London lambskins, Manhattan is the place to find them. Really, love, it's enough to make you stop wondering why they put the United Nations there!

Normally we're not the ones to be found slumming in department stores. But New York's are magic... Bendel's, Bonwit's, Bloomingdale's... not another city in the world has anything to compare.

As for the boutiques, can a city which spawned Adolfo *and* Halston be all bad? Of course not. Be it men's, women's, or children's clothing, the best the world has to offer is on the streets of Manhattan.

And where would we be without a bit of sable and an "important" stone to set it all off? Right back in our faded jeans, that's where. But no need to worry about that, Manhattan thoughtfully provides Harry Winston and Ben Kahn to set those unjustified fears to rest.

New York shopping... in short, it's a girl's best friend!... and men like it, too!

DEPARTMENT STORES

Bergdorf Goodman	754 FIFTH AVE. 10019 753-7300

There are certain things you *won't* find at Bergdorf Goodman—bargains, for example. But really, the things you *will* find there so far outweigh the ones that are missing that you shouldn't give them a second thought. If you're looking for real silk stockings (you know—like grandma used to wear) rush right over. And it's positively the last place in town that's ready to supply you with kid-lined 16-button opera gloves. Of course even Bergdorf's will sell only two pairs to a customer—the supply's a bit limited, you know—but if you're careful while sipping your Dom Perignon, a pair should last all season.

You could bump into John Chancellor getting a haircut or Nan Kempner ordering a fur. And if you get invited to the store's top floor penthouse you'll meet Andrew Goodman, son of Edwin, who founded B-G at the turn of the century. The site was originally used for the great Vanderbilt mansion, but the only hint of a Vanderbilt heritage that's left is Gloria running in for an occasional shopping spree.

Even that's rare—when Gloria's busy, which is more often than not, she simply rings up Jo Hughes and tells her to start planning. Jo has her own private offices and fitting room on the second floor. You'll want to stop in and see them at least once, just so Jo will get to know a bit about your looks and lifestyle. But from then on, all you need to do is ring her up and let her know you're coming into the city, and by the time you've arrived she'll have shopped the store from top to bottom looking for things to suit your special needs. If you happen to be in the neighborhood, you can drop in to try them on—but if that's too much of a bother simply tell Jo and she'll arrange to have the best of Bergdorf's delivered to you. It's a VIP treatment that's saved for the special clientele—like you! Well, this whole arrangement works so nicely that you'll not only be ecstatic with her choices, you'll have saved enough time to run out and spend a few thousand elsewhere!

There are, of course, other special features that keep the old guard coming back to Bergdorf. You can have hats custom made, with gloves to match if that's your style. Handmade silk lingerie will be delivered by messenger to your door, and alterations are a matter of course; hands that once fit Balenciaga suits work today to make Bergdorf's ready-to-wear fit as well as custom clothing.

Loyal customers can also have fur showings right at home. The Bergdorf Goodman staff is only too happy to spend a few days in Cleveland if that's what's required to slip you into a full-length chinchilla. Naturally, it would be a bit much to insist that they fly in just to turn your old fur coat into a glorified raincoat lining ($1,200 to $2,500 for this little Emeric Partos innovation)...but perhaps for a sable or two. The Partos tradition is still evident in Bergdorf's timeless furs—but then a man who was lining Gloria Vanderbilt Cooper's raincoats in sable, when he wasn't using it to cloak the Duchess of Windsor, isn't easily forgotten!

If you'd rather shop for furs right in the store, use Givenchy's Nouvelle Boutique as an excuse to come into town. Directress Madame Elieth Roux will be sure to send you invitations to their twice-yearly showings if you ask nicely. And just think how lovely that new Givenchy will look when accented by a little something from Bergdorf's Van Cleef & Arpels boutique!

By the way...if you asked Jo Hughes to set aside size 8s for you, only to discover that your recent visits to Caravelle have helped you to blossom into 10s, you'll be happy to hear about Bergdorf's seventh floor BodyWorks Salon. Not only can you exercise, but you'll do it with Frank Wagner, the director of International Dance for Carnegie Hall. All this for just $80 for ten lessons!

There may be bargains at Bergdorf's after all! While the men are waiting for the classes to end, they can have their hair clipped in Jerry's barber shop right on the mezzanine floor. John

Lindsay enjoys Jerry's $20 facial and the president of Ford has been known to have his sideburns shortened there to meet Detroit's standards (the better to satisfy Ralph Nader!). Jerry refuses to let us in on which of his customers take advantage of the coloring treatments, but he *does* confirm that they're all in love with the phones and food his barbers supply on request.

Well, now that you look so nice, you'll want to capture your beauty in a portrait. Why not slip into that new Givenchy and run right up to Nena's Choice on the fourth floor, where portraits by Zita Davisson are featured along with Nena's own soft florals and frosty landscapes. No one, we hear, knows how to capture a Givenchy better than Zita! She's done portraits for the likes of Polly Bergen, Princess Grace of Monaco, and Glenda Jackson. Maestro Leopold Stokowski and the Maharani of Jaipur have each invested $3,000 for a Zita portrait—but there are others, like the Henry Bryers III and Skitch Hendersons, who have been more clever and taken advantage of the family rate. At just $1,500 for each additional person, you could even afford to throw in a dear friend or two! The Rockefellers commissioned Zita to do six *separate* portraits, including one of Winthrop. Oh well, what's an extra $7,500 to a Rockefeller?

By the way, gallery owner Nena is the great-niece of one of Pablo Picasso's closest friends and confidants. Whatever it was that Pablo shared with Uncle Pedro must have rubbed off on Nena—her gallery is frequented by private collectors from all over the world.

Bergdorf's. With all of this, it's almost worth staying at the Plaza so you'll be next door!

Bloomingdale's 1000 THIRD AVE. 10022
355-5900

On Monday and Thursday evenings, young materialists spend hours ogling each other there. It's a sure bet for any model, actress, ad-agency secretary, art director, or security analyst who doesn't have a Saturday-night date. Some weekends, it's difficult to tell if the crowds are shopping for clothes or just looking each other over. But there's never a moment's doubt that without these eight stories of temptation, many New Yorkers would manage to live a more frugal existence.

Bloomingdale's is the hub of New York department-store shoppingdom. If you want it, they have it. They also happen to have just what everyone else in the city wants, which causes it to be the busiest store in Manhattan. Going into Bloomie's past noon is pure madness. You'll struggle to find a salesperson, and you'll fight to keep her. We must admit that for the few moments you manage to capture her attention she'll be polite and well informed. Take advantage of it—the average sales attention span is two minutes, and once that noon whistle blows in Bloomingdale Country, even Emily Post would forget her manners. Literally thousands of salespeople aren't adequate to help the throng of shoppers in the 59th Street store once that magic hour arrives, so *do* shop in the morning.

Of course everyone shops there for a reason—the same reason that every major retailer and designer has for frequent Bloomie visits: to see what's new. Just about everything that is or was anything got its start at Bloomingdale's, from YSL's Rive Gauche to Pet Rocks.

Halston's first department-store boutique was in Bloomingdale's. Ralph Lauren just sold ties until the store's late, great Kate Murphy decided to make him a star (now his boutique sells $4,000,000 annually—how much of that goes on your back?). You'll find domestics like Anne Klein, Bill Blass, Scott Barrie and Calvin Klein, as well as imported Missoni, St. Laurent, Issey Miyake and Sonia Rykiel, each in separate boutiques planned to display a good range of their collection. Be ready to bump into Diana Ross as you round the corner between Missoni and Rykiel; she wouldn't dream of coming to New York without a Bloomie break. Sometimes she just can't wait—in case of emergency, she shops by phone from California.

On any one day you might find the likes of Gloria Vanderbilt showing her sheets and her skirts, while Craig Claiborne cooks in the Gourmet Shop (where, we might add, they have the finest housewares selection in the country). You could spot Walter Matthau outfitting himself in something suave. As for Catherine

Deneuve, if you spot her, it will probably be testing the scents in the perfume department. They're all Bloomingdale's devotees.

We are too, particularly when it comes to the furniture floor. Dina Merrill says it's too expensive up there; as for us, we say that makes it all the more fun. We rather liked the attitude of the Frenchman we saw there one day who fell in love with one of the store's model rooms, bought it, and had it shipped to Paris. One $460 fireplace, a $7,900 tapestry, and $3,000 worth of flooring, and he had his own little Bloomingdale's Country right in the heart of Paris! Don't feel upset about losing that model room; the store carries everything from African ethnic to antique English. You're sure to find something you like.

If you don't spot us in the furniture area, try the Delicacy shop. One whiff of the pastries plus a sample of Bob Gumport's 300 cheese varieties insure that you won't go home empty handed. Bob's so concerned with the quality of these taste treats, he's even been known to fly to the caves in Roquefort to complain about over-salting in the cheese. Every bit of Brie is made especially for Bloomingdale's, and even the color of the package of Droste chocolates was customized before it was allowed on the Delicacy shop counter. Not only is Bob demanding, he knows the prestige his store commands.

If you can't bear the thought of hassling the crowds, keep in mind that Bloomingdale's has been known to open its facilities on special evenings for worthy charity affairs. If organizing a group of 500 seems a bit much just to get in an hour or two's unhassled shopping, it can only mean you haven't been there lately on a Saturday. Believe us, finding 500 who are willing to put on formal dress can be easier than finding sales help on an average day. Naturally there's a less extreme solution (though it's not nearly so entertaining). You can use "At Your Service," the store's personal shopping service. It will buy for you from all departments, let you pay with a single check, then have your purchases shipped in one package anywhere in the world. Convenient, isn't it! It's those little conveniences, plus those big fashion names, that make Bloomie's so addicting!

Numerous jokes have been made about Bloomie-holic wives, but our favorite story is no joke. At a fund-raising dinner we attended not so very long ago, one affluent New Yorker promised a major donation equal to his wife's yearly bill at Bloomingdale's. Now *that's* what we call generous!

Bonwit Teller   FIFTH AVE. AT 56TH ST.   10022
355-6800

What Bergdorf's is to the old guard and what Bloomie's and Bendel's are to the avant-garde, Bonwit's is to the new guard. It's where you'll find Nancy Kissinger, Paul Newman, and Virna Lisi when they're in Manhattan. You might just see Rose Kennedy shopping for her offspring; we swear we see her there almost every day she's in town! And why not—what with its Fifth Avenue location, it's ever so convenient to get to.

Bonwit's is fresh and trendy. The first floor is accessory heaven. We go there to find the truly unusual, and we're never disappointed. The buyers spend a great deal of time traveling and bring home treasures from Brazil, Africa and Europe. Things aren't necessarily expensive—we loved a $4.50 wooden bracelet (until we realized how underpriced it was)—but some are even beyond the reach of *our* daily budget. We simply couldn't justify $35,000 for that 18-karat gold cosmetic box, even though it *was* wafer thin and had ample room for eyeshadow, lipstick and other necessities. Rather than leave empty-handed, we found elephant-hair rings in the Hunting World Boutique on the first floor for only $7.50 and marvelous jackets made in China for $18.

Like all the other major stores, Bonwit's has its super shopper, Connie Buck, who will coordinate your head-to-toe wardrobe for that next trip or the coming season. She'll make a special call at your hotel if you're just in for the day, or she'll come to your home if you're planning to stay. Stop in at her sixth-floor office and she'll save you the trouble of traversing all nine floors looking for that perfect outfit.

Lucky you! Missoni has a whole department on the first floor. And the S'fari Room on four is fair game for anyone who wants to find a hint of exotica. Giorgio Sant' Angelo and Christian Aujard are mainstays there. So is almost every name on fashion's best-dressed list.

The design salon on the sixth floor carries well-edited collections of Galanos, Stavropoulos, Bill Blass, and Adele Simpson. Children's clothes are on the ninth floor, but most of those little people really go to nine for Mr. Jennings' charming old-fashioned ice cream parlor, where banana splits taste like they did when *we* were kids. It's a favorite spot for very-new guard (never much older than six or seven) birthday parties.

Bigger folk might want to wait out the festivities at Café Orsini's, where the light, airy atmosphere makes a great setting in which to nibble on a spinach salad or a marvelous mini-hero with a mini-eclair and cappuccino to follow.

And if you're not hungry at all right now, just stop by Carol Guber's food section and prepare yourself for a later date. Now, now... none of those stories about it being the cook's day off! Not only will Carol give lessons, she's a former James Beard student. Once she's through with you, you'll be ready to give that cook a month off!

Henri Bendel   10 W. 57TH ST.   10019
                     247-1100

Isn't it nice to know that New York has one store where you can always get your money's worth... providing, of course, that you're carrying that $500 a day allowance! Henri Bendel is so exclusive that even Buster, the doorman, is a classic! And for good, chic, avant-garde fashion, Henri Bendel makes it simple to buy a whole wardrobe with one-stop shopping. If Chloé has a brand new look in raffiné silks, it's at Bendel's first. When Zandra Rhodes produces yet another fantasy, it becomes Bendel's dream. And as for the accessories to go with them, all we can say is that it's almost as good as a trip to Paris!

Bendel's gets interesting before you even cross the threshold. Bob Currie started the trend to controversial window display a couple of years ago, and while every major store has now picked up on the idea, none are as habit-forming as Currie's. New Yorkers look forward to his sidewalk art—windows packed full of pasta and panties were just one of his traffic-stopping ventures.

The inside of the store always lives up to Currie's dramatic introduction. It's hard to pass through those first-floor accessory boutiques without stopping to admire the detailing on at least one Carlos Falchi bag. Further down their little London street you'll run into cosmetics, jewelry, scarves and the Shoe Biz area. People from all over the country look forward to stepping into the new season with Shoe Biz on their feet, despite the fact that their price tags set budgets back a step or two.

No one passes by the paper shop without picking up some of Bendel's wonderful embossed stationery, or at least a postcard or two and a wicker backgammon set to keep them entertained during that long limo ride back to the country house. Any bedroom benefits by your visit to Scentiments with its potpourri, candles, and pillows planned to be olfactory delights.

As if you really care, Bailey-Huebner maintains that kitchens can be chic and functional at the same time (what do you mean you can't even remember what yours *looks* like!). The special little housewares shop is loaded with Lucite, baskets and enough gadgets to keep any new-fangled cook content.

Other main floor attractions include Peter Barton's men's wear (what could be more Continental than a Barton walking stick?) and Tabletopping—mats, napkins and cloths that make entertaining festive. Our favorite hostess gift, to give *or* receive, is a set of eight larger-than-lap-size napkins—the better to protect you from that straying soufflé, my dears.

Bendel's is always so packed with new items, it makes sense to cultivate a special salesgirl who'll let you know as soon as the newest goodies arrive. Vivianne takes care of us on the second floor. She's a typical Bendel salesgirl—pretty, smart, and dressed so stunningly you'd feel embarrassed if you didn't live up to her. Besides, she's truthful. If something doesn't look right, she lets us know. Devastating, to be sure, but helpful in the long run. Besides, what with Jean Muir, Holly Harp, those new travel-planned crepe separates by Zoran and the fur perfection of Viola Sylbert to choose from, she's sure to find *something* that will make you look divine. And she's right, you *do* look better in sable than you do in muskrat!

Look for classics on the third floor. That's where you'll find Sonia Rykiel and Ralph Lauren. On four, you can make small investments in both European and American ready-to-wear pieces, or large investments in whole outfits. And of course, our favorite fourth-floor stop is Beauty Checkers, where Amy Green gives makeup lessons in her salon. An hour with Amy, and you can face anything, even trying on shoes at yet another Shoe Biz boutique, where the crowds are just as big as they are on the first floor, and the prices are smaller.

On five you'll find lingerie and at-home wear designed by the likes of Willi Smith, Carol Horn, Holly Harp, and Fernando Sanchez. Plus there's always a good selection of swimsuits for those of you who resort to resorts when the city skies are gray.

By the time you reach the sixth floor, you'll welcome the idea of turning yourself over to the master of head-to-toe pampering, Jean Louis David. You can be washed, cut, dried, waxed, manicured, exercised, and pedicured all on one floor. Isn't it nice to leave feeling like a million dollars when you've only spent a few thousand?

Lord & Taylor   FIFTH AVE. AT 38TH ST.   10016
                     391-3344

We never shop at Lord & Taylor without lunching with William Palmer at the Soup Bar on the tenth floor in the men's department. His Scotch broth is always delicious, and his apple pie is so much in demand that now it's all he serves for dessert. We also make it a point to look for any new additions to the Waterford crystal collection, which just could be the largest in New York. For about $300, some of those larger Waterford pieces can be made into spectacular lamps.

Personal shoppers are available who speak Spanish, Portuguese, French, Italian, Yiddish, and German. Some customers have been dressed by personal shoppers for years and have never even been seen in the store. Many are just another card in Theresa Orlando's 30-year file; as head P.S. she has catalogued each customer's needs and purchases. She sends things to Americans living in the Orient who can't wear Japanese sizes and sends furniture to South America, as well as keeping in-store customers content and well garbed.

When you plan your next outdoor gala, remember that you can special-order a striped party tent from Lord & Taylor for only $2,500. It will take two weeks to arrive, so don't hope for last-minute magic. You'll find everything else you need for a fine fandango on eight and nine. On your way down, stop on three to pick up a little something to wear to your party. Maybe a Valentino or Basile if you like to look tailored, or an Oscar de la Renta if you want to look tantalizing.

Saks Fifth Avenue　　FIFTH AVE. AT 49TH ST.　10017
　　　　　　　　　　　　753-4000

Obviously you know where that is. If you haven't been to the store at 49th and Fifth, you've at least been to one of the 30 other branches across the country, so you know Saks quality. It's the only store in the country where you'll find a $100 Panama hat, a teddy bear that drinks water and wears a lorgnette, a vicuna bath robe and a chinchilla-lined cashmere sweater—all under one roof.

If you took our advice before going to London on $500 a day, you probably bought your Vuitton luggage at Saks. Some people listened to us; in one day Saks sold two steamer trunks at more than $3,000 each. Now there's an excellent Vuitton zippered dog case which allows you to take your dog on the plane and still gives him enough room to work out. If you've a yen for the sporting life, you'll also find Vuitton ski and racquet covers, golf and duffel bags, seamen's bags, shooting cases and the ultimate: a Vuitton mailbag for the yacht. That's all in the luggage department, which has the most extensive collection of fine luggage in New York.

Trunks for $3,000 are nothing new at Saks, however. At the official opening in 1924, the windows displayed a $3,000 pigskin trunk, a $1,000 raccoon coat, chauffeur's livery, and foot muffs for auto trips. In those days the store featured an electric number-ing system which was installed above the 50th Street marquee so that chauffeurs waiting across the street could be called in time to pick up weary shoppers. The numbering system is gone now and so, we regret, are most of the chauffeurs. Today those special ladies don't want to fight those main-floor crowds.

Instead they phone Tommie Ritter and ask her to plan a whole season's wardrobe at once. Some call from as far as Texas and have the box full of Adolfo and Revillon furs sent out. Tommie dressed an entire Detroit wedding party without ever being questioned. One of New York's most famous fashion connoisseurs trusts Tommie enough to shop for Chloés by phone, even though most average around $700. If you choose to come into the store see Sarah Mittleman, who operates the Connoisseur Suite where you'll find those Karl Lagerfeld designs. In the Private Island, directress Lily will help you to choose Blass, Beene, and Adolfo.

Saks' Fauchon Boutique is the most extensive in the United States. You'll find coffee at $5 a pound, asparagus at $11 a jar, and an array of marvelous pâtés and sweets to fit any budget. At Christmas those prepackaged food baskets make lovely gifts. For $225 the Cuisinart machine will grind pâté and steak tartare, chop vegetables, and make flaky dough in 15 seconds. If you can't end your dinner *without* a cup of espresso, you can special-order an espresso machine for $1,500.

In the Linen Pavilion, Rebecca Convisor will design rugs and toss pillows to match the exclusive African Bakuba linen designs. Do remember that the rug will run around $600 and throw pillows are $100 each, so budget accordingly.

If you carry your puppy in a Vuitton dog case, you'll want to visit the Dog Toggery. Mr. Merlo will be happy to make a mink coat to keep your chihuahua from shivering. Perhaps your poodle needs an evening dress; it's a mere $30. A set of full dress tails will run the same price. Doesn't your St. Bernard deserve a cosy ski parka with rubber shoes to match? If you're gift giving and are confused about the proper size, consider a sterling silver or Porcelain de Paris dish for the Alpo.

Grandmothers love to shop at Saks. Some think nothing of spending $200 for the exclusive French christening dress by Nanouchka. And how convenient to have a separate file on each grandmother's darling so she can always send just the right size.

Every luxurious fur in the world is sold by Miss Burke in the

Revillon Salon. The last full-length sable was sent to Southhampton, a pretty little cape number for $100,000. You can get something more economical—a sporty lynx coat at $27,500 or a sweet street-length chinchilla for $12,000. Revillon mink blazers are becoming extremely popular at $8,000.

Remind your friends from out of the country that language is no barrier at Saks. The International Shopping Service speaks dozens of languages, including Arabic and Japanese. The Shah of Iran's sister bought a perfectly beautiful set of linens and had no difficulty communicating her needs to the multilingual staff.

BOUTIQUES/TAILORS/ACCESSORIES

For Men and Women

Bottega Veneta 655 MADISON AVE. 10021
371-9218

If what you're looking for is the most beautiful leather in the world, do add Bottega Veneta to your shopping list. All we can say is thank heaven this Italian store came to New York. We were getting a bit fatigued what with having to run over to Italy every time we needed a clutch purse! Now not only can we stop in to visit them on Madison Avenue and East 60th, we can get a Bottega Veneta "fix" at I. Magnin, Neiman-Marcus, Bergdorf Goodman or Korshaks. With what we've saved on air fare we can almost afford their luggage!

It's a small shop, replete with replicas of antique Venetian furniture and positively overflowing with great shoes, sweaters, and accessories. From the moment you open the door, it smells of good fabric and leathers.

There are frames crafted of mother-of-pearl, ivory, or burled wood. There are kidskins, woven leathers, plain leathers, and suedes. There are silk scarves in a variety of rich Italian designs. The selection is so varied that you'll be glad there's a staff of seven fashion-conscious sales people to help you make your choices. And if you happen to have manager Peter wait on you, you're luckier still!

Claude Manet	131 E. 57TH ST. 10022
Fashions	752-6197

Claude's specialty is fine Italian gabardines—the best in town. He has skirts, pants, jackets, and trenchcoats paired with washable silky shirts. And to insure that everything is perfect, Claude keeps a tailor on the premises, and keeps an eagle eye on those dyed-to-match separates to make sure that a beige is a beige.

The clothing is structured, but the atmosphere is relaxed. Nestled in a neo-Georgian building, the shop is furnished in rich brown carpeting, birchwood paneling, and touches of brass and mirror that emphasize the natural beauty of the structure. Isn't this the way all stores should look?

Ellen is waiting to help you put the pieces together. And even if coordinated classics in silk and gabardine aren't your style, stop by the shop for a look. It's worth seeing.

Gucci	689 AND 699 FIFTH AVE. 10022
	826-2600; 753-0758

As if it isn't enough that you have to put up with seeing the same Gucci bag being carried by everyone everywhere, you have to put up with those perfectly horrid expressions on the salesclerks' faces, too! Honestly, you'd think those dour glances would be enough to tarnish their double G's! We did see one or two manage a smile the week after *New York* magazine devoted an entire article to their glum and somewhat irritating attitude, but it wasn't too long before Gucci customers had to readjust to service without a smile.

Nevertheless, nothing seems to discourage the crowds. Even two shops can't handle all the New Yorkers who want to add more GG's to their belt rack. They're mobbing the handbag, luggage, jewelry, and ready-to-wear store. They're standing in line at the shoe, bag, and scarf store. We sometimes suspect they've been hypnotized.

While the attitude of his clerks might leave something to be desired, we must admit that Dr. Gucci is a thoughtful man. How considerate of him to think of putting solid gold buttons on his $1,500 vicuna blazer. How sweet of him to remember to waterproof those $69 canvas loafers you've been buying by the dozens.

Speaking of loafers, it's time for you to add a new style of men's shoe to your Gucci wardrobe. In addition to the traditional moccasin, Dr. Gucci is turning out a brand-new style, perfect for day or evening wear, terribly sporty, available in a myriad of materials and priced at just $110 to $140 the pair.

They're just part of the good Doctor's move to produce fewer initialed pieces in the future, and more limited-edition pieces. What could please the status seekers more!

Jackie Rogers   787 MADISON AVE.   10021
            744-7303

Jackie Rogers is one of the few women we know who have the nerve to call the late Coco Chanel an old battle-ax. Not that Coco would have cared—she'd have realized it's just Jackie's ex-model's way of covering up just how much she worships her old fashion doyenne. It shows in everything she designs and sells in her Madison Avenue boutique.

Jackie's place is silver on gray ... metallic leaf screens plus muted carpet and walls. And though her New Man jeans and silk ski underwear T-shirts ($25) might be the items that draw Dustin Hoffman and Joel Gray in, it's a cinch that Lee Radziwill is more likely to be attracted by the classic women's suits at $300 to $375. Not too many men have snapped up Jackie's quilted Chinese jacket lined with sable, but we're sure that Bob Currie, the man responsible for Jackie Rogers' understated decor, will give one a try.

If you really want to get clipped, try Jackie's chic little men's barber shop. Bill Blass and Herbie Mann elbow each other out for the privilege of spending $18 for a shampoo and cut.

And when in Southampton (often, we hope!), try Jackie's Pizza Parlor. Just don't try it enough to outgrow those slim-cut trousers you bought at her boutique!

| **Jaeger** | 818 MADISON AVE. 10021 |
| | 628-3350 |

Well, well. You'd think that after being in business for 150 years, Jaeger would have come up with a new idea or two. They haven't, but dedicated customers don't seem to care. Most New York Jaegerians are just as pleased as punch that it's no longer necessary to go all the way to Regent Street to get the real thing, though some still insist on the trip just for the pleasure of spending some time wearing their new blazers in the Connaught dining room. These staunch London lovers really needn't worry. Not only is the Madison Avenue shop the first American retail outlet Jaeger's started, the stock isn't nearly as complete as that you'll find in London. Isn't it nice that there's still an excuse to take that long distance shopping trip?

There is *some* younger clientele at Jaeger these days, though the vast majority of their business still consists of East Side wives and their matching husbands spending their Saturday afternoons buying camel hair and gabardines. That's togetherness. If you want to add a classic or two to your wardrobe, pick up a blazer at around $175 and coordinate gabardine pants for $80. Once you buy a pair of slacks for him and realize that the price tag is only $65, you'll want to round out the investment by adding a $290 suit. Greg in the men's department will be happy to help you find the perfect one.

Jaeger's not really the place to go shopping for dresses, but it's a wonderful spot for locating that slim, rain-resistant trenchcoat you've been searching for. It's just $250, but then it isn't lined. You'll also find a good selection of shirts in both silk and cotton in the $40 to $60 range, as well as some luxurious scarves priced from $16 to $30.

You may not be overly impressed with this classic haberdashery, but it's worth a stop just to feel some marvelous camel hair, gabardines, and linens.

Jag	21 E. 57TH ST. 10022
	751-9522

Oh, dear... the things one must go through in order to get a good pair of jeans these days! First you have to pick your way around Bianca Jagger diapering her child on the plush chocolate carpet, and as if that isn't inconvenience enough, then you have to fight Marlo Thomas for that perfect size six jumpsuit. Just stand up for your rights and tell her that you had your eye on it first. After all, owner Adele can always order her another pair from their Australian warehouses.

Jag originated in Australia, but since their migration from the continent to the Big Apple, their status rating has been moving straight up. In an era of status jeans, that silver and black Jag label (yes... it *is* supposed to be worn outside) is the *pièce de résistance*. If Jag can't contain your curves, it's time for you to consider spending your allowance on a trip to Nicholas Kounovsky's exercise classes instead. A poor substitute for trendy denim, it's true, but you'll thank us in the long run, when you're in great shape.

At Jag you'll find more than the finely made, finely fitted jeans and denim separates which have gained them U.S. fame. You'll also find a bevy of silk shirts, velveteen pants, and tapestry blended with other fine fabrics from around the world. Call on shop manager Jennifer to help coordinate and accessorize them. If she can make you look just one tenth as young, comfortable, and with-it as she is, it's money well spent!

Jean De Noyer,	219 E. 60TH ST. 10022
Inc.	838-8680

Since you summer in Southampton, you already know De Noyer. Jean Pierre thoughtfully arranged to open a Manhattan branch so you don't have to suffer withdrawal during the off season. But you'll still have to get your tennis togs in Southampton... the city store is geared a bit more to street wear.

De Noyer is a combination of French cuts, Italian sweaters

and a very tattered carpet. If only they could spare five minutes and stop people from rushing through the front door, they'd have time to change it! Shop De Noyer for young classics—nothing faddish, just good blazers in cotton, velvet or denim, New Man jeans for men and women in velvet, cord, and cotton, and cashmere sweaters in ultraclassic crew necks for $125.

For men, a sporty suit sells for about $295, and most are appropriate for fathers and sons alike. For women, tailored white cotton and silk suits for summer sell at about $395. Margaux Hemingway drops in to pick up $12 T-shirts and wraparound skirts, claiming it's a refreshing change from all the trendy boutiques in town. Dustin and Anne Hoffman find it another good place to shop together.

The clientele is generally young, but it's not unusual to find some businessmen in their mid-sixties coming in for a regulation blazer or two.

La Seine 221 E. 60TH ST. 10022
593-3800

La Seine is a long, narrow shop which caters to long, narrow customers of both sexes. This immediately qualifies Cher and Diana Ross to wear their things. They do. It immediately disqualifies any man with a waist over 38. And though they do alterations, we can't imagine you asking them to do anything other than taking things in!

The clientele is composed of a fashionable, loyal group drawn largely from the fields of advertising, public relations and the theater. They love the $300 suits and $45 sweaters Danielle brings back from France on her six annual buying trips. Obviously the stock is up to date! It's composed of classic looks by Christian Aujard and dresses by Renata. Cashmere and silk frocks will set you back $300, a good pair of gabardine pants a mere $60.

Candice Bergen shops here for the simple hand-knits she wears for her Polaroid commercials. Danielle put men's wear in the front, but women's wear isn't far behind. Go straight to the back of the store, and maybe if you're very lucky Candice will be there with her camera and agree to photograph you in your new outfit.

Mario Valentino 5 E. 57TH ST. 10022
  486-0322

We can't vouch for his men's shoes, but Mario Valentino's women's shoes are the most comfortable walking styles we've ever worn. We've worn our stacked-heel loafers with every pair of slacks in the closet (about 147 at last count)—$75 is a small price to pay for *that* brand of versatility. The pumps and ankle-strap styles have been worn by the likes of Barbra Streisand and Mrs. Joel Grey, but they're as likely to have picked them up in Naples, Rome, Florence, Milan or on the rue du Faubourg St.-Honoré as they are to have bought them in good old New York.

The sales staff, especially Claudio, like to brag that it takes 312 light bulbs to brighten the main room of the store alone. The better to see that wonderful Italian detailing with, you know. In among the chrome-encased bulbs and plexiglass displays you'll find the finest herd of antelope in the city. They're not on the run; they're stitched into blazers, coats, skirts, and suits. Our favorite was piped in woven leather—an incredible touch for just $600!

If you're wondering where to pack all those new shoes, take a peek at the Valentino luggage. Some of those pieces are so cleverly constructed that one of those dear Italians might just have to show you all the extra features. Simply make a request to see Claudio or Pietro and ask to see the leather duffle... so perfect for weekends, and with everything designed and made in Milan you're assured of excellent workmanship. Now, aren't you glad to be able to say good-bye to those crowds at Gucci!

Riffs Men's 1075 THIRD AVE. 10021
Boutique 688-6826
Carina Nucci

Riffs is the perfect place for super-together couples. While he spends a couple of hours picking out things for himself, she can try on exquisite shoes and boots at Carina Nucci. Both stores are creations of Jean-Luc, who cleverly realizes that the under-40 New Yorker wants more out of clothes than coverage.

Most of the clothes are imported from Italy and France, so they have that marvelous continental look. You can take the suit approach at Riffs and find a fabulous Rafael for about $300 or, for summer, a three-piece Egyptian cotton gabardine. If you prefer separates, Jean-Luc can show you a navy cashmere blazer at $195 which could easily be teamed with one of the 15 colors of wool gabardine slacks (we loved the burgundy). Add a crepe de chine shirt for $75 and a lightweight $60 cashmere pullover, and the look is fabulous. We don't believe you can walk out of Riffs without looking dapper, since Jean-Luc has such exquisite taste. The thing we all like is that Jean-Luc has a strong range of small sizes, but larger men needn't be disappointed, he does have some 46's too.

In Carina Nucci, ladies will find shoes priced about $70 and boots about $150. We must mention the bags you'll find here, since they must be some of the best in the city. Our favorite was a lovely daytime bag in rust kid with removable straps that made it a wonderful evening bag as well. Double duty for $195. You'll see your favorite Judith Leiber bags, too, but do shop often; they move quickly.

Salvatore	717 FIFTH AVE. 10022
Ferragamo	751-2520

If you are on your way to Steuben Glass, you must stop in at Ferragamo. No doubt you've seen Ferragamo shoes in the better departments of Saks, I. Magnin or Neiman-Marcus, but this is the only place you'll find such an extensive collection of handmade shoes for both men and women. Talk to Mr. Slocum, who will tell you more about shoes than you ever dreamed you'd want to know. Somehow all that knowledge makes it worth a woman's while to spend $120 for those little lizard shoes. Men's shoes are reasonably priced around $80. All the shoes are made on American lasts to accommodate our longer, narrower feet.

According to the lovely red-haired Celeste, who once worked across the street at Gucci, Ferragamo clothes are typically Italian and tend to be more conservative than trendy. Ferragamo features wonderful Italian knits, but it's their silks that captured the American fancy. American women aren't into knits the way the Italians are, explains Celeste, and would much rather spend $500 on a silk suit than $150 on a knit. Customers buy the signature silk blouses by the handful at $170 and think nothing of taking home two silk dresses at $500 or $600 each. But do try at least one of the Italian flat-knit sweaters. Once you've felt its lightweight luxury, you won't hesitate to call in for more.

San Francisco	975 LEXINGTON AVE. 10021
Clothing	472-8740

Any store that's sold Greta Garbo a mackintosh has got to be on the most-recommended list. If it's a store that's also frequented by Andy Warhol, it gets extra status points. We're not too sure whether Andy does his own shopping there or stops in to pick up things for his cohorts (well, they *do* stock things for men *and* women, you know!), but we have it on the best authority that it's one of his favorites. Owners Howard Partman and Michael FitzSimmons have also had the foresight to keep English tea biscuits in stock (just $5 the tin) so that if you don't happen to fall in love with one of their cuddly lambswool robes you can still walk away happy.

Actually, you can stay there happy, too. Just make yourself at home in one of the comfortable armchairs that are scattered throughout the Persian-carpeted, parquet-floored boutique. With its warm, dark walls, it's as much like a gentleman's library as a boutique.

The shop owners have definite preferences—for natural fibers and superb cut. You might find a tweed hacking jacket for $175 in other stores, but where else will you see a pure silk dressing gown for only $95? Or a genuine badger shaving brush? Or deerskin gloves? Whether imported from England, France, or Italy, there's one common denominator: everything is well bred and the best of its kind. And even if you don't happen to feel like nestling into a $150 Harris tweed blanket or watching Jack Nicholson shop, it's nice to know that there's one little corner of Manhattan where a gentler sort of atmosphere has managed to survive.

Ted Lapidus 666 FIFTH AVE. 10022
582-5911

1010 THIRD AVE. 10022
751-7251

Paris wouldn't be complete without Ted Lapidus...so why should New York have to do without? Luckily, it doesn't! Ted's Fifth Avenue shop is stocked with all the things you'll find in his main shop on avenue Pierre-1er-de-Serbie in Paris. The only thing that's missing is Ted, and if you're lucky you might even find *he's* just flown in on the day you arrive.

If he hasn't, ask for Arnaud Thierry, who'll guide you through the best of the Lapidus world. Coordinated sportswear for men and women, dresses, coats, accessories...anything you need is right there. You remember those wonderful leathers you fell in love with at Ted's Paris shop? Well, he's offering you another chance to snap them up in New York. His luxurious wools and wonderful silk shirts are here, too. Even if you've already finished your New York boutiquing, it's worth a stop at Ted's to pick up that perfect hat or belt to round out every outfit. Our only advice is that if you're planning to stop in, consider paying your hotel bill in advance. Heavens, you wouldn't want to find yourself all spent out, would you?

We heard about one young lady who stumbled into the Fifth Avenue boutique and was thrilled to find the beautiful knit cocktail dress she'd been looking for for just $40. Why, it even had its own matching chiffon flower. Then she realized the $40 price tag was just for the flower. As for the knit, we're afraid to tell you. The French and Middle Eastern customers who pass through the doors seem better prepared to deal with Ted's rate of exchange. And he does try to make it easy; the staff is fluent in French, English, Spanish, German, Chinese and

Arabic. Perhaps you should drop in and brush up on your Arabic before you buy those next oil stocks!

For Women

Adolfo 538 MADISON AVE. 10022
688-4410

When Barbara Walters, Betsy Bloomingdale, Mrs. Armand Deutsch, and Gloria Vanderbilt Cooper all show up at a luncheon wearing identical suits, one thing's for sure: it's an Adolfo. After all, why be concerned with exclusivity when you can count on Adolfo's innate good taste to see you through?

His customers are the doers, the movers, the women who can't be bothered shopping around when they're in the mood to spend $800 or $900 for a suit. So they simply drop in to visit Adolfo and invest in a bit more of his dependable quality. Of course they know by this time that there's no stock available at Adolfo—but they're also smart enough to realize that if they really need something, he'll have it done overnight. Play your cards right and he'll do the same for you. Just look him straight in those sparkling eyes and tell him you love his skirts as much as you used to love his pillboxes.

And how pleased you'll be with all that special attention he gives to perfect fit. But if he happens to be on vacation the week you're in town (really... how could he!) you'll find Miss Elizabeth waiting for you among the Chinese screens, gold Empire chairs, satin couches, and throngs of feathers. Not only is she a delight, she'll also give you all the Tender Loving Care that Adolfo normally lavishes on his special clientele.

Barbara, Betsy, and Gloria agree that your Adolfo wardrobe won't be complete without one of his three-piece suits at $775. For evening you'll probably like the velvet skirt with chiffon blouse at $550. Once you've become accustomed to spending big for his investment clothes, you may never have to shop anywhere else again—except of course at Saks Fifth Avenue, which has an exclusive on his designs. But then that wouldn't be any fun, would it?

Alaine Goodman　　225 E. 57TH ST.　10022
　　　　　　　　　　421-1636

We've tried to keep this name a well-guarded secret. Our own little fashion coordinator with the uncanny feel for what's happening. She keeps a constant stock of up-to-the-minute designer goodies—sportswear, evening clothes, costume jewelry, furs. Best of all, everything is available at a discount, and at the price of Adolfos these days, it won't be easy for you to stay on your budget if you don't find *some* good buys.

Of course you have to have an appointment to visit Alaine's apartment. But if she doesn't have just what you want hanging in her closet, you can talk her into taking you on a shopping spree at the better garment houses in New York.

Alice Schweitzer　　739 MADISON AVE.　10021
　　　　　　　　　　861-3350

Run right on over to see what new things Missoni has come up with this season. Alice Schweitzer has a better selection of their things than anyone in town (yes, Bloomingdale's, we do mean you!). Not only that, she's willing to impart to you the secret of mixing last season's separates with this season's new pieces. Think how much *that* handy little lesson can save you! Not only can you walk out with a totally new look, you can even afford to tip the doorman.

Mrs. Leonard Bernstein swears by Alice's French imports. Alice's two- and three-piece Chanel copies enchant Mrs. Henry Fonda. And even *we* don't mind that the $350 price tag is a good $500 less than a *real* Chanel once manager Valentine finishes explaining to us all the quality that's sewn into every seam.

It's the kind of shop you'll want to frequent, as Alice constantly has new treasures coming in; and you *do* want to keep on top of the new Missonis, don't you? Take a quick look at the accessories, too. Was that cinnabar brooch really tagged at just

$23? Oh, well, you can make up for it by taking home the Chinese jade mirror for $310!

Art Bag Creations 735 MADISON AVE. 10021
744-2720

If you found some beautiful cobra skins on your last trip to Bahia, do go to Art Bag Creations to have a wonderful handbag custom made from them. Or if you could kick yourself for not buying that super little velvet clutch you saw in Paris last month, draw a picture of it for Lou Rosenberg, and chances are he already has the pattern for it. If not, he'll have one of his European-trained experts style something just for you. Art Bag specializes in the one of a kind handbag using fabrics from their genuine paisley collection or exotic skins such as hand-painted whipsnake, python, or cobra. Don't worry, nature lovers, they will not use the skins of any animals on the endangered species list. These *un*dangered creations start at about $100, but you'll also find some stock bags around $30. Don't despair when your other old handbags need restoration and rejuvenation. Art Bag has all the facilities to take care of them.

Arthur's 27 E. 61ST ST. 10021
Dress Shop 838-3482

Arthur, Arthur, Arthur... how could you! The largest size that man stocks is a ten, so if you're anything over that, you might as well prowl elsewhere. If you've been having trouble finding a chic size four, you're in luck!

Let's just say that Arthur's hand-picked stock of European imports is a bit on the conservative side. Wives of board chairmen melt into Empire chairs when they enter these doors. Not only are the clothes authentic, the furniture is, too!

Despite all this, Arthur manages to discover new designers and keep a wonderful variety of interesting sportswear, evening and daytime styles artfully displayed in his magnificent 61st

Street town house. It's definitely worth a stop if all the good advice we've given you on New York restaurants hasn't already put you out of his league!

Austin Zuur Ltd.	835 MADISON AVE. 10021
	861-1211

We've heard some women complain that the clothes at Austin Zuur are too much like Halston's. But since the prices are so much lower, isn't complaining rather mad? Especially since the clothes at Austin Zuur *are* so much like Halston! Why, Nan Kempner says the black satin jumpsuit she bought there for $300 is simply the most useful thing she's ever owned—and you just *know* how practical Nan is! She and Nancy Kissinger have the same go-anywhere black linen dress. You know, the one that Nancy wore to the Shah of Iran's lawn party. But if you'd rather not share the same looks with them, opt for your own reversible full-length cape at $450 or a suit of beige angora: skirt, shirt, and shawl for just $325.

One of the nicest things about visiting Austin Zuur is the warm greeting you'll get from Huibert Zuur and Edward Austin (almost as warm as that beige angora suit you're buying). They'll even stage a mini-fashion show if you request it. Nice service, considering the prices start at just $125, isn't it!

Betsey, Bunky &	746 MADISON AVE. 10021
Nini	744-6716

Sounds as if they might have been the girlfriends of the seven dwarfs... doesn't it? Well, before you get carried away with images of Grumpy, Sneezy, and Happy, we might as well tell you that this triumvirate isn't as Walt Disney as it sounds. What we really have here is the latest incarnation of Betsey Johnson... you were wondering what ever happened to her after Paraphernalia, weren't you? Paraphernalia designers don't fade away, they just move on to hand-stenciling walls in their own little boutiques.

It wasn't so very long ago that Betsey, Bunky and Nini was simply everyone's favorite store. On the other hand, it wasn't so very long ago that everyone wanted to look like an overgrown little girl. How cute! There were weeks when you couldn't *see* the varnished floors for all the "Mary Janed" feet tramping over them. Oh, well, times change and so does Betsey. Today she pleases a slightly more eclectic clientele—like Berry Berenson Perkins (you know ... Marisa's sister) and the McCartneys, who had the girls fashion them matching capes for an album cover.

Everything that isn't imported from France or England is made right on the premises, with Betsey still heading up the design team, doing such things as a skirt and blouse made out of kitchen toweling. All the new and trendy things of the moment are here. T-shirts are only about $12, but if you try, you can add up a $500 set. Don't overlook it for one-of-a-kinds and specialty items.

Courrèges 19 E. 57TH ST. 10022
755-0300

Ho-hum ... one more Courrèges shop. If you want to look like everyone else on the block, do stop in. We really hate to be picky, but when it comes to Courrèges, give us Paris. Not that the basic hospital decor changes. Not that the rows of "C" insignia sweaters are different. It's just that the salespeople seem to have been gifted with a touch more imagination in Gay Paree. It was all the 57th Street girls could do to put together a red skirt with a red sweater and battle jacket the last time we stopped in, and we just *know* that André had more than that in mind when he shipped them over.

Though we've chatted with Liv Ullmann in the Beverly Hills store, we've yet to see Marlo Thomas browsing through the sweaters in the New York shop, *despite* the fact that we've heard she shops there. No doubt she tries to stop in when she can be alone. The shop's so tiny that she'd get claustrophobic if there were another body on the premises. Why not wait until you get to Paris?

| **Evelyn Byrnes, Inc.** | 480 PARK AVE. 10022
355-0480 |
|---|---|

Have you gotten a bit bored with shopping at Martha's for the past 20 years? You'll be happy to hear that we've found you a lovely alternative—one of New York's few remaining couturier shops—Evelyn Byrnes.

Evelyn and her daughter Harriet preside over a shop that's been carrying on quietly and successfully for over 20 years. It's a simple combination of black floors, ivory walls, and magnificent crystal chandeliers. It's also a place where you'll find eight dressing rooms and enough personalized service to make you feel catered to for days. They sit you down, bring everything out—assist you in the dressing room—help you to decide—and will even call you when something comes in that they think you'll like.

In the front boutique area you'll find moderately priced Bill Blass and Dior, but you'll want to do your serious shopping in back. Ask Kay Pettingill to show you the newest Galanos if you like Jimmy's style. We picked up a super sportcoat for just $1,300 last year, but his newer versions may run a bit more. If you have something dressier in mind, look at their selection of Trigères, or splurge on a Norell. But think carefully... at $500 a day, that whim could set you back a week!

| **Halston** | 33 E. 68TH ST. 10021
794-0888 |
|---|---|

We really do have to give him credit. He's come a long way from those days as a millinery maestro to his current reputation as *le dernier cri* of American fashion. Why, you can hardly even get into bed any more without finding his name splashed across the sheets. Oh, well, it *does* keep one from getting lonely, doesn't it!

There's so much Halston in the world today, it takes four floors on Madison Avenue just to show it all. Of course they're all classically pure floors—subtle combinations of beige carpeting, chrome, and stark white walls that go ever so perfectly with his clothes. Snuggle down into the off-white Ultrasuede sofa if you really want to get that Halston feel.

Although the atmosphere is purely tasteful, the windows *can* give you a few shocks. The last time we stopped in, they contained half a dozen bald models. In any event, the windows are constantly changing, so they're always worth a look.

Having gotten by them, you can waft into the shop on an air of Halston scent. For $70 you can make an ounce of it your own. Better yet, bottle it in $69 worth of Elsa Peretti silver made to be worn around the neck. That's the way that Halston likes it best.

Three steps down on the street level, you'll find an incredible array of sweaters, skirts, slacks, men's wear, hats and scarves. Peruse it quickly, then establish yourself with Pam Abinet, the manager, and let her know that you'd really rather not dress in ready-to-wear. Naturally, those $280 cashmere dresses are lovely —but you already have three at home. And how could she possibly doubt that you appreciate Halston's $300 Ultrasuede shirtdresses when you've gone to all the trouble of buying a special bottle of Woolite just so the maid can wash them properly. But isn't it time you graduated to *real* Halstons? The ones he designs just for you? Of course it is! Ask Pam to introduce you to Sassy and Sherry in the third-floor couture department. But they do insist on appointments.

Once they know your taste, Pam will meet you anywhere in the world, swatches, samples and tape measure in hand. After all, she does it for Liza Minnelli, why not for you, too?

We've heard that once you've had six mentions in the *WWD* "Eye" column, you may even meet Halston himself. You'll recognize him by the chrome and glass desk and the basic black uniform, the eyes masked by sunglasses no matter what the weather outside, and the essence of Halston drifting from the candle by his side. We're sure he'll be cordial, and take as much trouble suggesting styles for *you* as he has for Mrs. William Buckley, Elizabeth Taylor, and Marisa Berenson Randell. And if he seems to be selling you an overly extensive wardrobe, don't worry a bit.

He'll be glad to supplement your purchase with enough Halston luggage to get it all home.

Pack a little something for the man in your life in that duffle bag, too. How about some Ultrasuede jeans for $135? A matching jacket would be nice, also. And don't forget the cashmere sweater and scarf.

If you're generous enough, he might even decide to get you something, too. The cashmere caftan at $400 would be lovely on you in shocking pink (and since it fits everyone, he wouldn't even have to worry about the size). The black velvet pantsuit is a steal at $380, or for $1,000 your *amant de coeur* can woo you with hand-painted chiffon pajamas. If he has taste, he'll add Elsa Peretti's solid gold mesh bra to be worn underneath. Make sure you wear it with your favorite silk shirt, unbuttoned, of course, to show off your $4,000 chest.

And, by the way, if the couture prices that Sassy and Sherry were quoting sent you into a faint, stop on the first floor where the Halston show samples are sold. All you'll have to do to pick up that lovely brocade pant and coat outfit from the last show is manage to slip into a size eight and then still lift your arms high enough to hand over $950!

Helene Arpels   665 MADISON AVE.   10022
                     753-1581

Don't you ever accuse *us* of not appreciating the simple things in life! The shoes at Helene Arpels are some of the simplest in New York. Some of the most expensive, too.

Helene whiles away her hours in Paris, designing every shoe you'll find at the salon. If it hadn't been for a little prodding from Rose Kennedy she might have been content to just go on year after year making the list of the world's best-dressed women. But that Kennedy drive is contagious, and before Helene knew what hit her, she was dressing the feet of the rest of the world's best dressed ... slipping slippers on Fran Stark and Harriet Deutsch, and giving a boot to Mary Wells Lawrence and the rest of the Kennedy women.

So if you have a yen to make that list (you mean they didn't name you last year!), stop in and try on one of her classic beach loafers ($75) or a pair of evening pumps in satin (starting at $275). If you *insist* on having rhinestones Helene will try to discourage you; if she can't, she'll have them sewn on by hand to your design. We're afraid to tell you what the price is for *that* little whim. Boots are available in leather, antelope, or satin, ranging in price from $250 to $325. Beware: if you ask for a pair in suede, the salesladies might just wash out your mouth with saddle soap.

If you'd like a bag to go with your new pumps it can be special-ordered in snake, kid, or velvet—but since one of Helene's rules is that shoes should never match accessories, don't be unhappy if you get a surprise. At $250 to $350 per bag, we hope it's a nice surprise. Maybe you'd be better off just asking manager David Scoggins to hand you that nifty little Panama straw in the corner for $350.

Henry Lehr 1079 THIRD AVE. 10021
753-2720

Henry Lehr's New York shop is young and groovy. Not quite as young and groovy as during those London days when he originated tie-dye suede and fashion-right metallic leathers... but trendy nonetheless. The tasteful little cork and bamboo shop can't be more than 1,000 feet in toto, but by the time Henry finishes giving you a guided tour complete with explanations of how each piece of clothing can be worn several ways, the place seems three times its size. He'll take a Castelbajac vest and show you ten different ways to wear it over Kenzo wrap skirts, Jag jeans, or one of those wonderful cashmere turtlenecks he has stacked in his bamboo cabinet at just $55 a sweater. At *that* price, you'll *want* ten!

Henry likes to think of his shop as the equivalent of a designer's workshop. You'll find the latest French looks from Kenzo and Castelbajac, as well as a selection of Lighthard designs to give the Americans representation (don't worry, we hadn't heard of him either—but once Henry showed us his things, we were sorry we hadn't discovered him sooner). All the store's merchandise is trendy, yet sophisticated.

The merchandise is displayed in a happy combination of good lighting, healthy plants, and blessed peace and quiet. Lehr believes that if you're going to be spending money, you should be able to hear yourself think. Really—that could change our lifestyle, couldn't it! He also believes that smoking is hazardous to your health, so put out that Virginia Slim before you cross the threshold. While browsing, keep an eye on the other shoppers; you might run into chic New Yorkers, such as Beth Rudin De Woody, up from her loft in SoHo.

If Henry's out when you arrive, ask manager Joan to help you decide between his blazer cut from navy surplus trousers and his coat cut from an army blanket and trimmed with fatigues. For $225 the coat can be yours, but *do* watch out for M.P.s. You wouldn't want to be picked up for impersonating an officer, would you?

Julio 867 MADISON AVE. 10021
249-2904

You say you're going to Régine's tonight and you haven't a thing to wear? Don't waste a moment—tell the driver "Julio's, please." You might also mention to him that it's on Madison, though by this time we're sure he's as familiar with its location as he is with his own front door. It just *has* to be the most popular after-dark boutique in town!

Julio came all the way from Barcelona just to sell dresses to Peggy Lee and Lena Horne. He was already a star by age 20. Some say the reason he understands evening wear so well is that he's young enough to have a real feel for today's disco and club scene. Evidently the appeal is universal—his things are snapped up by Bloomingdale's, Bonwit's, Bendel's and Beverly Hills' own Georgio's almost before they have a chance to hit the racks in his own Madison Avenue boutique. Practice one-upmanship and surprise the folks back home by arriving at your club in a new Julio before they've seen it featured in *Vogue* magazine.

Ellen, the manager, will help you choose something that's just right for you. Actually, it isn't too hard. Lucky you—everything is made in a one-size-fits-all manner so you can stuff yourself on caviar and still never outgrow that latest Julio. But as long as you manage to restrain yourself, you'll be able to slip into his young-at-heart silk chiffon jerseys, theatrical crepes, and soft, billowy styles. Take the trouble to choose something in aubergine and you'll not only look smashing at Régine's for dinner, you'll get a good table to boot. It *is* her favorite color, you know!

Part of the fun of shopping at Julio's is the painful indecision of choosing between his double-faced kimono sets in red and black and his tie-dye silk shirts. It's a pleasure-pain experience. The other part of the fun is guessing what the store is going to look like. Bendel's own Bob Currie designed it in a way which allows all display nooks and dressing rooms to be moved. As a result, every time we go in the store it has a new floor plan. Not that it ever loses its chic brass, bronze, and gray flannel sophistication. Simply hope that they don't move a wall while you're in the dressing room and leave you stranded sans chiffon!

Julio's has a constant stream of trendy New York shoppers, who readily part with $500 per outfit. Don't be surprised if you turn a corner and bump into Babe Paley or Joanna Carson.

Kamali, Ltd.   785 MADISON AVE. 10021
                    879-3228

Norma Kamali is always good for something unique—that is, if your business manager is not piqued by paying $800 for a jumpsuit made from an actual used silk parachute (jump cords still intact, of course!).

While ordinary folk have managed to find a few things here, the taste level runs more to Bianca Jagger than the Main Line. The faint of heart and over-35 crowd are warned away from Norma's shop, and not just because they have to handle a flight of stairs to the second floor before they arrive. If you're the type who'll faint when asked to pay hundreds for an evening dress cut from gold lamé curtains, you're probably better off with Bergdorf.

Even the decor of Norma Kamali is offbeat. The glitter-coated gray laquered walls are decorated with moon-shaped mirrors. If you feel like taking a nap when you see yourself in her cocoon coat made of old sleeping bags, by all means stretch out on the quilted gray satin platforms that are scattered throughout the shop.

When Norma Kamali isn't shooting the rapids on the New England shore, you'll find her in her New York or Beverly Hills boutiques. She'll tell you to sit down and make yourself at home before you buy. We couldn't agree more. It might be simple to spend $28 on something like her Savage swimsuit, but paying $800 for that parachute getup is going to require some clear thinking!

Koos Van Den Akker	795 MADISON AVE. 10021 249-5432

You'd think that for $500 you could get better than pieced-together fabric scraps. Whatever is the world coming to? These patchworks aren't really the result of inflation; they're the work of Koos van den Akker, that Dutch master of fabric collage.

People are calling Koos van den Akker the Rembrandt of ready-to-wear, since his stunning wool suits and coats have gained such an audience. Besides, how chic: everyone can have a favorite *French* designer—leave it to you to come up with a Dutchman!

Koos spent years with Dior. Now he's displaying his own designs in a second-story Madison Avenue boutique. If you don't find him in, it's because he's busy in his 38th Street workshop piecing together scraps into another design—he insists on never repeating a collage! Have Helene or Neil help you look through his collection if Koos is busy.

It's a medley of textures and colors, always combined with a fine sense of tailoring. Expect to pay $475 to $700 for a coat or suit, knowing full well that the look alone is justification enough! The last time we visited we fell in love with a reversible wool jacket and matching wraparound skirt, appliquéd and piped with contrasting fabric. We also thought his little blousettes (short dresses) were great for over pants, and at just $140, how can you go wrong? Besides, in your heart of hearts you know you've always wanted to own something made by the designer who fashioned Elton John's velvet robe!

Marion Javits and Nan Kempner move to the Koos beat, too, buying both clothes and those marvelous Carlos Falchi accessories. What could be more appropriate than a bag pieced together from lizard and snake? And at just $150 and up.

Lady Continental	836 MADISON AVE. 10021
Shoes	988-0110

Now that you've found your Chanel copy suit at Alice Schweitzer and your Chanel bag at Cache-Cache, you'll want a Chanel pump to finish the look. You'll find the best at Lady Continental. Edgar Hyman stocks that two-tone classic in every shade that Coco ever dreamed of, as well as a few that never entered her imagination. The best news is that these beautiful Italian shoes are only $62. At these prices you don't even have to worry yourself about making decisions—simply buy every color. That's what Ethel Kennedy and Rita Hayworth's daughter, Princess Yasmin, do.

Edgar styles beautiful boots, too, in the finest leathers at prices that range from $90 to $145. And in case you *haven't* picked up your Chanel-look suit at Alice Schweitzer, he has a select collection of imported sportswear.

By the way, if you'd rather pick up that suit in Paris (why not... that *is* the only place you can get an original, after all!), he'll be happy to run those shoes over to you at the Paris Ritz. He's done it before; he'll do it again. Of course we should warn you that it might up that $62 price tag a bit...

Lonia, Inc.	55 W. 55TH ST. 10019
	757-2655

One thing about Lonia: she has the highest-priced collection of nobodies in town. But then who's to say that today's nobody isn't tomorrow's Bill Blass?

The stylized shopper loves Lonia's flair for picking unknown designers who are moving in the right direction. Leave it to Lonia. With *her* eye for fashion she probably had Mary Travis tied up in a pair of harem pants before they were even a twinkle in Seventh Avenue's eye!

How far out of your way would you go to pick up the newest Tomotsu? Two blocks you say? Well, we're sure you'll walk at least a half mile once you see his beautiful fabrics in all their high-styled glory. And in all fairness, Harriet Winters' designs are looking very sharp, too.

At $50 to $75 for a shirt or skirt, you can always afford to throw them away if the look you buy at Lonia doesn't jell! She's also great for accessories—you'll see everyone from Ford models to Bernadette Peters stocking up on her summer bamboo bags at $32 or her hand-crocheted purses at $16.

By the way... the classic shopper still loves her silk shantung raincoats for $85. At prices like that, you can understand why they're singing in the rain!

Lorris Azzaro	733 MADISON AVE. 10021
	861-5155

It wasn't so very long ago that Lorris Azzaro was teaching the alphabet to French schoolchildren. Today he's teaching American women a thing or two. His dresses, to quote the *Daily News*, whose reporter panted over them from the day his Madison Avenue shop opened, are "so sexy they look alive even on the racks." They're now considered to be one of the fastest ways in Manhattan to catch a husband, or better yet, what with price tags ranging from $200 to $1,200, to latch on to a good provider.

Not every wife would have been so patient when it became apparent that her husband's secret desire was to stitch up evening dresses, but Michele Azzaro took it in stride, and today has been rewarded with a chain of nine French, Italian and American boutiques.

If your life could use a few changes, ask shop manager Gavin to show you the Azastrass in clinging jersey with a beaded bodice and open back. Just $780, and you've assumed a newly sensual personality. In order to avoid causing New York to have an even larger traffic jam than usual when you're out walking, buy one of his wonderful black and silver evening sweaters for just $275 and cover up. Then just pick out a pair of shoes to match, and you're on your way to causing total chaos in Fun City!

Lorris works primarily in jersey, though he also drapes petal-soft chiffons and gossamer crepe de chine. The last time we visited, his best seller was a shimmering silk style at just $600. No wonder it was so cheap; he'd sold 320 of them in six short weeks! If that doesn't cause a rush to the justice of the peace, nothing will!

Jacomo, Inc.   25½ E. 61ST ST.   10021
832-9038

This is probably the only place in the world where you'll find handmade pangolin bags. And no wonder. No matter how you pronounce it, it's just another name for anteater. Luckily, those scaly African creatures look a good deal better after Jimmy Kaplan fashions them into purses than they did when they were crawling around Kenya. With faces like that, we're not surprised you didn't bother to bring any back from your last safari.

Jimmy's breakfronts and vitrines hold the most fantastic selection of one-of-a-kind bags that we've ever seen. It reminds us of going to Tiffany's... it's almost too hard to choose. We're sure Elizabeth Taylor, Diana Ross, and Barbra Streisand have the same problem.

If you decide to pass up the $1,000 crocodile bag, you can always settle for a paltry something in fabric at $70. At least, sample the Jacomo perfume ... it's divine.

Mario of Florence	767 FIFTH AVE.　10022
	832-7931

Don't go to Mario and expect to find the perfect pair of shoes to wear this weekend. Or even next weekend. Go to Mario knowing full well that you'll wait about nine weeks for your first pair of handmade shoes (but only six weeks for your next ones). If you're patient, you won't be disappointed. Babe Paley never has been, nor has Mrs. Henry Mancini. Mario's shoes are so habit-forming that typical customers come in only twice a year and order 20 pairs per visit, which could be exhausting if it weren't for those comfortable white velvet chairs and that nice-looking Jean-Pierre. He could make any woman add one more color to her list of shoe "musts."

The initial last (foot form) will cost $150, with most shoes somewhere in the neighborhood of $80. Women like Mildred Natwick, Mrs. Biddle Duke and Claudette Colbert don't think that's too much to pay for a shoe that fits perfectly and always complements their outfit. And of course, James Galanos wouldn't think of having a fashion show without first consulting Mario about color-matched shoes for every new design.

You'll probably want to invest in at least one pair of gold or silver evening shoes and one pair of velvets. In the latter category we recommend a deep wine with a high heel and slim straps a la St. Laurent. Since this is the only store in the United States where you'll find them, you probably won't see these shoes walking nearby—unless you come toe-to-toe with Betsy Theodoracopulos.

Martha, Inc.	475 PARK AVE.　10022
of New York	753-1511

Personally, we can live without Martha's Dress Shop. It would be nice to find selections from all of the major designers—

Valentino, Norell, Galanos, Chlóe, St. Laurent, Zandra Rhodes, Thea Porter, Ungaro, Geoffrey Beene, Stavropolous, Halston, Hanae Mori, Trigère, Bill Blass, Mary McFadden, etc.—in one store. But with a little extra footwork, we can find most of the same things and get far better treatment.

Even though Martha's clientele are the richest women in the world, and her label is as sought after as any designer's, no one should have to put up with her brand of rudeness. So don't expect special treatment. You won't find that at Martha's.

If it's your first trip in, expect to be sized up—and we don't mean dress size. It seems that a customer has to prove her worth before she is treated to any of the special service Martha claims to bestow on everyone. Obviously, some women are well proven, and are treated accordingly. Without a doubt, the lady who flew in from Texas and asked Martha to wrap up a $12,000 windowful of Trigère was treated politely. And Martha herself admits that she prays for the health of the wealthy widow who invests $250,000 for Martha's special treatment each year. But unless you're in their league, you should probably be wary.

If you don't mind buying good service and can stand your ground in the face of high pressure, you may be challenged by Martha's. But *we* can live without it.

Ruth Matthews   767 FIFTH AVE. 10022
751-2037

Eleanor McGovern, Mrs. Winthrop Rockefeller and Betty Ford are Matthews devotees. You know how it is when you've been on the campaign trail ... more than one suitcase is a bother! So *they* stop in to see Ruth Matthews and walk out with a single suitcase that holds enough to dress them for the entire season. Skirts, dresses, suits, accessories ... they're all there. Ruth will even include sketches of how to put them together if you're totally unequipped to make decisions.

You're Matthews material if you demand a practical wardrobe, hate the thought of a crowded closet, and find dressing much more of a necessity than a pleasure. *Ruth* finds dressing a pleasure... dressing *you*, that is! So be nice to her. Put your wardrobe worries in Ruth's skillful hands and give her all the pleasure she wants. Though you'll get just a single suitcase four times a year, you'll find enough inside to get you cleverly through any occasion.

We've run into Mary Tyler Moore several times in the Beverly Hills store, and she frequents the one in New York whenever she's in town. Mary appreciates a decor that's more than just chrome, glass, and stark style, so she loves those Mexican tiles in Ruth's General Motors Plaza boutique. And all those fiesta pillows piled on the banquettes add a Southwestern flair that you don't find in the city very often. In between sitting on these colorful comfortables, you might take a look at Ruth's denim and Ultrasuede suit with ivory buttons... just $170, fancy that! Simple sporty dresses will run $130 and up, sweaters from $40.

The styles appeal to the Hepburns, both Audrey and Katharine, though you probably won't see them dropping in quite as often as Mary does. *They're* too busy using Ruth's clothes in just the activity they were planned for: traveling, my dear, traveling!

Montenapoleone   789 MADISON AVE.   10021
                      535-2660

Make a list of all the Italians you might consider ringing up to ask for advice on lingerie—Marcello Mastroianni, Giancarlo Giannini, Federico Fellini, really it just goes on forever—then add one more name to the list. Vittorio Truchi. He's been running the Madison Avenue branch of this famous Italian lingerie house since its inception, and he's been getting wiser every day. It didn't take him long to figure out that while silk and satin are lovely, travel-happy Americans would rather have something practical and wrinkle-free to tuck into their Gucci's. So while Montenapoleone lingerie regularly slithers up to the $150 to $300 mark, it does so in washable polyester satin or crepe.

The store has a very clean, slick line to it, with everything (including Vittorio) beautifully displayed. Merchandise is coordinated by color, and fabrics have a magnificently rich feel despite their drip-dry, packable personalities.

One of the best sellers here is a crepe polyester gown at $150. Jean Harlow gowns are popular, too, bias-cut with large gores in front and back for a fabulous flowing look. They run around $134. You might pick up a little something (and we *do* mean little!) for $45, but really, we have bigger plans than that for you.

Since you probably have as many ideas on sex appeal as Vittorio does, have your gown custom-made. If you specify hand-stitching, expect to pay at least $300 and expect to wait, as all the gowns are made in Italy. Don't quibble about the time lapse. Princess Aziz, Mrs. Laurance Rockefeller, and Mrs. Brooke Astor have all been patient at Montenapoleone, and they assure us that good things are worth waiting for!

Roberta	645 FIFTH AVE. 10022
diCamerino	355-7600

Any store that pays $500,000 rent can't be all bad, can it? Rumor has it that's what it took for Roberta diCamerino to join that Fifth Avenue Italian hierarchy and be reunited with her old friends Ferragamo, Gucci, Buccellati and Bulgari. Rest assured, the signora won't have any trouble meeting the overhead: a few $60 scarves here, some $2,180 cashmere coats there, a few $70 umbrellas for good measure.

Once you've seen the diCamerino store, you'll understand why it's well worth the half-million. Floor-to-ceiling diagonal panels of fine blond wood divide the slick, well-lighted facility into separate areas for leather goods, daywear, eveningwear, and outerwear. There's even a terrifically stuffy doorman thrown in for good measure.

The clothes are built for traveling, so most are made of either a lightweight wool jersey knit or a polyester knit with a special stitch which allows it to breathe and accept printing better than normal polyester would. Which is lucky, since

Mrs. diCamerino's specialty is trompe-l'oeil prints. Nothing is quite real—collars, cuffs, and sashes are printed right on the fabric (think of all the time and money *that* will save you when accessorizing; no wonder you can afford to pay $500 for a simple day dress!).

You'll love the leathers at Roberta diCamerino, too. Moccasins run about $80, with matching purses available from $78 to $500. And you'll want to pick up at least one of Mrs. diCamerino's famous trompe-l'oeil velvet bags. Does $800 seem a bit much? Well, if you can't make a snap decision about that one, rest easy in the knowledge that with 35 European diCamerino stores, you'll surely be passing by one again before the season's over.

Ask for Gina when you arrive. She has a wonderful flair for coordinating, and terrific patience when dealing with the B.P.'s. For the rest of the world, she has no patience at *all,* but we're sure she'll be happy to see *you.* When she brought out the Orologio leather coat on our last visit, she knew she'd found our weak spot. How could we resist that double-faced calf; it's so soft they didn't dare line it! It's the ultimate $950 leather. She added a simple dress for $650, doused us with a spray of the new diCamerino cologne, made sure the bold initial "R" was showing on our new velvet bag, and sent us out to face Fifth Avenue one more time.

By the way; if your Yorkie's been looking a bit disgruntled lately, you can treat him to one of the store's full line of carrying cases for man's best friend. If you bring him along to pick out his favorite, he can probably stay in the playpen that Giuliana diCamerino provides for her three dachsunds. After you pay $430 for the canine carrier, surely Giuliana won't mind dog-sitting while you look for something for yourself. In fact, she'd probably be delighted.

Rose Lash	58 E. 55TH ST.	10022
International	759-6213	

The last gift box we looked forward to receiving was from Tiffany's. But then that was before we met Rose Lash! We used to think that no one liked to be boxed into a corner, but Rose was just the lady to change our minds.

Rose has mastered the art of taking helpless males under her wing and helping them to assemble perfect gift boxes for those ladies they might want to impress. If they want to make only a $90 impression, she'll group French-cut pants with a striped T-shirt, signature scarf, straw fedora, and belt. If they're thinking more of a $210 impression (now you're talking!) she'll put together a "theater box": a combination of wrap sweater, black satin bias cut skirt and matching English cloche. And since she personally assembles a different box for every customer, you can even feel safe sending in that Austrian count who claimed he wanted to make a $500 impression on you.

Rose's boxes have made it as far as Australia and Japan—with so many being circulated, you're sure to receive one eventually. But if you're patience is running a bit thin, why not make it even easier on him than Rose will—just drop in, assemble your own box, and charge it to him!

Fiorentina Shoes   691 MADISON AVE.   10021
838-9098

Tasteful Americans like Mrs. Henry Ford and Mrs. Henry Fonda got so terribly tired of running all the way over to Florence to buy their shoes that they convinced Jacqueline Sappia to start selling her wares in New York. The shoes had hardly been unloaded from the boat before fashionables like Mrs. Tony Bennett and Mrs. Abraham Ribicoff joined in too.

Today Mary McFadden accents her favorite outfits with shoes by Jacqueline—she knows there just isn't a better place for finding variety of fabrication for day and evening shoes. Be it antelope, calf, satin, brocade, gold or silver—Merle and Marilyn can pull you out a pair handmade in Jacqueline's own Florence factory. Just slip into one of those marvelous little Florentine needlepoint chairs and put your feet in their hands!

Tony Anton	11 E. 54TH ST. 10022
	753-2577

Oh, Tony... how could you do it to us? Now that we've blown a week's allowance on the sleek silk knits at Veneziano, you've opened your own shop to tempt us with a whole new array of goodies. And to tell you the truth, our resistance has never been great.

Neither is Lee Radziwill's... she ran in the first week and picked up one of Tony's new French navy-blue double-breasted blazers. Tina Sinatra was hot on her heels, opting for two of Judy Hornby's new print dresses. And Nan Kempner couldn't help but walk out with two or three of those airy silk sets.

You'll see a few changes in Tony now that he's left Veneziano. The overly tailored lady is being fast replaced by a sportswear–conscious woman who'll select from his color-coordinated selection of silk shirts, shimmeringly feminine eveningwear, crew-neck and V-neck sweaters and gabardine pants and skirts. In addition to his own superb collection, there are carefully selected choices from his new French and Italian sources, with a more limited amount from his established sources in Milan, Florence, and Rome.

Colors are more vibrant, looks are less matronly, and all in all it appears that Tony Anton has a winner.

Tony still stocks his beautifully tailored raincoats. Not that we ever expect it to rain on your parades... but just in case!

Veneziano	819 MADISON AVE. 10021
Boutique	988-0211

Really. With all the traveling you do, shouldn't you drop that Dior and put on something a bit more packable? Veneziano can keep you looking great even when you've become a member of the million-mile club! There's nothing so terribly practical-looking about silk jerseys and silk knits, now is there!

We dislike those tiny little Veneziano dressing rooms, but we've seen Mrs. Neal Walsh and Nancy Ittleson emerge from them smiling. Even the Princess of Luxembourg has been known to drop her sable there and take a super sportswear look back home with her.

Ralph always keeps such a terrific selection of silk jerseys on hand that it's as easy to pop in and pick up the perfect shirt for St.Tropez as it is to find an evening look for Monte Carlo. Rest assured, not one of them will wrinkle. The skirt and shirts come in marvelous prints—and at just $250 the set, how can you go wrong? If you've overreached your allowance this week, avoid the silk dresses at $350 and take home a cotton T-shirt at $50. And if you *really* want the world to know where you've been shopping, be sure to pick up one of their appliquéd denim and velvet "status" pant suits. We've heard that Mrs. Vincent Astor always packs three—and you wouldn't want to be caught short, would you?

Valentino   677 FIFTH AVE.   10022
             421-7550

There he is...one block from Bonwit's, two blocks from Bergdorf's, and five blocks from Saks. Of course there *are* other Valentino devotees, Alexis Smith and the rest of the Kennedy women to name but a few, but it was Jackie who turned that famous Valentino initial into a V for victory.

Naturally, you've been to Valentino's Paris boutique; in fact, you've probably even visited him in Milano. Well, you'll feel right at home with his New York location. It's the same beautifully eclectic blend of travertine marble, wood, brass and mirror—even the same Valentino-designed bamboo fabric on the sofas. The same beautiful clothes, too. They don't call this Italian the pied piper of luxury for nothing! And though his things are extremely conservative, he has managed to turn classicism into class and has a wonderful way of looking extremely timely despite his confessed refusal to follow fads.

Besides, how conservative can you feel spending $450 and up on a simple dress? Have directress Eve Orton help you slip into a silk shirt for $225 or a soft little $200 sweater and you'll probably forget you ever knew the word "trend."

Valentino's mens wear is equally unobtrusive, but his choice of fabrics does reflect the luxurious price tag. If you manage to find a three-piece suit at Valentino for under $550, it's sheer luck.

Now we know how much you love your new Valentino shirt... and the suit's sheer heaven, too... but when it comes to packing up and taking them home, skip his black canvas luggage at $1,500 for four pieces. After all, even a Valentino devotee must be practical some of the time!

Yves St. Laurent	855 MADISON AVE. 10021
Rive Gauche	988-3821
Boutique for Women	

Yves might get carried away with petticoats and babushkas at times, but the *real* St. Laurent look is dependably classic. All those years at Dior had to show up somewhere, didn't they! As a result, the YSL cult consists of two types of women.

More conservative dressers like Lauren Bacall keep a standing order in for his new trousers styles as they're introduced; one that's new in every color, please. The fit's so consistently good at St. Laurent that there's really no need to keep trying on styles once you've found your size. So why waste the taxi fare down to Madison Avenue? Just phone in orders and have those wear-forever sweaters ($50 to $200) and classic capes delivered. Social butterflies who wouldn't dream of wearing the same thing twice follow the Christina Onassis/Florinda Bolkan approach and have fun with each season's new fantasy pieces.

Whichever way *you* look at it, one thing's sure: once you're hooked on Yves St. Laurent, it's difficult to be comfortable in anything else. There aren't many who'd trade their dependable YSL poplin suit for something by another designer!

In New York, Yves's signature T-shirts (the best bargain in the shop at $18) and costume jewelry are displayed in a muted beige, brown, and terra-cotta shop that combines stark track lighting with soft rock tapes. Things are so clearly displayed you probably won't need to call on Connie Uzzo to help you. But if you did, she'd be sure to recommend the garbardine blazer at $350 as a good first investment. Follow it up with at least half a dozen of his silk crepe de chine shirts at $130 to $205. Let's see; even if it's one of those weeks when the value of the franc has been floating downward, we've exceeded our daily allowance, haven't we! As Yves would say...*c'est la vie!*

Yves St. Tropez   4 W. 57TH ST.   10019
                        765-5790

                        251 E. 60TH ST. 10022
                        759-3784

It's not worth a flight over from London, but if you happen to be in the neighborhood, do drop in. Nestled in among the gray suede walls and carpeting and the rosewood ceilings you'll find semi-precious French clothes. Do not disturb them unless you're prepared to part with $495 for a suit, or $125 for a crepe de chine blouse.

Robert's managed to make Joni Mitchell and Goldie Hawn happy, though. They both like his women's wear, which in truth is much more avant-garde than the things he carries for men. It's a small shop, and since everything in it is manufactured in Paris you won't squeeze in unless you've stayed on your diet. Really...don't make us laugh! Perhaps you'd be better off investing that $100 in a good lunch and not worrying about staying slim for Yves St. Tropez!

For Men

A. Sulka   711 FIFTH AVE.   10022
                 980-5200

A man feels comfortable the moment he enters Sulka. Everything is neatly displayed in this tiny efficient shop decorated with glass counters, chrome trim, and wood paneling. It has the same ambience you'll find in Sulka stores all over the world.

Robes here begin at $250, but if you simply must have a custom cashmere or silk robe, be prepared to pay up to $1,000. For custom shirts, they feature the finest fabrics from France and England. Shirts start at $40 for cotton and go up to $125 for silk.

If custom pajamas are your thing, you'll find yourself paying upwards of $100 a pair. Custom undershorts are a bargain at $50 a pair. Custom suits start at $750.

The man who shops here keeps a low profile. He is not flamboyant. On the other hand, we heard of a man who comes in every six months to order $10,000 worth of shirts!

But you say you're in a hurry. Sulka to the rescue—they also have ready-to-wear shirts, ties, golf jackets, slacks, blazers and handkerchiefs.

Arthur Gluck	37 W. 57TH ST. 10019
Custom	755-8165
Shirtmaker	

Decisions, decisions. First Arthur makes you choose among 400 different fabrics, then he tells you that you're perfectly free to choose any style your heart desires. If you manage to walk out without at least a dozen shirts it can only mean you've a heart of stone. What's even more dangerous is the fact that you'll have to resist the remaining oxfords, chambrays, and silks every time you bring those shirts in for his custom laundering service. It would be better if you sent them in with the butler—just hand him at least $2.50 per shirt and tell him to ask for Room 403.

Arthur's been making shirts for the last 25 years, and his list of celebrity clients just keeps growing. Alan King and Robert Sarnoff button down in Gluck designs. Harry Belafonte wears his open to the navel, but we don't recommend that you adopt that style unless you've been keeping up with those daily sit-ups!

If a minimum of $45 per shirt causes you to choke up a bit, calm yourself with the comforting thought that Arthur will change collars when those old ones wear out. And just think how handy *that* will seem when you've put on ten pounds in those New York restaurants!

Battaglia   473 PARK AVE.   10022
             755-1358

Let Giuseppe Battaglia and Emilio face the Italian inflation and Communist demonstrations—*you* can get the choicest merchandise of the Italian ateliers without any of the bother! Simply stop into Battaglia and take advantage of their artfully handpicked choices. Giuseppe's taste is so fine you're assured of finding nothing but the best, and isn't it nice that once he finds a true classic he stocks it in every color imaginable. It's not surprising to find New Yorkers who own his wonderful silk and cashmere turtlenecks in a dozen shades—just $135 apiece.

Among them you can find Mickey Mantle and Joe Di Maggio, just two of the famous swingers who wear that Battaglia uniform of elegant basics. From ribbed cotton body sweaters to suits at $400, to magnificent handsome Italian leather loafers in black, brown, or rust at just $75 the pair, everything is distinguished by its stylish simplicity.

Battaglia offers an impressive selection of suede and leather apparel as well. We couldn't resist the $240 antelope suede shirt-jacket, especially when Emilio, with typical personal attention, showed us how fantastic it looks with just a simple featherweight wool shirt by Celli underneath.

Speaking of wool, Battaglia's shelves feature more than 300 Continental-looking sweater styles besides Celli's classics—enough so that even Joanne Woodward can slip into a little something if she gets bored waiting for Paul Newman fans to finish collecting autographs while he does his fall shopping.

Dominick	59 E. 54TH ST. 10022
De Steno/	355-1949
Crysteno Inc.	

Dominick's one of a vanishing breed—the custom tailor for men. No, no... don't blame their demise on the Big Apple. These greats aren't an endangered species just in New York; you'll find as few in Paris and Rome, and only a handful left on Savile Row in London, where bespoke tailoring got its name.

Which is all the more reason that you should take advantage of the likes of Dominick while he's still around. His atelier is on the third floor, but a suit from his needle is worth the trip up. Business magnates David Begelman and Leon Hess agree; $475 is a paltry amount to pay for a suit that's custom made for the discriminating man. If you feel obligated to spend more, you can commission Dominick to start on a tuxedo at $600, or a full dress suit from $750. Throw in an odd jacket or two at $350, and a wardrobe of slacks at $125 per pair.

Dominick's a friendly soul who's always there to greet you. But he's a busy man, too. If your trip is too short for him to fit you in, consult with Bernard Weatherill at 16 E. 52nd Street, or William Fioravanti on 57th Street, either of whom will be glad to furnish you with all the little niceties you expect after spending $600 and up for a suit (even more if you visit William), like perfect fit adjustments after you've broken in that new jacket. Isn't it nice to know you'll have a friend who can fit your wardrobe to your ever-changing waistline?

| **Dunhill Tailors** | 65 E. 57TH ST. 10022 |
| | 355-0050 |

It's a brown-on-brown masculine shop which caters to men with a conservative bent. Not boring, you'll note, just conservative. You know the type, a Paul Newman or George Hamilton. Paul and George *do* shop at Dunhill, but not in person—by phone. That's the nice thing about Leon Block's store; once they've fitted you into one of their generously cut European-styled suits, your corrected pattern goes on file. Then you can just call in and request Dunhill to work your favorite fabric into a suit so perfectly classic, you can't go wrong. Expect to pay upwards of $650 per suit for the pleasure.

Leon Block is the president, the designer, and the man to see when you decide to have *your* suit made. Don't be disappointed if Leon doesn't pop out of his office to help you; he's probably in Switzerland perfecting the new prints for his rich silk ties or wonderfully light and comfortable printed silk knit shirts ($90). Of his salesmen, Mr. Henry has been there the longest and can assist you with fabric selection. You'll want at least one of those Dunhill hopsacking blazers. With their gold buttons and circle-printed linings, they're a trademark.

Expect three fittings before you're a Dunhill man. Some days we're sure they do that just to lure you back in and tempt you with their wonderful cashmere scarves and imported leathers and suedes. For very special clients like you, Leon will coordinate an entire wardrobe around each suit, including tie, shirt, and additional blazers, and slacks. Leave it to him to dress you in good taste.

Yacht lovers depend on Dunhill for boat shoes. These rubber-soled wonders are lined with terrycloth for comfort, and finished with distinctive red or blue trim. We knew a couple of landlubbers who got so hooked on these $45 deckers that they bought yachts to go with them!

After years of requests, the store has added their own fur coats, and we think they're truly bargains. A $500 shearling lamb coat is a practical way to make it through any long winter —even if you *do* spend most of it in Rio!

R. Meledandri   74 E. 56TH ST.   10022
                     753-1520

Are there a few interviews you've been hoping John Lindsay would air on the "Good Morning, America" show? Well, why not drop into Roland Meledandri's men's wear den and tell him about it? He's just one of that clique of debonair New Yorkers who like nothing better than to spend a couple of hours hanging out in Roland's ever-so-masculine surroundings. They just seem to feel so comfortable in his wood-paneled den, settling down among those bare wood floors, red plaid carpets, and louvered, shuttered display cases. Besides, with the hundreds of fabrics he has for them to choose from, it requires at least a few hours of concentration!

Although he carries some ready-to-wear, Roland tells us that 60 percent of his business is in custom-made clothes. Two-piece custom-made suits start about $595, with their more contemporary three-piece counterparts costing an extra $100. Yes, for $100 the vest is lined!

R. Meledandri has a terrifically Continental flavor... he was one of the first to show wide ties. And he's the only store in New York to carry Testoni's Italian shoes, to boot! Trenchcoats start at $350 for wool and $375 for cashmere (how *could* you consider anything else!); silk shirts run about $125; and you can grab a bargain-priced cashmere and lambswool sweater for just $110.

Fifteen tailors are stitching on the premises to fill the needs of clients such as movie executive Dan Melnick and Robert Tisch of Loew's Corp. With that much custom sewing going on, it's no wonder that it's such a popular place for having a dinner jacket ordered—just the thing for your next dinner at Régine's! Order it from Meledandri manager Mr. Reddy.

Alexander Shields   484 PARK AVE.   10022
832-1616

Alexander's a seventh-generation American. He's listed in the Social Register. He's the tennis champion of the Oyster Bay circuit, and one of the most popular summer regulars in Marrakesh. His first shop was in Gloria Vanderbilt's town house, and his first fashion award the Coty. Would you buy a robe from this man? You bet you would!

Alexander is credited with innovations like the square-ended tie, the fly-front shirt, the caftan, and embroidered men's wear. But he's most famous for his robes. Every man's closet should include at least half a dozen (heavens, with all the colors of terry Alexander cuts, you could collect for years without repeating yourself). Choose from his basic wraparound or rajah styles at any of fifty Alexander Shields boutiques scattered hither and yon.

Then be ready to step out of your shower and wrap right up, secure in the knowledge that style is more important than fashion! Right, Alexander?

Pierre Balmain   795 MADISON AVE.   10021
  628-4260

Pierre Balmain has established a little haven on Madison Avenue, where he caters to American men who crave the European look and fit with the same savoir faire he's been lavishing on his Paris and Cannes customers for years. No longer will you have to run over to the rue du faubourg St.-Honoré to pick up one of his classic sportcoats in tweed, velvet or houndstooth with pleated pants to match. Pity, isn't it!

Housed in this small shop are the same chic velvet suits you've discovered in his European shops, as well as that favorite cashmere sportcoat at just $325. Not only has Pierre brought along monogrammed accessories and sweaters, he's gone a bit overboard and emblazoned his initials on the walls, too. Oh, well, since the rest of the shop's done in shades of brown and stainless steel, this bit of ego doesn't stand out too terribly. Besides, it's such a blessing to find one shop which doesn't have you keeping time to music in the dressing rooms, it's worth a stop even if you don't appreciate Pierre's touch. None of the customers seem to object to the ready-to-wear racks; managers J. M. Gabrielli and John Lazarow say that's because Pierre's reputation as a master tailor is reflected in everything he does.

He sells both evening and daywear. If your social secretary has scheduled a number of black-tie events, Pierre's one-button dinner jacket is quick and easy at $435. A muskrat coat could be the perfect topper for winter at $2,500. If you scrimp and invest only $900 in the leather and fur jacket as a warm-up, you'll probably have to supplement it with a few Shetland and cashmere sweaters to make it through the next cold snap. And be sure not to forget that obligatory New York trenchcoat; the Balmain version is $300.

Robert Redford, Dick Shawn, and Totie's husband George Fields are Balmain addicts. But don't be afraid of losing your own identity by buying the same suit they've just purchased. The key to Balmain is looks that maintain their individuality when worn by different men... though why you'd object to assuming Robert Redford's identity, we can't imagine!

Yves St. Laurent	543 MADISON AVE.
(Men's)	371-7912

We used to think of Yves St. Laurent as the fashion prophet of the century; now we just think of him as dependable. Don't misconstrue that—it can be perfectly wonderful to be dependable in a world of overnight fashion trends and planned obsolescence. When you buy a suit by St. Laurent, you know you'll be able to wear it for years and always look just fine.

Why, just last week we found a pinstripe model that will be a basic for the next ten years. Keep a good tailor on hand to adjust the pant legs, and it will amortize to a mere $56.50 per year. The same goes for a two-button herringbone suit at $530. A few new Rive Gauche ties each season will add on more years and subtract only $30 from your profit-and-loss statement. And even though they'll become dated a touch sooner, it's hard not to warm up to his toggle-buttoned ivory cardigan sweaters at $160.

Thirty minutes in this chic brown and rust shop with its geometric carpeting and leather-curtained dressing rooms, and you'll probably have stretched today's budget to the limit. It's time to have Max Sarina show you to the boutique area. There you'll find the same YSL flair at mass-produced prices. Compared to a *real* Rive Gauche, that $200 three-piece suit looks a bit common, but we know you'll want a few of his $100 blazers for knocking around.

You'll see a number of women shopping for their men at Rive Gauche—it's a wonderful gift shop. A new set of hand-stitched sheets striped in wine and white is $150. And what better way to send him off to Tahiti than with an Italian YSL beach towel? Only $55. To guarantee that he comes back, buy him the cossack shirt in silk. So marvelous for relaxing if you don't get him all tense by telling him it cost $135. Less intimate friends will appreciate the YSL attaché case filled with toiletries.

But not *all* those women are shopping for their men; some, like Alexis Smith, are so narrow that they can fit into Rive Gauche men's pants. Don't you just hate them! We wish *we* could get into that marvelous cotton poplin suit; it was a bargain at $225, considering all those YSL details!

Furs

Here it is... time to shop for your third-biggest lifetime purchase. Furs... warm, wonderful, and expensive. Right in line after that new Bentley and the house in the country. Try to choose wisely, but don't despair if you can't quite make up your mind. How far wrong can you go in a town that has Ben Kahn, Maximilian, and the Ben Thylan Corporation to choose from?

Ben Kahn　　　　150 W. 30TH ST.　10001
　　　　　　　　　　279-0633

　　　　　　　　　　4 E. 52ND ST.　10022
　　　　　　　　　　838-7387

For 70 years, Ben Kahn was the king of the New York fur business. Today you'll want to sidle up to son-in-law Ernest Graf, who took over the presidency of the firm in 1947 and continued to run it after Ben's death.

Ernest's biggest sales are to women between 40 and 60, who tend to order $60,000 Russian sables while the 20-to-40 set picks up raccoon. While their older sisters spend $8,000 for a diagonal mink cape, or a marvelous little Black Diamond A-line trench coat, the youthful set is choosing between mole, lynz, and nutria for $1,250 to $4,000. We've even heard of one young lady who managed to pick up a Pepperton lamb cape for a mere $250—but at the age of one and a half, we're not sure she really appreciated the bargain she was getting!

When Muhammad Ali wanted a mink that would take the punch out of Joe Frazier's, he immediately jogged to Kahn and came out with an Emba Lunaraine in size 46. Pelts being what they are, you can be sure his large size cost him more. Ali's power being what it is, though, no one at Kahn is saying how *much* more, but we do know that a smaller version sold for $6,500. Nobody's quoting prices on Walt Frazier's famous round fur bedspread, either, but we're sure he didn't loose any sleep over the price tag. After buying those first ten coats, how expensive could one little round bedspread seem?

By the way, if it's celebrities you're looking for, you'll be more likely to see them in Kahn's West 30th Street location. Even if the other store is closer, this crowd is worth the walk!

| **The Ben Thylan** | 32 E. 57TH ST. 10022 |
| **Corporation** | 753-7700 |

The Ben Thylan Corporation encompasses seven of the greatest talents in the fur world. Biggies like Alice Rainer, Irene Spierer, Mr. Fred, Mr. Narins, Joseph Kit, Harold Russek, and Georges Kaplan. The two floors on 57th Street give them just enough room to spread out and work with their own styles and flair. Between the antique- and flower-bedecked setting provided by Thylan and wife, and the individuality and reputations provided by their pet designers, you're likely to find yourself excited by anything from a $1,950 chiffon scarf with fox trim to a $35,000 natural Russian sable coat. And just think of all the fun you'll have making that decision!

| **Maxmilian** | 20 W. 57TH ST. 10019 |
| | 247-1388 |

Anna Maximilian Potok likes to keep her salon terribly elegant; it's a combination of velvet chairs, mirrors and snob appeal.

Surprisingly, this aloof interior has managed to attract a younger, sportier crowd than that found at some of New York's other furriers. Not that the bluebloods don't frequent it too—Anna draws people like Mrs. Guinness and the Duchess of Windsor.

Naturally you'll want to have an invitation to her twice-yearly shows, although ever since *Harper's* and *Vogue* became so terribly interested in her, Anna's shows have been mob scenes.

The fact that she keeps $1,000,000 in stock at any one time guarantees that you'll find *something* to set your heart aflutter. It might be that cute little fox shrug in the corner for $2,500, or that cunning little mole jacket at $1,500, or perhaps it's that floor-length Russian sable for $50,000. Just as we figured! You'll *never* learn how to budget, will you!

For Children

Some of your friends insist that it's necessary to have children in order to ensure that you'll have good reason for studying the latest wrinkles in inheritance tax law. As for us, we're sure the reason the patter of little feet is heard so often is because parents simply want an excuse for exploring that wonderful new breed of children's boutiques which is proliferating in New York. What better excuse could there be than having a five-year-old clinging to your hand? If the thought doesn't appeal to you as a full time job, perhaps you could just borrow one for the afternoon. After all, we wouldn't want you to miss...

Cerruti, Inc.   113 55TH ST.   10022
                      753-5247

When John and Yoko wanted a complete layette, they shopped at the same place Charlotte Ford Forstmann and young Nelson Rockefeller do—Cerruti's. It's a haven for parents, grandparents, and parents-in-waiting. The Cerrutis will outfit any child from day one to adolescence, in imports from France, Germany and Belgium. They'll also make things to order, as they've done for Anne Ford Uzielli and Paula Prentiss Benjamin. One of the favorite special orders was the embroidered dress which Mary Martin ordered for her granddaughter. "My heart belongs to Mary Evan" it sang out... and we don't doubt it for a moment!

Cerruti's is one of the few spots in the States where you'll find pint-sized versions of the famous Izod alligator on tennis shorts ($8–$10) and tops ($12). Also look for tennis dresses and monogrammed tennis sweaters for tomorrow's pros.

Just to be sure that the kids don't feel left out, Cerruti's carries New Man pants and terry cover-ups that would do any Palm Beach sun worshipper proud. For more formal occasions, check the Florence Eisman dresses and boys' dress pants. As for evening clothes... they're yet to be found.

Little Bits	1036 THIRD AVE. 10021
of the Sixties	838-5961

Little Bits not only has star-studded jeans... they have a star-studded clientele. Cher was a good customer when there was only Chastity to shop for. No doubt she'll be in twice as often now that Elijah Blue has joined the family. Wouldn't he look adorable in those chino army fatigues that Little Bits does so well?

Tatum O'Neal's given Ryan the word that she's too old now for Little Bits. Even Little Bits' special expandable suspenders which allow for a year's growth can't lure her back now! Before she got her curves (and her Oscar), though, she was a favorite customer.

The specialty here is color and detail. From the patchwork quilts on the walls ($35 for a crib-size version) to the monogrammed tie-dye T-shirts on the racks, that old-style pink-and-blue baby chauvinism is dead. Designer-owner Patsy Campkin likes kids to have fun, so she adds a dash of whimsy to every functional design. We loved the $65 Charlotte's Web blazer embroidered with every character E. B. White and your child ever dreamed of. And how nice that little matching jeans were only $50! Some styles are so popular with mothers that Patsy's asked to copy them in big people's sizes. She's glad to oblige—at big people's prices!

Pat-Rick   930 MADISON AVE.   10021
Children's Store   288-1444

No child should have to suffer an identity crisis; Pat-Rick personalizes anything for $20. If the name has between 3 and 5 letters, that is. Don't give your child a long name unless you're willing to throw in an extra $1 for every letter. It wasn't too long ago that the Kennedy children were all outfitted by Pat-Rick. The store still caters to the silk-stocking set, waiting patiently for that next generation of Kennedys to come along.

No doubt they'll want to be dressed in Pat-Rick's famous brother-sister outfits, although they're strictly for the under 6X range. You'll find matching vested suits and lacy dresses at about $25.

Or maybe he'd prefer wearing hand-painted jeans. So perfect for the park at just $23.50. The jumper at $6.50 is a wonderful bargain... at least until you add another $20 for the monogram. And for keeping out the winter cold, the $58 English duffle coat complete with toggle bolt buttons is a Pat-Rick favorite.

VI. NEW YORK JEWELRY
It's Sparkle City

INTERESTED in a little something in diamonds that will help you to stand out from the crowd? Feeling a touch drab in that new Halston without a ruby or two? What better place to take care of the necessities of life than in New York City!

Breakfast at Tiffany's... lunch at Cartier's... Bulgari, Buccellati... Van Cleef & Arpels... Harry Winston... really, this page is getting so expensive even *we* can't continue. So let's just plunge right in and connect you with the right settings!

Artwear	28 E. 74TH ST. AT MADISON 10021
	535-6260

You'll be happy to know that if you own a piece of Artwear you're in the good company of galleries, museums and collectors throughout the world. You'll also be happy to know that it's possible to get some of their large, colorful polyester resin pieces for under $100. You'll be less happy to know that it's more likely you'll be paying something in the thousands for a bit of gold.

The jewelry ranges from belt buckles to bracelets, from pendants to earrings, from necklaces to whatever the imagination of the world's most creative artists can conceive. A Picasso pendant in gold might run anywhere from $5,000 to $7,000... small and finely crafted, though primitive in motif, just the perfect thing to wear on a tiny gold chain.

You'll see other favorite artists represented here, too. If you're lucky, when you're there they'll be displaying Alexander Calder's brass pins or gold earrings with a serpentine sort of feel. And his torso-encompassing necklace is a handy thing to wear if you're planning to walk through Central Park late at night. Max Ernst does things for the gallery, so don't be surprised to see his work on display, as well as that of Roy Lichtenstein, whose enamels have a special appeal.

Man Ray's lips can kiss you in gold... Louise Nevelson can sculpt you in an art deco feeling... really, there's no end to what you might find, and since the collection varies from day to day or week to week (the pieces being largely one of a kind), it's worth stopping by regularly.

Artwear is a cozy shop, and you'll get a thumbnail sketch of the things you'll find inside just by looking in the window. But since the pieces are actually works of art, most are best explained by an expert such as Marion Ferrara. You'll recognize Ms. Ferrara by the Robert Lee Morris neckband or knuckle ring she'll be wearing. Or perhaps she'll be wearing a kinetic sculpture ring: a forest of tiny rods that move as you move your finger or hand.

In any case, she will be happy to share her things with you as well as to point out that jewelry such as this is a very good investment since it's very rarely stolen. Understandable! It is a bit more difficult to dispose of a pair of golden lips than it is to cut up the normal hot diamond. In addition, as art, the pieces tend to appreciate more quickly than they would if they were just gemstones. And if we haven't given you enough excuse to buy something, we're sure when you see Art to Wear you'll be inspired to think up a few of your own.

Buccellati 703 FIFTH AVE. 10022
755-4975

Everything within Buccellati is from Italy... the beige brocade on the walls, the Oriental carpet on the floor, and the owner, Mario Buccellati, who shuttles back and forth between his factory in Milan and the store in New York. It has been said to be the most elaborate shop in the city, though as anyone knows there are a few in the running for that particular title. At any rate, we're convinced that it's one of the most personalized.

In order to keep his service as personalized as it was when his father founded the business, Mario has resisted enlarging and keeps the store in New York as beautifully compact as possible. It is hard to believe that everything from jewelry to silver to china and small gift items are contained within its walls.

Service is so personalized at Buccellati that not one piece Mario sells is ever duplicated. When a customer came in to purchase the $10,500 gold-and-diamond cuff bracelet that the store advertised only to find that it had been picked up by another New Yorker, her disappointment was severe. There simply wasn't another copy available—the mold was broken as soon as that first perfect casting was completed.

So imagine how we felt when manager Robert Philipson showed us that wonderful ruby, gold, and diamond carry-all on our last visit—$29,000 ... well over the day's budget ... and there we were, faced with the fact that if we didn't grab it up right away, we'd never have another chance. Ask us to show it to you the next time we see you at the theater. It has eighteen rubies surrounded by full-cut diamonds, textured engraving and hidden hinges. At Buccellati, they believe that shining gold is unattractive, so everything there is softened and the hardness relieved with a fabriclike texture.

Unfortunately, we couldn't afford the necklace he brought out next—a practically weightless diamond bib with the flexibility of lace. Four rows of diamonds set in white gold, at $36,000. We also saw some golden pearls at $45,000 and immediately hurried out of the jewelry department before we were carried away with a spending spree.

It was at that point we stumbled into the silver department. Luckily, the manager, Mrs. Vardela, was in and cheered us up with the sight of a silver giraffe reclining on a piece of gray rock, complete with a dignified expression (and a $9,200 price tag). Also among the menagerie were an amethyst-eyed frog at $720 and a hammered and chased elephant with ivory tusks at $8,700. At these prices, you could own the entire Central Park Zoo!

We have jealous pets, though, so we moved on to Tableware, where we prepared the setting for an entire dinner party before we left: a soup tureen with fluted bowl at $7,500, a silver-scaled fish for a centerpiece at $6,800 and "Prochon"-patterned flatware at just $310 the setting.

Well, by the time we left, there really was a dent in the Buccellati merchandise. But rest assured—they'll be fully restocked in time for your visit. Do drop by... it is quite an experience!

Bulgari PIERRE HOTEL, 2 E. 61ST ST. 10021
486-0086

At last... a fine jewelry store that's not done in period French antiques. Of course, the fact that it's not French might have something to do with it. Leave it to those Italians! Bulgari has a wonderfully slick modern look; the walls are covered with beige carpet or rattan and the lighting comes from plexiglass cubes which run along the top of the walls. If you're young and fresh, so is the store, and you'll feel quite comfortable in it. The furniture is made of bentwood and rattan (bye-bye Louis Quinze), with an updated European sophistication.

You'll also feel comfortable with Mr. Smith. He's as young and fresh as the store itself, and he has the extra added attraction of being the man who chooses the jewelry for *Bazaar, Town and Country, Vogue*... heavens, simply all the magazines. He'll be happy to tell you what Lauren Hutton is wearing for the upcoming Revlon ads.

But to get the most comprehensive look at the collection, you might want to have Nicola Bulgari himself wait on you. He's in New York for seven or eight months out of the year when he's not traveling with the collection, so your odds of finding him in aren't bad, particularly if he's expecting you. Feminists will be happy to note that Bulgari also has chic, young, pant-suited Natalie there to help them. You'll recognize her by her blond hair, tall stature, and her ever-so-tailored combinations of pinstripes and silks. She really typifies the ideal customer for the Bulgari look: sporty but expensive.

The clean look of the store is also typical of the jewelry, which has a more tailored look than some of the fussier French fashions. One Bulgari trademark is the use of antique golden coins which have been collected by the family over the years. You might find these dangling from heavy golden chains for as little as $2,000 or $3,000, but since they just discovered a coin which by itself is worth $80,000 do stop to look before you offer to add it to your coin collection!

The last time we were in, Natalie showed us a sapphire and diamond choker with the diamond set in a heavy, linked chain. Then she gave us the bad news: it had sold for $350,000 just before we arrived. Another nice necklace look was a colorful, festive combination of turquoise and amethyst with a huge cabochon emerald, just $100,000 (now Natalie is coming down to our price range). Bulgari typically uses silver, although they do use combinations of gunmetal and gold for some of their very sporty jewelry looks—for example, a chain made of gunmetal and gold without diamonds for just $1,200. Another nice look is little round discs of mother of pearl surrounded by gold and linked together into a necklace. They are also very well known for their enamels done in the style of Fabergé. Throughout the collection you'll see masculine links combined with enamels and gold, as well as Fabergé cigarette cases, evening bags, and other accessories.

The Bulgari trademark in rings is the cabochon stones. The stones are shaped in three-dimensional pyramids, typically mounted in trombino fashion with baguettes and pavé diamonds surrounding them. If you have a particular stone you love and would like to see treated in the Bulgari manner, their designers will work in Italy from a casting of it and within about two months (one, if you're in a rush to make it to that special party) will have a design worthy of you.

Cartier

FIFTH AVE. AT 52ND ST. 10022
753-0111

The younger set is shopping the Cartier boutique, but then look again... so is the fur-coated set! Little old ladies in sable coats come in followed by trendy 20-year-olds in blue jeans—and the doorman is really beside himself trying to decide who to be polite to.

Of course Elizabeth Taylor has that famous Cartier diamond right now, and Cartier is not likely to part with the Hope Diamond just yet, but we're happy to report that there are still a few acceptable baubles left over for you at this bastion of French tradition.

A simple marquise-cut canary diamond ring is yours for about $140,000. Or you may prefer the black onyx and diamond necklace priced at $9,700. Original art deco Cartier clocks are available too, and Cartier also stocks more mundane timepieces (the watches run in the $7,500 range).

As for the blue-jean set, they're shopping for lighters at $65, swizzle sticks in gold at $100, diamond wedding rings in the $250 range (complete with microscope to detect the diamond), and sterling hoop earrings at $22.50.

And you have the luxury of doing that inexpensive brand of shopping in a truly luxurious setting, the mansion of one of the founders of New York society, Morton F. Plant, who was a financier and a yachtsman. The mansion resembles an ancient palace, and has remained substantially unchanged since Cartier acquired it in exchange for a two-strand, black and white Oriental pearl necklace. Before you decide that Plant was completely dotty for making such a trade, consider that the pearls were valued at $1,500,000. We're happy to report that they enabled Plant to afford a new home with a little left over for dinner out à la *New York on $500 a Day*.

During the Christmas season coffee and tea are served on the second floor near the silver and jewelry department, which was Mrs. Plant's bedroom. And even in this rushed season you'll enjoy sitting in the wood-paneled sitting room while you wait to have your packages wrapped.

Some of the salespeople have been at Cartier's almost since Mr. Plant originally sold his mansion. Mrs. Wainwright, the personal shopper, will ensure prompt delivery of your purchases. Carlo Colonna, the head engraver, will be happy to put your family crest on everything from silver service to blazer buttons. Cartier's in-house designer, Alfred Durante, will take your family jewels and refashion them in any one of hundreds of interesting ways. Vice president William Cordes, who has been with them since 1932, is one of the favorites, as is Walter Kroehnert, who has been a Cartier clockmaster since 1936 and has the distinction of being one of the few men alive who can still assemble a watch from scratch. In the stationery department, ask for Mildred or Phyllis; they've been here since 1930 and 1928 respectively.

We've heard some nasty comment lately that Cartier's just isn't what it used to be ... that they're so busy catering to the middle-of-the-road shopper they've lost some of the appeal of their special brand of exclusivity.

We think the snobs are wrong: The last time we had it in mind to look at a trinket or two, Cartier's put them on a plane and flew them all the way to Monte Carlo—complete with salesman!

David Webb 7 E. 57TH ST. 10022
421-3030

David Webb should at least be seen. It's furnished with Louis XV antiques, taupe fabrics, taupe carpeting, and three guards. After all, you can't be too careful when you've a shop filled with jeweled wildlife! His golden frogs with sapphire eyes, his lapis panthers, his monkeys with white enamel faces and little diamond earrings, are enough to tempt anyone to turn to a life of crime.

Some people called David the Cellini of the 20th century, and his creative genius is still carried on in the salon he created. The jewelry designs are unique. In his day, David mounted a

Chien Lung coral frog intricately worked with 18-karat gold and emeralds for President Kennedy, and had the late Charles Revson's replica of his boat, the *Ultima II,* interpreted in gold and mounted on malachite. Last time we were there, we fell in love with an evening box of gold encased with diamonds and emeralds.

You say it's not exactly the kind of thing you had in mind? Well, don't fret. This store, which was started by the late David Webb, stocks everything from $125 cufflinks to $300,000 necklaces. Surely there's *something* there that's you.

But if you want to pay by check, be prepared to prove your identity and to wait while the store checks with your bank. The tale is told of a stranger who was enchanted by a $40,000 necklace and wanted to write a check for it. The store insisted on calling her bank, whereupon they quickly learned that the stranger was not only a Vanderbilt, but she was also an Astor. She left the proud possessor of a new necklace, and we're sure you will, too.

Fred Leighton	763 MADISON AVE.	10021
Madison, Ltd.	288-1872	

If the air at Harry Winston got a bit stultifying, try the bright, light look of Fred Leighton for a refreshing break. Murray Mondschein has managed to highlight his oak-planked shop with some perfectly fabulous antique jewelry. And to frame those wonderful old pieces, he's imported clothing that might range anywhere from a Greek blouse at $30 to a Turkish or Moroccan dress for $800. Whichever appeals to you, be sure you're prepared to take it home in a status carry-all—after all, this is Madison Avenue, isn't it?

You might want to fill that Louis Vuitton with necklaces of Georgian silver. You might be entranced by anything from ancient Egyptian beads to well-aged pieces by Fabergé or Cartier. Be prepared to fight your way past Faye Dunaway and Judy Collins to get to them.

Golden Nonsense   580 FIFTH AVE.   10036
                     247-6477

Where did Lauren Bacall go to buy those tiny clapping, golden wire hands for producer Larry Kasha when *Applause* became a hit? Where did Liza Minnelli stop in to order a diamond-studded "Chita" for her friend, Chita Rivera? And where would you run off to if you wanted to have anything from "outrageous" ($100), "dynamite" ($50 for a small explosion), or "bitch" ($55 for a large explosion) spelled out in 14-karat gold or diamonds?

Golden Nonsense, that's where! Don't be put off by the non-sensical name, just call Lois Sasson, Susan, or Joseph Abitabiale at their showroom at 580 Fifth Avenue or at the Cul de Sac at Bloomingdales.

In 1968 Lois Sasson and Arlene Altman had a hobby—they made gifts for friends. It might have been a tiny solid gold kite or a set of golden jacks for the girl who has everything; it might have been any little amusing whatnot. But as soon as they finished putting together a chess set of solid sterling and gold with lucite and discovered that that little flight of fancy was going to cost $50,000, it stopped being a joke. And that's how businesses are born!

They first opened in the Jewelry Mart on 47th Street. Lois left the real estate business and they began designing and manufacturing almost anything that couldn't be found in normal stores. They were possibly the first boutique designing gold and silver jewelry, although their most famous first item was a gold greeting card, 2-½ by 2 inches, on which they engraved one-liners, valentines, special messages or original poems composed by their client or written by co-owner Susan Goldenthal, which were sold for about $350. Now let's see ... what would you want to say for $350? A bit more than sending a telegram, isn't it! You'll be pleased to know that the famous Golden Nonsense greeting card turned silver and at the same time turned into a $35-and-up item.

Of course Lois will do *any* special commission. But if you

don't have that much time to wait for a custom-made order, you might consider a lapis and diamond bracelet for $700 or a tiny pavé light bulb for $1,000. Eureka! Isn't that a good idea?

Harry Winston 718 FIFTH AVE. 10019
245-2000

If you're going to get engaged while in New York, do your level best to have it happen while you're walking past Harry Winston. As they so nicely put it, "We're known for having 'important' jewelry."

First there's a locked door. Behind it (don't worry, they'll let *you* in) you'll find a sea of black, white and gray, from Empire desks, to carpet, to fabric-covered walls. By the way, be careful not to trip in that carpet—it is a bit deep. You'll also find a simple little emerald and diamond necklace for $2,000,000. One thing Harry is not known for is thinking small.

If you don't have enough in your checking account to cover that necklace, perhaps Harry will let you work off the difference. There's a school in the building that teaches diamond sorting, and that isn't the worst way in the world to spend eight hours a day, now, is it!

Winston stones are so special that they very seldom allow them to be sullied by having gold or semiprecious stones touch them. Nothing but the best platinum here, and the less, the better.

Harry has stores in Paris and Geneva, as well as cutting factories in Antwerp and Amsterdam, but he still manages to be on the premises in New York at least eight months a year. There's a good chance that if you're in the market for an "important" stone (and please, don't bother to get engaged in front of Harry's if you're not) he'll be there in one of those wonderful little private rooms on either side of his subdued gray corridor to help you. And do be comforted by the fact that if he doesn't happen to come up with something that pleases you immediately, the entire fourth floor is filled with rough diamonds, emeralds, rubies and sapphires, so that given a little bit of patience you can't help but be satisfied.

Tiffany & Co.	FIFTH AVE. AT 57TH ST. 10022
	755-8000

It has been just a little more than 20 years since Walter Hoving bought the controlling interest in Tiffany & Co. He must have known that Elsa Peretti's gold and silver bean-shaped jewelry would turn into a household staple; who ever dreamed of diamonds by the yard? The store that used to mean emerald-studded cigarette cases and diamond brooches now features everything from precious jewels to playing cards. What was once strictly Fifth Avenue is now a chain of six stores; there's even one in Houston.

A gift box from Tiffany still gets opened first. There's something about one of those little blue boxes that evokes glee. Perhaps it's the hope that something silver from Elsa Peretti will be inside, or a diamond stickpin from Jean Schlumberger's mezzanine gallery. At $750 each, those pins are a popular addition to flower arrangements these days.

Some really do contain diamonds; sparklers are available in just about any size up to 128 carats. That's the Tiffany canary diamond, a one of a kind, which was originally offered for $5,000,000 on a first-come first-served basis. There were no takers, but if you are in the market for the 128-carat version or even something somewhat smaller, the man to see is Mr. Schramm.

Tiffany's star diamond salesman has been selling diamonds for 60 years and claims to have sold more than anyone else in the country. He treats his customers with extra care, making sure that no well-meaning fiancé buys a duplicate set of earrings for his favorite lady. In the engagement ring case Mr. Schramm can show you styles ranging from $139 for a diamond so small that the bride should think twice to $490,000 for a 15-carat diamond that indicates how much the groom *really* cares.

In the Jean Schlumberger gallery on the mezzanine, Fabergé-type enamel work is displayed beautifully. Jean's following started with the Duchess of Windsor and now when one of his openings is scheduled, you'll find Kennedys flying in from all over the world to see the new pieces. A typical bracelet will cost around $5,000, but its timeless qualities make it a fine investment.

For more eccentric customers, the sterling silver frypan is becoming more popular, especially as a hostess gift. If your favorite puppy is ill, how about a china dog dish to get his tail wagging. The Caughley pattern is available in blue, yellow, green, or tortoise, depending on the dog's preference. A sterling silver computer at $150 is sure to please any scientist, and for indefatigable tennis players a crystal frosted tennis ball is only $25. If life is getting just too humdrum, why not pick up a simple set of gold bands for $35 each and throw a wedding? Don't forget to sign up at Tiffany's bridal registry—ask for Flora Danica china. At $675 per place setting, you'll want to set it off with one of Tiffany's 21 active silver patterns. Isn't that a romantic idea—everybody loves weddings!

Van Cleef & Arpels, Inc.
744 FIFTH AVE. 10019
644-9500

Classic perfection. From the time that the Arpels designed two diamond tiaras for Napoleon to give to Josephine and Marie Louise, to today's flawless 28-carat diamond ring and ruby necklace at $1,000,000 each, perfection has been the byword. In New York it's stressed by soft-spoken Claude Arpels, who carries on with quiet dignity the Van Cleef & Arpels tradition that started in America after the New York World's Fair.

He'll spend hours explaining to you the care with which Van Cleef sets stones to create a three-dimensional effect, then assembles them from the back so that not the tiniest bit of mounting is visible. It may take up to a year to assemble and cut enough small stones for a ruby clip at $65,000, but you can be sure that no matter how long the time or arduous the work every piece of jewelry which starts out as a twinkle in the eye of one of the Arpels is completed with perfection.

Crowned heads have been loyal to the firm since the late 19th century, the most famous crown being the one which was commissioned for the wife of the Shah Pahlavi, Empress Farah of Iran, which contains an emerald which weighs 150 carats. Not all the crowned heads are so lucky, however. Claude recalls that he has been to India ten times to buy stones from famous maharajahs who are more in need of money than of emeralds.

Though you can still find a more than ample stock of $250,000 sapphire barrettes and $10,000 passe-partout necklaces in snaky gold, you'll be able to get a measurably more carefree air about you shopping in the Van Cleef boutique, where all items sell for under $1,500. Each piece is still copyrighted and numbered for the customer's protection, but each piece is also a bit more "fun" than the opulent luxury of the traditional Van Cleef jewels. You might find golden blazer buttons at $65 or $75 each, or gold rope cuffs at $1,100. Or you might find something a bit more precious just by talking with Claude Arpels ... a philosophy of living. "I am a designer and jeweler. But one has to build quality from all meaningful interests in life." That's the spirit of Van Cleef & Arpels.

VII. MANHATTAN
Anything Goes!

WHILE New York is known to be a city that can supply the unusual, even *we* were shocked by some of the things we ran across, and *we're* not easily surprised! Why, we even found ways to get exercise without leaving mid-Manhattan. You can put on your ice skates, pick up your tennis racquet, or make use of those golf clubs and that fencing foil you've been carrying around in your Halston luggage.

If you're looking for something a little tamer, you can choose among sheets that take three months to embroider, florists who'll serve you chrysanthemums in a beer mug, silk flowers from France, buttons from the 18th century, and cakes with your picture painted on them (yes—we'll make sure it's your good profile!).

On second thought, you may not thank us for all this inside information. After all, it's difficult when you lose your excuse for not being able to find the perfect gift to bring to all those friends who are waiting for you back home!

FLOWERS

Bouquets	222 E. 83RD ST.	10028
à la Carte	535-3720	

Bouquets à la Carte is just perfect for piquing your sense of whimsy. It's even piqued Frank Sinatra's. It's just the place to drop into when you want something to give a friend a chuckle along with his chrysanthemums.

Patricia, Harry, and Roy keep their brownstone courtyard overflowing with plants ... just a hint of the wonders to be found within. Under the cloud-papered ceiling lurk three-foot balloons waiting to be anchored with ribbon streamers over an arrangement of fresh and paper flowers spiked with a split of champagne. A word of caution about this particular arrangement: the last time we tried to use it, it was barred from a hospital elevator by nurses who couldn't fit patients in around it. Plan to have the balloon blown up *after* arrival if it's going to be beside a hospital bed or taken on board the *QE 2* to celebrate the beginning of a friend's round-the-world cruise.

If you can't find someone willing to blow up that balloon on board, you might settle for their famous paper carnation with puzzles and candies. It's not nearly so dramatic, but it does have the advantage of being welcome almost everywhere.

Bouquets à la Carte will send their wares anywhere in Manhattan; or, better yet, they'll send themselves simply anywhere at all to do your next party. You might have seen them arranging centerpieces for the duPonts of Delaware. And yes, that *was* Patricia putting paper flowers on Navajo tablecloths for President Sadat's dinner at the White House. You know how fond he is of Western Americana!

One of our favorite gifts is their sturdy Lucite cane, decorated with paper flowers, ribbons and a miniature brandy (just $20). We use it every time one of our friends reports they've just broken an ankle during their ski trip. And no matter *what* you might say about paper flowers ... they do stay fresh all the way to St. Moritz!

Ethel Rogers 802 MADISON AVE. 10021
737-5522

You'll be happy to know that Ethel Rogers is still energetically turning out the ice cream soda arrangement of carnations that made her an institution 25 years ago. She's added two strawberries for flavor, as well as some wonderfully colorful new customers to spice the atmosphere of her Madison Avenue shop, but basically she's still the dynamic little lady who started collecting lilies so very long ago.

Her collection of small antiques, wicker, pillows, and silk and paper flowers plus her inimitable personality keep them coming in as decades go by: John Lennon, Gwen Verdon, and Chita Rivera all choose between her *Euphorbia protea* and her *alstremia*.

The last time we dropped in we solved that pronunciation problem by limiting ourselves to mums. She uses them quite cleverly in a beer mug topped with yellow blooms, imitation foam, and a pretzel for good measure (just $20). Unfortunately, what we saved by selecting a small arrangment, we spent by falling in love with an old English plaque she had hanging in one corner. But really—do you think that $1,020 is a bit much for one trip to the florist?

Ronaldo Maia 27 E. 67TH ST. 10021
288-1049

We never send our New York hostesses a floral gift unless it comes from Ronaldo Maia. Ronaldo is to flowers what Edison was to electricity: a true inventor.

Ronaldo came from Brazil to start in the New York flower business in 1970, and in the short intervening space of time has put daisies into laboratory glass, madonna lilies into terra-cotta ginger jars, and just about everything into the little fabric-covered Kinchaku carrying boxes that were designed by his assistant, Seto. His ultimate dream is to carry nothing but white flowers in his 67th Street shop, but in the meantime he makes concessions and carries everything from roses to sculptured moss animal shapes that are a favorite with neighborhood children.

One of the best reasons for stopping by Ronaldo's is his potpourri. It isn't just the traditional rose-scented version; he carries a range of seven scents which can be purchased in baskets or porcelain bowls or old-fashioned ginger jars at $250. Not only do they look wonderful, his refresher oils make the arrangements last for years.

Vincent Astor and the Duchess of Windsor buy blooms from Ronaldo. Beth Rudin (of the Rudin Realty family) used his madonna tulips and votive candles in terra-cotta holders for her wedding to James Carlton DeWoody II, and Charles Wrightsman gave him a year and a half to research the 18th century in order to plan floral arrangements for the opening of the two rooms of period antiques which they donated to the Metropolitan Museum of Art.

But if you're not prepared to wait 18 months for your bundles of roses with rosemary, don't worry. With a snap of the fingers and an investment of $400, you can have one of his extravagant leaf-filled vases. And if that's leaves, just think how much it would be with the flowers!

CRYSTAL

| **Baccarat** | 55 E. 57TH ST. 10022 |
| | 826-4100 |

Baccarat. Steuben. There, we've done it! Most people can't bear to mention the two in the same breath. They love one, despise the other. We say *de gustibus non disputandum est* (loosely, whatever turns you on). According to dear Mrs. Knowles at Baccarat, there is really no difference in quality; just in design and country of origin. When a maharajah had to make a choice, he commissioned Baccarat to create a crystal love temple and all the crystal furniture necessary to make it lovable. The French crystal has also been the choice of kings, czars, emperors and even presidents (like Teddy and Franklin Roosevelt) since it was founded in 1765 in the small town of Baccarat.

If you've kept your eyes open at estate auctions, you've seen Baccarat snapped up; 19th-century pieces are already collectors' items. A Baccarat paperweight dated from 1840 to 1860 is a fine investment.

Though there's an ark's worth of lead crystal animals and a collector's paradise of paperweights, the real Baccarat treasures today are the stemware and candlesticks. Most of the patterns are replicas of ones which graced the tables of kings, sultans, and sheiks. Mrs. Knowles informs us that men are buying the majority of the wine and brandy glasses these days. Seems they've finally learned to appreciate crystal the way women have for years. You can own a Baccarat glass for as little as $15 or as much as $100. All are the same fine-quality lead crystal that will cause your great aunt to hear bells when she taps the glass to test your taste. You can begin your collection with just one, or order 10 dozen for your next little party.

A caviar bowl at $167 is a luxury, but who can live without it? A mustard or jam pot with its own little spoon is a necessity. So for $23 why not consider buying two? Once you've developed a taste for Baccarat, you'll want to branch out. Perhaps candelabra, or a magnificent chandelier. They're remaking those seven-foot candelabra that were once made only for the imperial courts of Russia. That could be the perfect accent for your ballroom.

Steuben Glass FIFTH AVE. AT 56TH ST. 10022
752-1441

Of course, you all know about Steuben. And most of you have probably considered at one time or another buying their spectacular glass design—the Hull—for just $65,000. But have you ever considered commissioning Steuben to do a special piece for you or a friend? It's really quite simple; just hand them $25,000, and they'll come up with a choice of three variations (traditional, avant-garde, and middle-of-the-road) on the theme of your choice. Of course you *will* have to pay them a bit more for completion of the piece depending upon the complexity of the design, so be sure to set aside another $10,000 or $20,000 for the day when *that* bill comes in. But just think of all the occasions this will suit: birthdays, graduations, anniversaries, weddings. There's an idea that's just right for everyone. And since the Steuben designers have included Matisse, Cocteau, Dufy, Noguchi, and Georgia O'Keeffe, your comissioned piece also stands a chance of appreciating over the years.

Well, if we haven't made this wonderful suggestion in time, and that special occasion is just around the corner, you'll have to limit yourself to something that's already prepared. Just drop into Steuben's Fifth Avenue showrooms and ask for the Red Room, the gallery where their most spectacular exhibition pieces are housed.

You say this occasion isn't exactly *that* special? You might find something a touch less expensive in the Green Room, where major ornamental designs are housed. Steuben's store manager, Clifford Palmer, will be happy to show you through. If he happens to be out to lunch, ask for Miss Ryan, who also gives an enthusiastic and knowledgeable tour. She might even show you some of their inexpensive pieces during that tour— if she doesn't realize just how rich your tastes are. And it is always nice to know that while a Steuben special commission is fine enough to serve as a presentation piece to the pope, you can still pick up a frog paperweight at $62.50 or a bud vase for $85.

HOME DECORATIONS AND FURNITURE

Carole Stupell, Ltd.	61 E. 57TH ST. 260-3100	10022

New Yorkers who pride themselves on setting the perfect table know Carole Stupell Ltd. It has been almost 50 years since Carole opened her first shop at the Barclay Hotel, hardly more than a little gift shop catering to the carriage trade and assorted dukes. Today she still caters to dukes, and her 57th Street address has come to be known as the couture house of table fashion.

You'll find table appointments and home accessories that

blend with almost any decor, but there's an explicit emphasis on luxury. Carole hates reaching for the salt and pepper, so she has one of the largest collections of individual miniature salt and pepper shakers we've ever seen. They range from $12 to $27 a pair.

Her stemware selection is magnificent, elitist though it may be. A starlight-patterned water goblet priced at $540 a dozen would make a beautiful gift for your favorite new bride, but do check in Carole's bridal registry to make sure she doesn't get too many.

You may prefer a gift that is a bit more sophisticated; if you are a classicist, don't worry about finding the right china pattern—Carole carries over 400, in addition to crystal from Lalique, Val St. Lambert, Daum, Orrefors, and St. Louis. The silver flatware collection is equally impressive. To complete the table and protect it, table mats are available in 60 different styles.

If you'd rather just enjoy a completed table than coordinate it, ask Carole to do it for you. She may be off to Europe when you visit, so do ask for her son Keith, who inherited the family panache.

Diane Love 851 MADISON AVE. 10021
879-6997

Do we hear some of you tsk-tsking at the idea of spending exorbitant amounts for quickly fleeting flower arrangements? How *terribly* practical of you! Far be it from us to remain rigid in a changing world; we'll give you flowers for your money that will be with you for years. It's as easy as a walk to Madison Avenue and a talk with Diane (her friends call her Deeane) Love.

Diane imports and arranges wonderfully realistic fabric flowers. From $2.25 for a sweetpea to $14 for a columbine, you can satisfy your whims with one of her arrangements. Most are done in baskets—either antique, imported, or simply done. Her Japanese baskets (from $45 to $400) are the finest, and so perfect for *ikebana,* the Japanese art of flower arrangement. With the quality of container Diane seems to gravitate toward, it's not unusual to find some of her arrangements wearing a $300 to $500 price tag. To round out the figure, she also offers accessories such as ceramic plates and laquered rattan and bamboo furniture.

Diane's Madison Avenue shop also stocks her own *Flowers Are Fabulous* book at just $7.50. Let's see, now ... $7.50 for the book, and $2.25 for the sweetpea, if you're in a frugal mood, you can come up with something quite great by yourself and still save enough for dinner at Lutèce.

The Magnificent Doll	209 E. 60TH ST. 753-7425

Looking for a way to tell her "Oh, you beautiful doll"? Look no further. When Patricia and Helen planned their wonderful new doll store, they decided to stock dolls for people with taste and style. No newfangled dolls here to embarrass you by suddenly wetting their pants or saying "Dada" at the most inopportune moments. Helen and Patricia have found dolls which are old enough to have been spared that sort of progressiveness. All they do is sit at home waiting for you to dress them in fine old lace.

Not only are the Magnificent Dolls antiques, they've been chosen for their innate beauty, not for just their age; for their style, not for just their historical value (you know, somewhat in the way that *WWD* chooses Gloria Vanderbilt). The shop carries elegant music-box dolls, fabulous French marionettes and clowns created by two French artists, French-inspired clay bisques by a young American sculptress, wooden Pinocchios from Italy, and an American rag doll that makes Raggedy Ann look like she never had any taste.

If you still think you're too old to play with dolls (killjoy!), we'd like to point out that the Magnificent Doll also carries lithographs and original watercolors of dolls, as well as a few clothing trunks and cradles. *Do* be careful though ... some ladies we know would much rather receive a quiet little French bisque dolly than a baby cradle for their birthday!

Woolworks 838 MADISON AVE. 10021
 861-8700

What ... you don't have a bellpull? But really, however do you call the butler? The situation must be remedied at once! We recommend that you start needlepointing one immediately. Besides keeping the help in line, it will fill those idle hours you've been spending under the dryer at Kenneth's.

Naturally, you wouldn't want to spend your time stitching unless you were able to do it on something rather exclusive, so don't pick up a needle until you've stopped in a Woolworks. Inman and Daren used to be industrial designers, but they were bitten by the needlepoint bug over a dozen years ago. Today the Dorothys (Hammerstein and Rodgers), Mary Martin, and even Hugh Downs (yes, he needlepoints too) come in to pick up their custom designs. Countess de Rochambeau doesn't make it over from Paris quite that often; she has hers mailed out.

Now we really don't recommend that you start out by trying the Coromandel screen which Inman and Daren have designed. Admittedly its 6' 3" height and 8' width would look perfectly charming in your dining room. But it is a bit heavy for the chauffeur to tote around while you're working on it, and if it happens that you find you don't really enjoy needlepoint, you're left with a $5,700 investment on your—or should we say his—hands, and that's not even counting the yarn and mounting.

Perhaps it would be wiser to start with a modest pair of slippers. You can have them designed with the school seal of your favorite man—so perfect for him to wear while he watches the Sunday football games. If you'd rather do a pillow or chair seat, you can choose from over a hundred different flower designs and a hundred geometrics. Even the wools are dyed to order, and so they are almost unlimited in colors.

Well, it's so confusing to an amateur you'll probably need help. Call on Gloria, Lee, or Lalitte to help you choose the colors for your canvas, then wait around and look helpless and they'll give you lessons. Or on the other hand, you might consider bringing in the butler and letting them give *him* lessons. It's only fair that he should be working to the tune of a bellpull that he really enjoys, isn't it?

LEATHER

Mark Cross 645 FIFTH AVE. 10017
421-3000

Why limit yourself to Italy or France when Mark Cross stocks leathers from France, Italy, Germany, Belgium, England, and Switzerland, and manages to find the best of the artisans of each country? Besides, after being GG'd and LV'd to death, it's refreshing to come up with a pair of initials that isn't recognized by every status seeker in the country. You can still find that basic $300 gold-fitted wallet or that $900 piece of handy wheeled luggage at Mark Cross. You just won't be telling the world where you got it! Though if you're in the midst of an identity crisis and good, luxurious workmanship simply isn't enough to please you, you *can* still find some MC-identified pieces around.

Once you graduate from a longing for vinyl-encrusted canvas, you can get spoiled by the fantastic leathers you'll find at Mark Cross. We'll never forget that hippopotamus hide suitcase for $1,300—how could we—it's still in our closet today! And the way things seem to be going, it will never wear out! Naturally we haven't let that stop us—we've been supplementing it with Mark Cross's wonderful lightweight luggage and classic two-zippered handbag (at just $100, you can afford one in every color).

Their fresh, young leather designs have such a sense of style, it's hard to choose favorites, but we don't think any home should be without at least their $1,000 desk set, a ladies' briefcase or two at $180, and a complete selection of that practical little traveler's raincoat designed to pack in a pouch. Even the

Princess Aga Khan owns six of those little $60 wonders. One for each of her jets? Oh, yes... you'll want a guest register, too. Why not get yours from the shop that provides them to the White House?

Then on to Mrs. Simian's department, where you'll find a tremendous assortment of travel accessories. She can show you clocks, mirrors, slippers, and jewel cases—all light enough to make that nasty airline limit.

Some say the best advantage of having the Cross habit is Angela Hawkings. Angela came in to work over Christmas 23 years ago—she hasn't left yet. Angela's specialty is rearranging lives. No... not like Dear Abby, silly! Angela heads up the small leathers department and manages to make anyone who buys a wallet from her a devotee for life. There's no room in her life for bulging wallets or messy purses. She'll find a slim-line billfold for even the most avid charger, then code his most-used cards with Mystic tape. She'll take possessions that require six containers in that purse and fit them neatly into three. Now, if only we could persuade her to come home with us and work on our closets, too!

LINENS

D. Porthault, Inc.   57 E. 57TH ST.   10022
688-1660

Porthault's just the perfect place to visit. You'll have the treat of stepping off the sidewalk and right into a bedroom. And how often does that happen to you in the middle of New York?

Now, tell us the truth... how would you feel about paying $2,800 to go to bed? A bit more than the price tag you're used to? Well, at least with this one you get a few touches of lace and hand embroidery thrown in with the bed. And you just *know* how much longer those will last than some of the more transient pleasures in life.

Oh, by the way, the $2,800 applies toward your purchase of a set of new white Porthault bed linen. Not that the investment will stop there; with that much at stake you'll want to insist on putting a French laundress on staff. Noblesse oblige, you know!

Not in the mood for lace and frills? Maybe just a simple pair of pillowcases will do for today? Have no fear; Albert Aferiat always has time to step away from his manager's desk to help. He'll show you cases in Porthault's cotton prints at $110, or in linen at $180 the pair. If you want embroidery, plan to spend upwards of $200. But don't be swayed by that soothing French accent—you're liable to find yourself buying trousseaus for people you've never even met!

Now that you're settled down for the night, how about dreaming of a starter set of Porthault towels? Just $166 for two bath-size, two hand-size, two washcloths, and a bath mat. Now that's a bargain! Of course, you won't mind paying a bit more for custom-designed prints—but you might mind the six- to eight-week wait while they're finished in Paris. After all, you do have to wait until they've finished the Mellons' latest order. A simple terry robe is only $180, but if you have a yen to express yourself, you can design your own.

Porthault's so thoughtful. Not only have they gone to the trouble of stocking a complete selection of table linen, they've even arranged to have their shop opened right above Baccarat. That new appliquéd tablecloth just wouldn't look right without a few pieces of the world's most expensive crystal sitting on it, would it? Of course not!

Be sure to have Albert help you pick just the right one. In his 25 years there he's dressed beds for everyone from Lee Strasberg to the Whitneys. He'll confide the bedroom secrets of royalty, embassies, and famous homes. He'll also encourage you to visit the Porthault boutique on avenue Montaigne during your next Paris visit. Just jot down the address in your new Porthault address book (a steal at $14) and make a mental note that it's a must-see. And while you're there why not invest $5 in a Porthault handkerchief for your laundress—just think of how bored she must get caring for everyone *else's* Porthaults!

Léron	745 FIFTH AVE. 10022
	753-6700

The help is stuffy, but astute. Which makes it the perfect place for you to drop off your maiden aunt while you have your hair done at Kenneth's. You know, the aunt who's been simply crying out for a set of Madeira linen sheets. Just tell her to ask for Mr. Foster, and to be prepared to spend $69 per single sheet.

Mr. Foster takes pride in his pointe de Beauvais embroidery. For just $350 he'll wrap up a service of placemats and napkins for four, and he's so original, not one piece will match. Don't worry... it's supposed to be that way! If your napkin has a sparrow, your placemat will sport a robin. If your doily has a snapdragon, your tablecloth will have a rose. Oh, well, at least it keeps the embroidresses from getting bored!

If you really want to keep them busy, why not order a complete set of pointe de Beauvais bed linen. Those sheets with the ruffled fluting and ribboned lace trim will be ever so perfect for your Louis XIV guest room, but do plan ahead. It takes three to four months to complete a set—by the time they arrive the guests might have been gone for weeks!

Though the French pointe de Beauvais is heartbreakingly expensive, and the appliqued Portuguese pieces well above average, Léron does have a heart. Not only do their American workrooms quickly whip up modern tricolor sheets at just $25 apiece, they do wonders for keeping the country's employment rate up. They'll even initial a six-piece starter set of towels for just $68.

Order them from Mr. Foster's assistant, Ann. Or if you can't manage to make up your mind on the spot, ask her to put you on their catalog mailing list. Of course she will ask you to pay for the honor of receiving that glossy four-color order form, but she'll kindly refund the purchase price as soon as you write from Palm Beach to send in your order for that first terry robe... and with styles labeled "frankly feminine," how could you possibly resist?

Pratesi Shop	829 MADISON AVE. 10021
	288-2315

We used to think our favorite thing Italian was a well-tuned red Ferrari. Then we ran across Pratesi. What more can we say after we tell you it's the Gucci of bed sheets? Oh, well... we'll find more, we assure you. It takes only a few hours spent with Pratesi's Adelaide to remind you that beds are meant for more than just sleeping!

Pratesi's pretties are made in Pistoria, just outside Florence. Every piece is hand-finished and custom-colored. Our special love was San Gallo—just $290 per sheet and $109 for a set of matching pillowcases. It's enough to make you want to stay awake all night and enjoy it, isn't it?

If you value your sleep more than that, opt for an undistractingly white sheet at $89, with pillowcases at $32 a pair. Just luxurious enough to insure pleasant dreams without being so rich you'll have trouble settling down to sleep. Or you can choose from the more than 30 prints which are available, with matching pique blanket covers for $290. Heavens! If Pratesi sells enough of these, we can all but forget about divorce Italian style!

Naturally you'll want your set to include towels as well as bed linen. You'll be able to get two for less than $75 if you forgo monograms—and why not! If they don't already know who you are, why should you tell them! Matching terry robes can be had at $106 for his and $96 for hers.

Now you've done it—one set of sheets and you've overstepped the whole day's budget! Just for that we're punishing you by sending you to bed early! On second thought, just how much repenting are you likely to do curled up in that new set of San Gallo sheets? Not much, we're afraid!

POTPOURRI ELÉGANT

Caswell-Massey Co., Ltd.	LEXINGTON AVE. AT 48TH ST. 10017 755-2254

Naturally we always do our shopping in those places which are recommended by prestigious personalities—in this case we're following the advice of George Washington. He found their spicy Cologne No. 6 during a pre-Revolutionary trip to Newport, Rhode Island, and became so enthusiastic he not only wore it himself, he also sent bottles to Thomas Jefferson, James Madison, and John Quincy Adams.

Caswell-Massey still makes Cologne No. 6, as well as a seemingly limitless number of other quality nostalgic products which range from ivory hairbrushes to Swedish birchleaf soaps. Ralph and Milton remain staunchly faithful to their formula of natural ingredients, perhaps because their mother remains staunchly in the shop, supervising the preparation of those century-old recipes.

It's an apothecary-filled corner in the Barclay Hotel, paneled in solid walnut and smelling of soap from France, Japanese brown sugar soaps, snuffboxes (yes, one more bad habit you can now start cultivating!), and bottles of cologne. Mouse-shaped pumice stones vie with badger shaving brushes ($59 to $70) for shelf space. They still have straight razors, as well as the cucumber cream that the great Sarah Bernhardt had shipped to her Paris dressing room in 1887. Today it's used by Mary Martin for removing her makeup.

Caswell-Massey doesn't like to promote the obvious things which can be bought anywhere; they look for little-known preparations from other countries, those which have special merit. Thus they have become the agents for Floris of London, as well as Pompeia and Floramye perfumes and soaps from Piver of Paris. Imported potpourri comes in seashells or bowls, and swansdown powder puffs sell today for $25. There's a marvelous face pack for dry skin made by Christy's ($3 per tube), and a Manidama hand cream of vitamins and lemons ($3.75 per tube). There are old-fashioned hot-water bottles in four popular colors, and Dylon Quick-Wash for rinsing things out while on the road. Their old-fashioned store even supplies premoistened travel towelettes to the jet set in lavender, verbena, and tabac.

There are so many assorted wonders at Caswell-Massey that you can't possibly absorb them all in one visit. No wonder there are 25,000 requests for their catalog! Put in yours and make it 25,001. And by the way, if all you came in for when you saw the sign "Apothecary" was to have a prescription filled, don't worry. They've done over 13,000,000 to date, and will be happy to fit yours in between the selling of chic black mouches for ladies who have always wanted a beauty mark, and pewter snuffboxes!

The Gazebo	660 MADISON AVE. 10022
	832-7077

If your eyes still light up when you go to F. A. O. Schwarz, you'll be intrigued with The Gazebo. Personally, ours are more likely to light up at Harry Winston's, but the first time we walked into this little fairyland for adults it was Christmastime and we were won over, too. Everything's a blaze of color, spirit and gingerbread houses then, but the joy of the shop is that it doesn't have to be a holiday for it to make you feel like celebrating one inside.

Quilt collectors love Virginia Marple's collection of Early American masterpieces, some of which start as low as $100. You'll also find a nice selection of new quilts, some as reasonably priced as $45 for a king size. And it's always fun to commission the store to make a personalized appliquéd quilt. At $25, can you think of a better baby shower gift for your social secretary?

If she already has a family, a nice birthday present would be The Gazebo's family pillow with appliqués of mom, dad and the kids. If it's a close family, Rover can be appliquéd on, too. A family of four runs about $50. And if you want to add on the butler, it will run another $10. If you haven't brought home anything for the cook lately, consider a bowl full of papier-mâché vegetables. What could be more perfect—the price is under $50, and she'll never have to worry about peeling them. On the more practical side, you might buy her an appliquéd potholder for $7. They're so unique that she wouldn't consider using them on anything less than a French soufflé dish.

For your next dinner party, take a hint from former First Lady, Betty Ford, who commissioned The Gazebo to decorate the tables when Emperor Hirohito visited the White House. We got it from reliable sources: those chrysanthemums and dried fruits left a most honorable impression.

Hammacher	147 E. 57TH ST. 10022
Schlemmer	421-9000

If you don't find what you want at Hammacher Schlemmer, you're probably out of luck. If you do, we wager you're a bit of an eccentric. For 125 years this has been a haven for hardware, based first in the Bowery and now on 57th Street. You'll love all the gadgetry, like the turnpike toll gun for $9.95, so handy for shooting quarters out of your Ferrari, or a pocket peppermill that you can carry on the plane with you. For $10,000 take your choice of a silver carving cart or a mahogany pub. Either is the perfect addition to your dining area.

The store is on several levels, but it's the main floor where you'll find the preponderance of gifts and gadgetry. The Plummer-McCutcheon shop, which features porcelain, metals, crystals, china, linens, and silks, is on the second floor. Plan to spend a great deal of time on three and four, where you won't be able to resist an Italian marble sink, complete with gold-plated fixtures, for $3,000. Prefer to save a whole day's allowance? Order the sink without the gold fixtures.

If you've always wondered who designed the closets and bathrooms at the White House, you've found the place. You can copy them or design your own fabric-lined closets, complete with electric-powered revolving racks. With shoe bags, clothing bags and other essential accessories, the electric closet is only $350.

Create your own spa at home with exercise equipment and a portasauna. A single sauna is yours for $550, but for $895 you'll have a pair—after all, what good is a sauna without someone to talk to?

On the fifth floor you'll find a six-speed electric car that wouldn't be out of place on Main Street in Disneyland. For $3,750 your child can challenge any Porsche on the block. If you think his first auto should be a little less snappy, check out the giant pink and purple hippo for $1,695, with only one speed —slow. This is the same floor where you'll find an exact copy of Marie Antoinette's dog house for $595, a collapsible Indian elephant ladder trimmed in brass for $295, and a replica of Queen Victoria's sedan chair for only $2,500.

The sixth floor is delicious. Every cooking gadget imaginable is waiting for the right buyer: a stacker to keep crepes neat for $350 (you can also pick up the crepe maker for only $595, if you don't already have one), a cappuccino maker for $5,000 and best of all luxuries, a self-stirring saucepan that won't let anything stick while you take your bubble bath.

Tender Buttons 143 E. 62nd ST. 10021
758-7004

Button up your overcoat, but don't do it with anything costing less than $225. Far be it from us to keep out the winter chill with disks of mere modern plastic when we can as easily do it with engraved art nouveau silver at just a few hundred dollars for a set of six. There's no better place to make such a find than at Tender Buttons, and while some may say that Gertrude Stein would be taken aback at the thought of the title for her collection of short stories being converted into the name of a Manhattan button shop, we prefer to picture her thoughtfully commenting, "A button is a button is a button . . . "

Kitty Hawks would not agree. She's hopefully waiting for the hawk button to appear which will be the perfect closure to her basic blazer. And of course the girls (Diane Epstein and Millicent Safro) are bound to find a set for her. Be it with a bistro in Paris or a rabbi in Brooklyn, no button remains unturned.

They stock 1875 English enamels with brightly colored Japanese ladies at $40 each. For the more modest in taste, they carry handpainted plastics in the shape of any fruit or vegetable which might conceivably whet your tailor's palate. Gold or silver blazer buttons can be chosen from over a thousand styles—fishing, boating, golfing, tennis, hunting, motoring or even family crests (you do have one, don't you?). There are horn buttons from deer, elk, cow, and buffalo. Styles come in papier-mâché or tortoise shell. Metal buttons can be found in brass, silver, copper, pewter, or cut steel. There are buttons of Wedgwood, Meissen, Satsuma, camphor glass, and even some fashioned from the skin of Mexican chickens (so perfect for your next trip to Pamplona!).

Diane and Millicent's buttons have made all but the most blasé shoppers snap to attention. Jasper Johns went through 72 shades of green before he found the perfect target. Bill Blass, Carol Horn, and Oleg Cassini zip in to buy for their personal wardrobes. Glenda Jackson realized that the Tender Buttons cow belt buckle and matching buttons gave her a real "touch of class" and proceeded to wear them for the movie. Even Paul Newman asked Diane to button him up—her heart said no, no, no, but she did it anyway!

Diane will be happy to explain to you that her collection of buttons falls just one style short of infinity, so if you plan to make a thorough investigation of her wares, set aside a few hours. Travelers have been known to bring in a complete suitcase of clothes, requesting that she personalize them. Probably your needs will be a bit simpler—perhaps you just glanced down and noticed that a button has popped off the bottom of your full-length sable. Diane can fix that for you in a jiffy with a perfect match. Or for something a bit more camp, would you consider a Betty Boop garter button?

STATIONERY

Ffolio 72	888 MADISON AVE. 10021 879-0675

She may be considered a newcomer to the stationery world, but Muriel Glaser has been producing her handmade papers since the mid-sixties. It's obvious from the moment you walk into her red-walled store blossoming with stationery samples, which run the gamut from sporty to dressy, that she's succeeded in interjecting a touch of fashion into a traditionally staid field.

Ffolio 72 not only has a wide selection of fine papers, but the store will happily print your own design, or one of their making, on one of their handsome marbelized papers which have been crafted by hand and perfected for use as bags, files, writing papers, gift enclosures, or calling cards.

Everyone appreciates a Ffolio 72 gift. Generous New Yorkers select from hand-dipped pencils, boxes, pads, and English end papers. And don't forget that when you finish your autobiography, Muriel stands ready with extraordinary hand bookbinding—nothing but the best for your life!

Mrs. John L. **Strong**	699 MADISON AVE. 10021 838-3775

Been wondering what stationery to use to thank Gloria Vanderbilt for that last dinner party? Want to make a marvelous impression without stooping to the depths of using that ever-so-common Tiffany's engraved? It's time to call Mrs. John L. Strong.

Mrs. Strong is a tiny lady in a tiny stationery shop which is approached in a tiny elevator, but she thinks big. Having designed stationery for everyone from Barbara Hutton and Truman Capote to the Duke and Duchess of Windsor during the past thirty-odd years, she's just the one to put the stamp of quality on your social correspondence.

Don't worry about asking her to custom design or custom color for you—she's used to filling special requests. Truly, yours won't fluster her a bit—she does 40,000 Christmas cards at a crack for Thomas J. Watson of IBM. Obviously your note pads are going to be a breeze for her. They'll run you from $20 to $50 for three pads. Paper will cost you another $35 per hundred once you've had your custom die made, an initial investment which might range from $18 to $100. And like magic, you're pen pals with Barbara Walters, Ethel Kennedy, and the Javitses, all of whom send their salutations on Mrs. Strong's best. It's enough to inspire you to use nothing but commemorative stamps, isn't it!

VIII. ANTIQUES AND GALLERIES
Growing Old Gracefully in Manhattan

Next to the European capitals that produced many of the antiques sold here, New York is the busiest center of antique trading in the world. Also one of the most difficult to shop, because there are so very many stores to browse through. Decisions, decisions.

From collections of dealers like the Manhattan Art and Antique Center, to those extravagant independents like A La Vieille Russie and Stair & Co., New York can fulfill your every wish. But wherever you're shopping, there are a few rules you'll do well to observe. Although they cost more, works of superior quality are really the soundest investments. After all, remember how long that last black Bentley lasted you? So take your time and comparison-shop, and be sure to know your dealers and their reputations—the art market has its thieves as well as its princes.

ANTIQUES

The Antiques Center of America	415 E. 53RD ST. 10022 486-0941

For those of you with as much time as taste, the Antiques Center of America on East 53rd Street is a must. Imagine the ecstasy of

106 antique shops at one address; it's a shopping center for the civilized set!

If you collect anything out of the ordinary, there's sure to be a shop devoted to your passion here. All things American are sure to be found. Take napkin rings, for example. Just what you've been looking for? Well, Meta Belier features them at the Silent Woman Antiques. If vinaiegrettes—those beautiful little bottles for smelling salts (and all this time you thought it was something to put on salads!)—are your love, you'll find them at the House of Poncee for $75 to $450. And the Odd Ball Antique is one of those country store memorabilia haunts with everything from old paper clips and Camel ads to rare biscuit tins and a smattering of antique furniture.

Now we know you're the type who's used to being asked for your autograph, but you'll have to forget that when you visit Henry Gerskum Nazlen. He'd much rather sell you a copy of Eleanor Roosevelt's, Abraham Lincoln's, or George Washington's. Unless, of course, you can convince him that yours will be at least as valuable in the future. Then he might consider a trade.

If you simply need the proper accessories for your next high tea, join the decorators who frequent Anteccache looking for all sorts of British bric-a-brac. Then trot on to Ambergris, where you'll be able to select from a fine collection of American and Georgian silver, as well as from a few paintings and small bronze pieces. We picked up another bronze or two, as well as the best hatpins we've seen anywhere, from Objets d' Art, where prices range from $45 to $350. Then on to Valerie McCallagh, who specializes in 18th-century enamel boxes ranging in price from $100 to $2,000.

We just loved skimming the rare books at Collector's Antiques, where you can also find fine bindings, some pieces of fabric (so perfect for an overpriced patchwork!), and an assortment of Russian enamels. If your tastes are still being acquired, a marvelous place for beginning antiquers is Good's Antiques, where match safes and old boxes come in every size, motif, and price range. A wonderful way to wrap that next hostess gift, wouldn't you say?

As for Joanne Blum, she's been in the rare Wedgwood business for over 25 years—just long enough to become one of the country's leading appraisers of ceramic ware. Of her hundreds of anecdotes, the one we most love is when she tells of how Wedgwood started out making dishes for the poor. My, how times did change!

We've mentioned only a few of the treasures to be found at the Antiques Center of America; with 106 stores to choose from, you're sure to find something you'll just love. But bear in mind that all these stores have one thing in common: like a London marketplace, bargaining is expected. And no... we don't mean that you're supposed to ask them to move the prices up!

STALLS:

Silent Woman Antiques
House of Poncee
The Odd Ball Antique
Henry Gerskum Nazlen
Anteccache
Ambergris

Objets d'Art
Valerie McCallagh
Collector's Antiques
Good's Antiques
Joanne Blum

| **The Antique Market** | SECOND AVE. AT 58TH ST.   10022
355-4400 |
|---|---|

Some days it's so troublesome getting in and out of that limo it's a welcome sight to view 50 or 60 stores in one spot. The Antique Market is one of these multi-store haunts for serious collectors, novices and just plain browsers. There are so many shops here that we can't begin to go into them all in detail (if we stopped for that, we wouldn't have any time for shopping, now, would we!), but we have picked out a few which are our favorites.

If your most recent fortune cookie from Pearl's suggested you invest in Oriental art, check the fine Korean and Chinese antiques at Continental Enterprises. Yong F. Yoo carries Chinese art dating from 221 and 265 through the China of 1911. The pieces are often so important they're all but priceless. You might have even better luck at Lucky Arts Enterprises. Check that fortune cookie to be sure.

Robert Edward Mann Antiques specializes in bronzes and ivories; then if you have the time (just check one of those wonderful antique clocks at Clock Hutt, Limited) stop in to visit the Port of St. James, where James Sobel will be happy to share his marine arts with you. Bernice Fried will be happy to give you a new look in one of her marvelous *old* mirrors, art deco wonders that run anywhere from $50 to $75. And if you're happy with the same old you, you can always settle for a bit of her antique jewelry. You'll find old gold jewelry at Mrs. Liebow's attic, too, where they buy and sell antique china, glass or furniture, as well.

Judith Andus features fine decorative silver and antique collectibles. For decorating bodies instead of tables, Maria specializes in antique jewelry.

See now, just another 45 booths, and you'll have met them all! Let's polish them off quickly, then run on to our next stop.

STALLS:

Robert Edward Mann   Mrs. Liebow's
Port of St. James   Judith Andus
Bernice Fried

French and Company   17 E. 65TH ST.   10022
                        535-3330

How many times have you gone to a party and had the urge to make the hostess's favorite painting your own? Well, before you slip it into your purse and run the chance of being accused of burglary, try soothing your acquisitive nature with a trip to French & Co. It's the perfect solution; for just $600,000, Martin Zimet will let you lift the Renoir from his dining room.

In point of fact, he'll be happy to sell you any piece of furniture he owns, which is saying quite a bit, as his Manhattan brownstone contains everything from a George III mahogany secretary by Chippendale at $130,000, to a magnificent Picasso at $1,800,000. Of course if you don't happen to like his blue period, you wouldn't be interested—but if you do, it will be just the thing for that empty corner in the living room. By the way, don't count on lowering the price by flashing your credentials and demanding a decorator's discount. Martin will merely refuse you.

Before he'll sell you anything, you'll have to get past his bull mastiff. Having conquered that particular obstacle, you'll then have to pick your way through a rather dark hallway. But what waits at the end is worth the effort. Martin's home was custom-carpeted by Edward Fields. The walls are paneled in dark brown cut velvet and mirrors. Stainless steel railings define the ramp which leads up three levels. You'll pass by Andy Warhol's portraits of the Zimets, and a granite-topped dining table that seats 14 (yes, the candelabra *are* nice; they can be yours for just $50,000).

The library and den are on the second floor. There you'll find a magnificent rosewood inlaid Louis XV lady's table with matching commode (just $130,000). Not only does the home contain a collection of 18th-century English furniture which rivals in quality any museum in the world, but each piece is in mint condition. We dare you to find a single scratch.

Besides all this, Martin is just the perfect host. So obliging and friendly, you'll wonder how you ever got along in the Big Apple without him. But be careful; he could prove to be one of your more expensive acquaintances.

A La Vieille Russie	781 FIFTH AVE. 10022 752-1727

We're not sure we agree that A La Vieille Russie is really the most expensive gift store in the world... but you must admit, when people come all the way from Van Cleef & Arpels just to try to buy a gift box to make that jewel they purchased look a bit better, it can't be far off. After all, most of those Van Cleef diamonds need so little window dressing!

Unfortunately for them, A La Vieille Russie doesn't allow their boxes to be sold. And they won't sell their gold and silver Alexander III samovar, either. Understandably—the Schaeffers had to purchase an entire room of the czar's palace just to get that goodie. So sorry you had your heart set on it for your next high tea; you'll just have to get along without.

Maybe we can make it up to you with a Nicholas I period gilt porcelain tea set, or if that fails, a stunning icon for just $15,000. You're still not happy? Well, with showcases filled with everything from cigarette cases to serving pieces, from 19th-century Russian porcelain figures to Fabergé, we're sure you'll find something to pique your fancy.

A La Vieille Russie is an elegant little gray-toned store set next to the Sherry-Netherland Hotel. Since the entire Schaeffer family works there—Paul, Peter, and their mother—it's not a problem finding one of the owners to pass enthusiasm for superb craftsmanship, elegant design and apparent richness along to you. While the store's merchandise might range from antique jewelry dated 1625 to singular little snuffboxes, it all has one thing in common—its only limitation is quality.

Russian objects are a specialty, but following the tastes of affluent pre-revolutionary Russians, the shop offers fine objects, jewelry, silver, porcelain, glass, and furniture from wherever opulence reigned. Fabergé connoisseurs will enjoy choosing from the nation's largest collection of his 19th-century works, while furniture fans will be able to choose from a selection of 18th-century French furniture crafted by Parisian court cabinet-makers in combinations of fine veneer, marquetry and gilt. Don't be surprised to discover an Italian Renaissance steel box next to a Louis XV commode; the entire shop is a mixture of treasures. With an average price tag of $1,000 to $5,000 for those little trinkets, we *can* consider them treasures, can't we?

Connoisseur Inc.   717 MADISON AVE. 10021
L'Antiquaire Inc.   838-3880

Ring the bell at 717 Madison Avenue and you'll be welcomed into two antique shops, and one will surely suit your taste or mood. The Connoisseur is operated by Ruth Costantino and caters to those who cherish the 18th century. L'Antiquaire, whose proprietors are Ruth's daughter Helen and her husband Nero Fioratti, handles 16th-century relics. This family team saves you the bother of going to those boring estate auctions. They bring back the finest pieces, and just think, you don't have to go through all those catalogs.

Even European collectors make it a point to deal with Ruth and Helen, since they've acquired an international reputation with both private parties and museums. Have them take you into the cellars where they keep 16th- and 17th-century artifacts like the Italian *cassone* (wedding chest) for $4,200. You'll find exquisite mantels, too. For $15,000 you can add a marble Louis XVI mantel to your living room. Who wouldn't enjoy a pair of Louis XV chairs covered in silk and signed by Boucault for $27,500? If you're in New York at Christmas ask to see that fabulous collection of pillows made from 18th-century fabrics; at $85 to $500, they make memorable gifts.

Frank Kay, Ltd.   232 E. 59TH ST.   10022
758-0917

Parrish Hadley, McMillan, Inc., and Jesop and Edward Benesch wouldn't dream of finishing a building without stopping in to visit Mrs. Kay. They try to time their visits around her twice-yearly overseas trips. Mrs. Kay is busy collecting scads of European and Oriental antiques for the decorators who frequent her shop. It's an intimate business, yet it draws clients from all over the country.

Mrs. Kay specializes in decorative accessories. You'll find her treasures in homes from Cape Cod to Carmel, as well as in the Morgan Bank, the Mellon, and the Sky Club. If you, too, have a yen for the Oriental, choose from her giant tea canisters at $1,800, or the polished iron grills she's had made into tables at $675. Kang-H'si panels dating from 1750 can be had, as well as a Chinese brush holder for a mere $180. But if you opt for something a bit more costly, you'll want to pick up that pair of polychrome temple guard dogs, too. Ooops! At $7,500, who's going to guard *them?*

Leo Kaplan   888 MADISON AVE.   10021
249-6766

What won't they think of next! Now we've managed to find a shop that's selling glass that's more expensive than diamonds! Well, at least no one will accuse you of being pretentious. Leo Kaplan sells antique paperweights from $200 to $35,000. You're right—that would have been a rather small diamond anyway, wouldn't it! No doubt you will be better off with a bit of 1850 Clichy or 1973 St. Louis.

Leo will be glad to show you his selection of hundreds of paperweights, Russian enamels, and English pottery and porcelains, as well as an assortment of accessories in the finest tradition. Together with his wife and son Allen, he'll go out of his way to make you feel comfortably at home as you pick between Baccarat bud vases and Russian cane handles. The shop is small and busy; yet the Kaplans are happy to take time to sit down and explain any piece to you.

Think about it... that antique French paperweight would be just the thing for holding down your stock certificates, wouldn't it!

Lillian Nassau   220 E. 57TH ST.   10022
759-6062

It's the Tiffany of Tiffanys. No, dear, not diamonds, cut glass. But don't scoff. A lampshade at $75,000 is nothing to look down your nose at! In fact, rumor has it that the next time the Lord says, "Let there be light!" he's going to insist that it come shining through a shade from Lillian Nassau.

Lillian started collecting her leaded-glass Tiffany originals in 1937, which wasn't so very long after the Tiffany studio's most active New York period—1890 to 1925. Today, as these period pieces become rarer and rarer, the celebrity shopping crowd becomes larger and larger. Catherine Deneuve and Marcello Mastroianni picked up pieces here, though who has them today we can't tell you. Even the Beatles used some of their rock earnings to invest in glass.

In among the Tiffanys ($2,500 to $75,000) you'll find American bronzes, with the Art Deco and Nouveau periods particularly prevalent. You might even run across such curiosities as a tea set at $25,000. Ringo passed it up, but your maiden aunt in Des Moines will just love it.

Ah, yes... if you don't love *her* quite that much, take heart. There's always a good selection of art glass for as little as $15 at Lillian Nassau.

Philip Colleck	122 E. 57TH ST. 10022
	753-1544

Philip Colleck is used to dealing with customers who are wealthy and willing to pay for the finest. And though he normally works by appointment with the buyers who come in to purchase for estate houses, the Blair House, and the White House, he'll be willing to spend a few moments with you if he doesn't happen to be booked. But be ready to pay attention—if he senses you're not really interested in learning, he'll simply tell you he's a busy man. Study hard before you attempt to talk to Philip about antiques; there's no need for novice collectors to do anything but browse. Unless, of course, they're willing to part with $4,500 for that perfect pair of 1810 English cockfighting chairs. How's that for a beginning! After that you can work your way up to his rare English mechanical desk with secret compartments just made for storing away all your loose change. If you happen to have any left after paying $14,500 for the desk, that is! If you do, you might want to pull it out for that wonderful lacquered chest we spotted last week for just $28,000.

Philip's collection is mainly 18th-century formal pieces rather than country looks. His shop is a delightful clutter of beautiful desks, tables, chairs and porcelains. But don't be frightened by his awesome stature in the antique market. People have been known to find lovely $150 tea caddies and such nestled next to his precious pieces.

Philip W. Pfeifer	900 MADISON AVE. 10021
Antiques	249-4889

Is there a doctor in the house? If so, we're sure he'd love Philip Pfeifer's collection of 18th- and 19-century pharmaceutical and medical instruments. Not that he'd consider using them in his ever-so-exclusive Park Avenue practice. But they would give his patients something to think about and be grateful for, wouldn't they!

If his tastes range afield, he'll also be interested in Philip's collection of instruments for astronomy, mathematics, and navigation. And while we think that Philip is an avid collector of some rather curious devices, they might be just what you're looking for.

Take his sets of antique architectural instruments: folding boxwood rulers, sophisticated brass arithometers, pocket sundials and automatic calculators. Or his 200-year-old drawing tools crafted by Vincard of Paris—complete with calipers, compass, and square with a level and a sector. Just what you needed... and only $2,250.

Still haven't interested you? Well, since his shop has everything from dog whistles to walking sticks, from magnifying glasses to coats of arms, we can't help but believe that you'll find some way to spend your allowance!

Rita Ford	812 MADISON AVE. 10021
Music Boxes	535-6717

It's hard to find someone who doesn't like music boxes. And it's even harder to find a music box not to like at Rita Ford's shop. Mrs. Ford is internationally known for her collection of antique music boxes, each tuned to its performance peak. Her favorite is an eight-cylinder box made in 1875 for the Earl of Linsbourne at $9,500, complete with letter of authenticity. Even George C. Scott has been known to sit mesmerized by its song. Perched throughout the shop are various mechanical songbirds, but surely her most conversational piece is a life-sized chanticleer perched on a brass pedestal. This 1875 feathered friend can keep you company for $3,500. It isn't unusual to find Harry Belafonte ordering a special song box from Mrs. Ford; she can have just about any song made into a music box in Switzerland. She's put so many songs into new boxes that she even has a catalog of what's readily available.

Stair & Co. 59 E. 57TH ST. 10022
355-7620

How good it is to run into old friends. We hadn't visited the people at Stair & Co. since the last time we browsed through their London headquarters. How nice to find that we can rely on Alastair A. Stair when in Manhattan, too. After all, having owned the company since 1912, who could possibly be better than Alastair at bringing us the best?

Since Stair & Co. is one of the better places in London to find 18th-century English furniture, you might well imagine that it's the best in New York for finding the same. And since most of the pieces are museum-quality, you can also imagine that this won't be the place for you to find that wonderful little treasure for next to nothing. Alastair is nothing if not knowledgeable about the value of his pieces. He's back and forth to London quite a bit, so call ahead for an appointment with him. If he won't be back in the country in time to help you, Miss Lampageau will give you a tour. Having been his secretary for over 25 years, she can almost give you the same tour he would have treated you to.

Though you can find 18th-century porcelains ($90–$180) and other small collectibles, English mahogany is Stair's forte. Serious collectors will want to snap up that host desk with cross-banded top, circa 1780, for just $24,000. If it's gone by the time you get there, comfort yourself with the fact that there are five full floors of similar treasures.

If that still leaves you disconsolate, keep in mind that Stair's Incurable Collector located nearby on 57th Street houses still another collection of decorative pieces, including a wonderful

1780 tea caddy we spotted on our last trip. But its $450 price tag led us to settle for a quick cup in the Russian Tea Room instead.

Stair also offers a restoration service—Oxford Antique Restore, Ltd.—which repairs, regilds, and polishes antiques as well as restoring your favorite paintings. Though with the quality of merchandise which is offered at Stair and Co., we can't imagine you'd need their services!

Sylvia Tearston	1053 THIRD AVE. 10021
Antiques	838-0415

When one of the curators of the Metropolitan Museum has a question about 18th-century and 19th-century Regency furniture, he calls on Sylvia Tearston. Six of her pieces were recently on exhibit at the museum, so you know that a purchase at Tearston means authenticity to the nth degree. She has fine taste in both Chippendale and Queen Anne.

When you go in (you'll need an appointment) don't hesitate to ask Mrs. Tearston to show you some of her favorite Chinese porcelain pieces. We remember a magnificent Chien Lung period vase from the Peking palace that was an unbelievable $7,500. For those of you who fancy Rockingham, she has a lovely dessert set for $3,500, including 22 plates and 3 tureens. Please don't quibble—what do you expect for 25 pieces?

GALLERIES

André Emmerich	41 E. 57TH ST. 10022
	752-0124
	420 WEST BROADWAY 10012
	431-4550

If you'd find it disconcerting to pay $125,000 for a piece by Hans Hofmann while standing in the midst of a gallery that's somewhere between a showroom and a roster of nearsighted accountants, avoid André Emmerich. If, on the other hand, you'd enjoy discussing that upcoming purchase with a struggling young artist over a drink at the Spring Street Bar, look him up immediately. Though André Emmerich has been safely located on 57th Street for 10 of the 20 years he's been dealing in art, we think his newer Soho gallery wins hands down when it comes to atmosphere.

André's selection of modern painting and sculpture is superb. His Helen Frankenthaler pieces are usually sold by mail even before her openings (with a mailing list of 5,000, there's bound to be a bit of competitive bidding!). A Caro sculpture will go for $40,000 to $50,000, and you might be able to pick up a little something by Morris Louis, Sam Francis, or Ed Moses for even less. David Hockney's prices, of course, are skyrocketing.

Despite the fact that André deals primarily in modern painting and sculpture, we've always been convinced that his real love is pre-Columbian pieces. He's written several books on the subject, and he has some of the finest pieces we've seen. We couldn't resist those tiny golden frogs for $100, and the bits of pre-Columbian jade at $500 (oops... another day's allowance shot!). Having lost our self-control when faced with those frogs, we just had to pass up his 2nd-century bronze boy. Frankly, we didn't have the necessary $500,000 left. Next time, we'll plan ahead!

The Hammer Galleries	51 E. 57TH ST. 10022 644-4400

A trip to the Hammer Galleries which doesn't include a chat with Victor is never quite the same. Of course, it does get a bit difficult to time your trips to New York around his Palm Beach and London jaunts, but believe us—it's well worth the trouble.

If you're a first-time Hammer visitor, you'll recognize Victor by his gray Sullivan and Wooley suit, white bowtie, and ever-present white carnation. He's as patient with browsers as he is with buyers, so don't be hesitant about starting a conversation. Ask about his dear brother Armand, and Victor will reminisce about the days when they ran the art concession for Gimbels, just one of the innovations he brought to the conservative New York art world.

Even though Armand is president of the galleries, it's Victor who makes things click. He's done everything from selling the contents of J. P. Morgan's yacht to putting price tags on paintings, which brought a blush of horror to the cheeks of dealers who were accustomed to hushing such information up.

People still talk about his "elegant piece of artistic surgery" back in 1959 when he found a canvas covered with oil sketches by Auguste Renoir, jigsawed around them, and transformed one salable canvas into eight little masterpieces. Total sale: $55,000. Quite a feat of creative salesmanship, we'd say.

The Hammer Gallery is renowned for quality. Whether you're looking for American, French Impressionist or Russian pieces, you can rely on the Hammers to offer the best for your dollars. You'll find everyone from Lautrec to Charles Russell, Renoir to Remington, Pissarro to Grandma Moses represented in their collection. And don't be shy about asking for prints. The lower gallery is full of them—many for $1,000 or less.

New shows are scheduled every two or three weeks, so if you time your New York stay correctly, you might be lucky enough to see two or three. And if with all this you still can't find anything that appeals to you, take heart. Since Victor owns the Knoedler Gallery, too, he'll be happy to take you there to start browsing all over!

Julie Artisan's Gallery, Inc.	687 MADISON AVE. 10021 688-2345

Oh, heavens... how would you feel if your Picasso started to shed? Well, that's the sort of thing you have to be ready for when you buy art to wear. Julie Shaeffer has every major artist who sculpts ready-to-wear hanging in her Madison Avenue gallery. It's just that she has them hanging on coathooks instead of in picture frames!

We can remember when she only had a few friends who stitched together feathers, fluff, and yarn. Then she showed in her apartment. But now that Elton John and Diana Ross are wearing her fluttery finery, she's qualified for an entire gallery. They weren't above the idea of buying beautiful pieces that made them look good, too.

Most of the muffs, masks, and capes which Julie's artists do are one of a kind, though you'll occasionally stumble across a series—such as a black satin evening coat with six variations of hand-painted and appliqued detail. We're sure that in such a case you'd insist on buying up the entire series, rather than see your original turn up in the next collection of Geoffrey Beene, Mary McFadden, or Bonnie Cashin. Oh, yes, they shop there too. Nobody ever said fashion was an easy business, did they?

If it's really against your principles to scrunch down into the back seat of your limo wearing your newest original work of art, you'll be happy to hear that Julie also stocks a terriffic collection of wall hangings, quilts, and pillows. We've run across her things in homes all over Europe, as well as New York.

The gallery is open 11 to 6, Monday through Saturday, and of course it's crowded every minute. After all, who can resist buying new clothes that are art, too?

The Pace Gallery   32 E. 57TH ST.   10022
                         421-3292

The Wildenstein is a bit too Old Master for you? What you're really hankering after is a simple little Louise Nevelson wall? That's simple enough—just tuck a quarter of a million in your pocket and trot on over to the Pace Gallery on 57th Street. We *know* there are two Pace Galleries, but no one chic would dream of going anywhere but the 57th Street branch!

Pace is the exclusive representative for Bell, Dubuffet and Noguchi. In their spare time they handle Kandinsky, Mondrian, Frankenthaler, and Stella. Isn't it really time you took home a Calder to brighten up those gray days?

The average price for a work from the Pace Galleries is between $25,000 and $50,000, but if you're in a particularly opulent mood we're willing to bet that you could pick up

Dubuffet's "Group of Four Trees" for somewhere between a quarter and a half-million (Yes—we do mean dollars). Of course it *is* 42 feet high. And it *is* currently rather permanently installed at the Chase Manhattan Bank Building. But Pace Director Arnold Glimcher assures us that it could be yours for the right price. There might be some minor problems involved in moving it, but isn't it the perfect solution for that dining room you've been thinking of redecorating? What could be better than a little polyurethane paint, fiberglass, aluminum, and plastic as an accompaniment to vichyssoise? If Chase Manhattan refuses to give it up, don't despair. There's always the Philadelphia Building's Dubuffet. If they were able to buy it from Seagrams for just $250,000, they'd probably be willing to sell it for a slight markup. Let's see now . . . did that include handling?

If what you had in mind was something a touch smaller, the Pace Editions Division publishes prints, multiples and posters which are executed by Pace Gallery artists, as well as such names as Ernst, Johns, Oldenburg, Picasso and Vassarely. The last time we were in we went rather mad for an untitled Nevelson litho at $950, but at the last minute decided that for that price she could at least afford to throw in a name! As for her plexiglass "Sky Cathedral Two" it was all we could do to rip it away from a dark-haired man in New Man jeans who insisted on thrusting his $10,000 forward first. Ah well, we were able to comfort ourselves with a modest pre-Columbian.

Besides being credited by the Art Dealers Association as one of the top three contemporary art galleries in the country, Pace is also listed as one of the top three representatives of ancient and primitive art. With one of the largest collections of African, pre-Columbian and New Guinea treasures to be found in the city, we're sure you'll find something to pique your fancy.

Primavera Gallery   808 MADISON AVE.   10021
                       288-1569

If rare Lalique is your favorite, Audrey Friedman is your lady. She has pieces ranging in value from $200 for clear crystal, to over $2,500 for multicolored collector's items. Don't be surprised if you run into Yves St. Laurent in this small, intimate shop—he's already given the royal fashion nod to Audrey's treasures. Andy Warhol bestowed the art world's accolade, and Elton John offered musician's sanction shortly after Dustin Hoffman and Jack Nicholson approved it for actors. As long as quality of merchandise rates as high as the celebrity register, Audrey's in business.

The entire Madison Avenue shop is filled with art nouveau and deco pieces, as well as a collection of rare American Indian jewelry. Her period furniture starts at $500; the graphics, ably managed by Ellen Oelsner, at even less. To really understand the pieces which are at Primavera you'll want to speak to Audrey, but be sure to call ahead and make an appointment. She's in Paris scouting collectibles almost as often as celebrities are at Primavera scouting purchases!

Sindin Galleries 1035 MADISON AVE. 10021
288-7902

Really, how lucky. To think that you could find a lovely outdoor sculpture garden and a $15,000 Miro litho both at the end of the same second-story climb. It's enough to leave you positively breathless. No wonder the Sindin Galleries are becoming such a special favorite of Madison Avenue gallery hoppers. It was opened in 1972, and already it's such an important place for you to see—not to mention be seen.

Though Sindin specializes in Latin American art, you can also find works by Miro, Picasso, and Chagall. But the Latin American collection is the most complete. Pity, the last time we were in we just missed finding that $80,000 Zuniga sculpture we'd been searching for.

Oh well, Cesar Andrade promised to keep his eyes open for another. We're sure he'll be glad to promise the same for you—we're just not sure whether he'll promise it in French, Spanish, Portuguese, English or Hebrew. He's polyglot and just full of surprises!

The Wildenstein Galleries	19 E. 64TH ST. 10022 879-0500

Isn't it worth a small fortune just to be transported to Paris for an hour or two? The Wildenstein Galleries are as good as being there. This five-story town house on East 64th Street is the epitome of understated elegance and beauty, from the rock-crystal chandelier which graces its 25-foot entrance to the marble floors and fresh flowers which abound, to the exhibition rooms replete with Louis XV consoles, cane-back chairs, and period pieces of all descriptions. If it weren't for the sound of Con Edison ripping apart the sidewalk outside as you ascend the filigreed, skylighted staircase, you'd swear you were in Paris.

By the way... Wildenstein carries art, too. In fact, the Wildenstein Gallery is one of the foremost in the world. As you cross the portal, insist on speaking to Louis Goldenberg. When you're spending $70,000 for a Fragonard, we don't see any sense in dealing with anyone but the man on the top.

For you he'll open the eight private viewing rooms on the exhibition floors, but don't limit yourself to that until exhibitions director Alberto Raurell shows you the entire gallery. Don't set your heart on buying that Millet in the exhibition room. It's only on loan. Instead ask about *The Gentle Rebel*. It's reputed to be Renoir's largest work... but we're sure it will still fit into that Brinks truck you have waiting to take you home.

The Wildenstein is open six days a week, which is quite lucky. After all, when you're making a decision as important as this one, you'll want to be deliberate. We know how difficult it is to resist being impulsive, but for $70,000 you're going to have to develop a bit of willpower. Ask Louis to put your choices in the vaults, and take a quick look inside as he tucks them away. Seeing that cache of treasure which isn't even displayed for the public is enough to convince you that the Wildenstein is all but a museum.

By the way, the Wildenstein Galleries are conveniently located quite near La Goulue. You *will* want to stop by for a glass of Dom Perignon to toast your new purchase, won't you?

IX. THE NEW YORK BEAUTY SCENE
Pretty Is as Pretty Does

PRETTY is as pretty does, so do be sure to do it right. After all, not only do you have to fight the rigors of New York city—dirt, traffic, snow, sleet, and humidity—you have to combat the fact that the nation's best-looking models and career girls are walking the same streets that you are. That's bound to keep you on your toes!

Luckily, Manhattan offers a full range of services to ready you for the fray. You can join Lauren Bacall for a coif at Kenneth's, then go on to Christine Valmy to learn the secrets of keeping skin healthy and clean in one of the world's largest cities. Lydia Bach will even teach you sensuous pelvic control between situps at her exercise haven—how's *that* for being equipped to make it in the big city?

You're right. You might be able to get by without the sensuous pelvic control. But for heaven's sake, don't skip the facial. After all, you do want to prepare the proper setting for those new earrings you're planning to pick up at Bulgari, don't you?

BODY TONING

Elizabeth Arden 691 FIFTH AVE. 10022
             486-7900

How terribly taxing for you to have to plan whether you'd prefer your massage before your manicure or after. How can one be expected to make such decisions day after day? Isn't it lucky that Elizabeth Arden came up with an easy solution; turn yourself over to them for a day, or a half-day "Miracle Morning," and they will do all the planning for you.

The "Miracle Morning" includes massage, hairstyling, manicure, face treatment, and daytime makeup. With a morning that good, just imagine what might happen during the afternoon! When you treat yourself to an entire "Maine Chance Day" ... five and a half hours and $80 worth of exercise class, steam, body massage, shampoo, style, cut, manicure, pedicure, facial, and makeup. They'll even throw in a touch of salad and coffee.

If you're still not satisfied with yourself, you might want to take one of Miss Craig's classes: a complete head-to-toe shape-up course based on a consultation with and analysis by Marjorie Craig. Miss Craig is famous for finding body exercises that move every muscle just as nature intended, as well as facial exercises that ensure a natural lift. Why not give one of her courses to the woman who has everything?

Another option is the one-day "Visible Difference" course. Since the exercise classes included in this take only six ladies, though, you'll usually have to book your spot around ten days in advance. This $70 bargain includes consultation with a hairstylist (Arden has 28; there must be one who'll understand you!) who will explore your lifestyle and plan your hairstyle around it, a one-hour face treatment by one of the 26 on-staff facial experts, a manicure, shampoo, styling, coloring, makeup lesson, makeup chart, and comb-out. Naturally, now that you've come this far, you'll want to make that difference really visible with a little something by Galanos or Bill Blass—just nod your newly coiffed head and they'll be glad to run a few designs up from the lower floors for your approval. They'll even accessorize them for you so you don't smear that new manicure flipping through scarves.

This brand of peaceful, pink pampering attracts such beautiful people as Arlene Dahl (who stops in not once, but twice a week), Shirley Bassey, Liza Minnelli, Maria Callas and Margot Fonteyn.

As good as all those preplanned days sound, you might be happier just choosing a selection that's all your own. Consider a makeup lesson with Constantine or Terry—just $30 an hour. Or a face treat, including muscle strapping, peel-off cleanser, thermal heat treatment, and an hour-long home treatment lesson on how to take care of yourself ($22.50). A shampoo and blow-dry in the cutting garden with Karina or Everett will run about $25, as will an hour of individual lashes. Then of course there's a complete selection of massage, paraffin baths, waxing, and manicures.

The most visible difference of all might be accomplished by Rafael, whose Elizabeth Arden wigs are justly famous. Three to four weeks of having him design you a new look of natural hair will cost about $600. If you'd rather accomplish something with your own hair, ask for Roberto Vega or Lewis. When Lewis isn't traveling with Sarah Caldwell and listening to operas, he's in residence at Elizabeth Arden. Either of them will be happy to send your hair-setting chart to an Arden salon in any other city if you like the results.

They'll also be happy to forward it to Maine Chance Health Spa in Arizona for you if you're so impressed with Arden that you'd like to follow their routines for a week. And after all, who could quibble about paying $1,050 for a week's board once you discover that it includes not only a personal maid and a chauffeur, but a 900-calorie diet, too!

Joseph Rottenburger   430 E. 56TH ST.   10022
753-9149

As if it weren't bad enough to watch Clara Pilates working out on the "Cadillac" at 95 . . . now we have to listen to Joseph Rottenburger tell us that he's been up doing push-ups since 4:30 in the morning! Has the whole world gone mad?

Oh well, at least with Joseph Rottenburger you have the comfort of having him shame you in private—he'll come to you at your home or hotel and give you an hour of calisthenics and massage for $35. He'll also give you the same workout at his own studio, but since the price is the same and the idea of being outdone by a man pushing 75 is a bit embarrassing, why not just let him come to you.

Rottenburger teaches stretches in *Vogue* editor Diana Vreeland's domain. He relaxes tensions for designer Adele Simpson. And he even claims to have been Queen Mary's Buckingham Palace masseur.

His credentials are obviously impeccable. He'll come over as late as 11 at night. And the cost is a mere $35. It's getting harder and harder to find an excuse not to exercise these days ... isn't it!

Katia Perret	65 CENTRAL PARK WEST	10023
Aubry	877-2616	

If your only excuse for not taking on Rottenburger was the $35 an hour, we've got bad news for you. Katia Perret Aubry will give you an at-home workout for a mere $25 ($20 if you promise to keep at it faithfully more than once a week!). Don't complain, it's really for your own good!

Katia thinks it's an exciting adventure to discover the unending source of energy that you can release or activate by moving. Obviously, she hasn't been around when we get up on a Sunday morning! She started as a ballet dancer in France, moved on to Spain where she became a flamenco dancer, then relocated in New York where she's been teaching body movement since 1968. Another one of those sublime-to-the-ridiculous stories, you know.

Katia moves to the rhythms of baroque, classical, and Indian music. In no time she'll have you stretching to the same strains which inspire Diane von Furstenberg. Initially it will require a consultation and the planning of a set of exercises specifically suited to your needs (just $30 for this). Then it's $20. Better yet, get Diane von Furstenberg to join you for a mutual hour of exercise, and you'll count as a small group and get by for just $10 per body.

As much as we enjoy exercising with Katia, we can't help but admit that our favorite portion of the lesson happens when she puts us into our yoga position and gives us a back rub. Almost makes it worthwhile to do those blasted exercises when you earn a reward like that!

Manya Kahn	12 E. 68TH ST. 10022
	288-1300

Manya Kahn is to New York bodies what General Motors is to cars—the largest producer of new models in the nation. The third floor of 12 East 68th Street is a quiet haven outside the traffic and noise of the city. The only disturbance you'll hear is the chatter of Pat Lawford comparing diets with one of the Rockefeller women or Mrs. David Susskind asking Mrs. Mike Wallace which facial she recommends.

Most of the women who come here are doers, intelligent enough to know the importance of exercise, proper eating habits, and planned relaxation. Manya Kahn guarantees them all. From the very first, she'll tell you that hard massage is wrong—if it causes pain, it will only cause you to tense up. Relaxation is the key word.

She's also attuned to the difference between men's and women's bodies and has developed exercise routines accordingly. Rather than recommending the sort of strenuous movements expected of an O. J. Simpson, she'll have you stretching to promote line, limberness, and proportion.

Hardly a month passes when she's not quoted in *Vogue, Town and Country,* or *Harper's Bazaar.* Among those most easily remembered is her heartless declaration: "There is no such thing as cellulite—it's only flabby muscle tone." How unfeeling of her to deprive us of our excuses!

To combat flab she'll teach you body rhythms: exercises that help you reshape and retone those soft muscles into firm ones. They help you to acquire the straight back and shoulders and elegant carriage that will make you feel slimmer and more energetic, while they make you relax from within. There are two different courses available: a one-hour course for the weak of heart, or a two-hour course for those of you who are gluttons for self-indulgence. The hour course is only exercise and heat therapy. The two-hour course is followed by an hour of heavenly massage.

Manya's been here for over 20 years, and has helped legions of women who have made their sessions with her not only a crash course, but a way of life.

| **Lydia Bach-** | 23 E. 67TH ST.   10021 |
| **Lotte Berk** | 288-6613 |

We wouldn't argue for a moment that certain survival techniques must be mastered by the modern woman if she wishes to get along in the big city, but we never thought we'd reach the point of having to study sensuous pelvic control in between situps. Only in New York would they call that exercise! Lydia Bach's sensuous pelvic control exercise method was imported from London, where it is said to have set typical English detachment back a notch or two. Frankly, it will take more than a few pelvic push-downs to upset the New York status quo, but since rumor has it that the method's developer, Lotte Berk, was still beating off thirtyish lovers at the age of 63, we're willing to give it a try. Just call us impressionable tourists!

The Lydia Bach salon is in a brownstone atop several art galleries. Get off at the fourth floor, take one look at Lydia and her teachers, and you'll be sold. As if it isn't enough that they have those perfect bodies... they insist on walking around with such contented smiles. Whatever could explain it?

Ms. Bach started her New York facility in 1971, and has proceeded to attract not only half the hottest models in town, but social circle names such as Nan Talese and Mrs. Joel Grey. They share the same ballet barre for exercise consisting of a combination of modern ballet, orthopedic exercise, and hatha yoga. The one ballet barre is the only equipment Lydia has.

You might as well stop looking for the massage and sauna right now—this is strictly work, girls! One-hour classes will contain six to eight people, so you can't sluff off for a moment without being noticed. Before you start slipping and sliding to Sly Stone and working out to the hustle with Pam, Rip, or Andrea, Lydia's going to insist that you hang out for a bit. No, we don't mean sit and relax in the lounge, we mean hang out! Literally! Grab the top of a door then just hang on for as long as you can keep your shoulders relaxed and down. Does wonders for the posture of ladies who normally walk with tense neck muscles rather than keeping their coiffed heads poised in natural balance on the tip of the spine.

If Lydia's classes tend to look inordinately shapely, it might just be because she's managed to convert almost every top model in town to her method. Not a bad advertisement at all! If you want to find yourself doing stretches between Eileen Ford's finest on the right and Pia Lindstrom on the left, just put together $95 for your first ten lessons ($190 for twenty).

Nicholas	25 W. 56TH ST.	10019
Kounovsky	246-6415	

If you're just flying in for the day and want to indulge yourself with a lunch at Russian Tea Room, do your penance beforehand with Nicholas. If you're planning to spend New Years at Vail and don't want to come home with an autographed cast, stop in and shape up with him ahead of time—Jackie O does! Either way, you'll be happy to learn that Nicholas' theory is that a little bit done at the right time is twice as good as quantities done at the wrong time—if he balances things correctly, you can achieve results in three minutes that couldn't normally be done in an hour. See—you won't be late to lunch after all!

By the way, if you recognized his name, you won't be surprised to recall that Nicholas is the author of *The Joy of Feeling Fit*. That's right, the silver-haired Russian who kept making Johnny Carson do push-ups! Nicholas was educated in Russia as an aeronautical engineer, so when he applies his skills to you it's a cinch that you'll either end up looking better or flying. Since he's whipped into shape God only knows how many pudgy politicians, actresses, jet-setters and corporation presidents, we're sure his magic will work on you.

When you enter his studio for the first time, Mr. Kounovsky will give you a physical fitness test. The first lesson, including this initial evaluation, will cost you a mere $25. Following these observations he'll give you a written program outlining exactly which sorts of exercise will be appropriate for your condition and body type, and will place you in a class of beginners, intermediates, or advanced students, according to that evaluation. Wherever you find yourself, it's a great way to overcome the atrophy and stiffness of the big city.

Nicholas has taught everywhere from Deauville to California. He's done nationwide push-ups with Dinah Shore, and whipped one model into such good shape that she ended up signing a $500,000 contract for a year with Avon (the real "Joy of Feeling Fit"?).

J. Pilates Gym   29 W. 56TH ST.   10019
974-9511

When you go up to visit J. Pilates, the first thing that meets your eyes is a barbell. The next thing to cross your vision might be the members of the New York City Ballet working out, or perhaps a professional figure skater or two. To say the least, this is serious exercise!

J. Pilates' methods are taught here on 56th Street and in Los Angeles at the Ron Fletcher studio. If you have any doubts as to its effectiveness, you should have seen the class his widow Clara taught before she died, at 95 years of age.

By the way, if you're yearning for the pleasant surroundings of Lydia Bach, you might as well forget about working out to Sly Stone, too. Though the Pilates studio is rumored to own a small radio, no one can really remember when it last went on. During the Olympics, probably! Where Lydia Bach is long on wall-to-wall carpeting and short on equipment, Pilates would be heaven to a machine-crazed exercise nut. From his famous "Cadillacs" through a variety of other equipment that positively boggles the imagination, there's the glitter of chrome in every direction.

But for beginners we've noticed that the most popular piece of equipment is the couch. We guarantee you'll need two or three trips to it during your initial sessions. Don't be shy about telling John you can't go on with a single more knee stretch or long spine exercise—it happens all the time. If you let Sari know that another short spine exercise might be the death of you, you can count on being couched immediately.

Pilates students range from 4-year-olds to 90-year-olds (just as you figured, the 90-year-old never uses the couch!), so you're always sure to find a full variety of figures huffing and puffing from 7:30 A.M. to 7:00 P.M. Now, are you ready for a test of courage?

HAIR

Cinandre 11 E. 57TH ST. 10022
758-4770

How nice! A hairdresser who doesn't insist on making you one of fashion's victims. No more brassy blond streaks, or flashy reds. Say bye-bye to ethnic influences and hello to the idea that whether you're working or playing tennis or going out in the evening, the important thing is still the individual face. And now that we've adopted their philosophy of tailoring volume and length to the wearer, we couldn't be happier.

Cinandre's three floors of clinically Courrèges white are run by André Marthèleur. Don't expect him to give you a cut—sacré bleu! André deals in concepts, not hair, though he does train all the stylists himself. He just doesn't happen to like to touch the customers himself! So ask for Jean-Louis, or take your pick of any of the other 30 stylists in residence. Since they've all received the same training, there's really not a lot of difference in their approach.

You can lock yourself inside Cinandre for the day and emerge at 6, having been washed, cut, dried, facialed, manicured, pedicured, waxed, and made up. By the end of the day you'll probably have been touched by hands that have earned credits in *Vogue, Harper's, Cosmo, Seventeen, Mademoiselle,* and *Elle.* They do so much work for the press that almost every member of the staff has contributed at one time or another.

A wash at Cinandre will run you about $5; $20 will see you through for a cut; set aside $10 or $11 for a blow dry, depending upon how long your hair is. While it's true that you can occasionally call and get a same-day appointment at this salon, if you're planning to come in on Friday afternoon or on Saturday, *do* call ahead.

Davian   833 MADISON AVE.   10021
535-1563

Be prepared to submit yourself to the discretion of the stylist, for he won't submit to your requests, and to have your hand slapped if you so much as say the word "roller." Davian does an easy-to-care-for Sassoon type of cut, and they do it for so many of the top New York models (including Margaux Hemingway and Kay Graham) that their shampoo room tends to look like an annex to Eileen Ford's agency. The styles are up-to-date, "now" looks; the names to ask for are David Daines or Ian Harrington.

The street-level shop is open and airy, and the second-floor coloring area even includes a garden. It's so wonderfully light that you can tell just what your new tint will look like in daylight.

By New York standards, Davian is a small shop: just a dozen stylists, two colorists, two manicurists, and a makeup artist. In prices, however, they live up to the level of the very best. Expect color to range anywhere from $23 to $65, and a cut to go from $21 to $40. At those prices you'd think they'd do it your way, wouldn't you?

Kenneth   19 E. 54TH ST.   10022
752-1800

We'd love to come up with the name of some wonderful little shop hidden on 76th Street where you could be assured of rising a cut above Kenneth's, but we have to agree with Rose, Pat, Eunice, and Ethel (oh, really—you know their last names!). After trying the rest of the best, when all is said and done we keep on coming back to Kenneth.

We know . . . it does look a touch conservative. But just be-

THE NEW YORK BEAUTY SCENE 245

cause these Empire rooms contain stylists in drab blue or black duly garbed with ties doesn't mean that creativity is stilted. Au contraire! Flip through the pages of *Harper's* and *Vogue* while you're waiting for your color consultation and just see how many credits that cute little Pamela Geiger got this month.

Naturally, you'll want to start at the top and have Kenneth do your cut (don't count on him to follow through with the blow-dry unless he's known you for years—you'll more likely be finished off by Mary). If you don't have an appointment already, your personal secretary should call immediately—it may take six to eight weeks. Of course if you're chummy with Lauren Bacall, she might be able to help you get in a bit earlier.

Kenneth is located in a Manhattan town house. Most New Yorkers would be thrilled to live there, so we're sure it will be comfortable enough to get you through a snip and set. But do be careful not to get trampled by the hundred people on staff as you make your way to Kenneth's domain.

You might want to start with the color deparment—you *were* getting a bit bored with that same old sable brown, weren't you? Ask for Al, Thomas, or Paulette and be sure to call a week in advance.

Next, the drying room. Any socialite worth her salt knows that you should insist on getting one of the spots with a chair-side phone. So much nicer to be able to receive your calls without being paged, isn't it? Besides, if you don't keep yourself busy with dialing, there's only the paisley-tented ceiling and Regency chandelier of Bristol glass to keep you entertained.

With all this elegance, it's sometimes difficult to remember that Kenneth started in the Navy, isn't it! Of course if you ask for one of the chaise-lounge dryers you can simply take a nap and not worry about whether Kenneth came up with his decorating ideas while serving his country, or whether he was inspired during the course of his work as a hairdresser in Syracuse.

For all this elegance you'd expect to have to hock the family jewels, but Kenneth is nothing if not reasonable. Despite his reputation and popularity, you can still have him give you a cut for a mere $35. His 35 stylists will do your cut for $20, and a blow-dry for $10. The set is $10 ($12 for longer hair—why not consider something short and sporty and save?), $4 extra for the shampoo. Add $3 for a lemon rinse and $3 for a cream rinse.

It would be a pity to let that nice new hair sit over the same old face—make a quick stop and have them design your makeup. For $30 you'll get a lesson with step-by-step instructions. But if do-it-yourself never appealed to you, you can have her give you a lovely new look and no instructions for just $15.

You're looking so lovely now, that French count you met last night at Régine's is sure to want to get familiar. Better stop by the waxing department before you leave. To the knee it's $12.50, but if you do the whole leg you can get a special price of $21. How could you resist?

Try as we might we can't find a thing to fault Kenneth on. Not only will he cut, wax, manicure, and make you up...he's even installed a shower and sauna. My dear, one could live here! You can buy your clothes in Mr. Snyder's downstairs boutique, then be entertained by Joan Rivers or Kay Ballard—and you just know how funny they are under the dryer!

So bon voyage and happy hairdo...just pick your way through the potted palms and you'll come out looking like a million!

Monsieur Marc 22 E. 65TH ST. 10021
861-0700

Most of Marc's clientele come to him through personal recommendation, then wait a bit for an appointment, but he might be willing to give you special consideration since you're in from out of town and your time is at a premium. Now all you have to decide is whether, between the rollers and the ratting, you *want* him to give you that special consideration. When Marc says he's looking toward elegance and refinement in beauty, rather than newness in image, he means he's styling for the 30-and-up ladies-who-lunch, rather than the trendy young. If you want the look you saw in last month's *Mademoiselle*, stay home!

But if you want the look that Babe Paley and Nancy Reagan

cultivate, rush right in (well, don't rush too fast. It *is* one flight up!). Mrs. William Buckley and Mrs. Jules Stein are Monsieur Marc customers, too.

You'll recognize Marc by the caribou head hanging over his mirror. If he happens to be too busy ratting to show off his trophies, you'll have to find him by looking for a dapper gray-haired gentleman. There he is now—right by the brown leatherette banquette in the middle of the salon.

Marc tries to give a quick check to every client passing through the shop, but of course the majority of his attention goes to the ladies he's cutting and styling himself. For this undivided attention, he'll charge you $30 for your first cut, and an additional $12 for styling. The second cut is $25, and he will trim you between cuts gratis. That tempts you to stay in New York, doesn't it! If you do decide to go home despite this wonderful arrangement, Marc will be glad to do a sketch of his roller pattern for your regular hairdresser. Pack it next to your hair spray. You wouldn't want to lose it, would you?

Vidal Sassoon   767 FIFTH AVE.   10022
                   535-9200

Everyone can go to Vidal Sassoon (at least, with 40 stylists and 40 assistants, we assume that they can accommodate everyone), but can just anyone arrange to be clipped in the V.I.P. room? Well—Candy Bergen and Julie Christie can. Mia Farrow and Diana Ross can. Maxime de la Falaise and Dionne Warwicke can. But it is much more fun people-watching in the main salon.

If they prove to be a bit stubborn about letting you into the V.I.P. room, go them one better and insist that Howard Fugler come to your hotel instead. Since he's the star's pet stylist, there's a very good chance that you'll be cutting out Raquel Welch if you book him first.

Don't even bother asking to have Vidal cut your hair. If you even find him in New York, it's an accident. And since he's all but given up cutting clients, he doesn't approach it with much enthusiasm. A demonstration for thousands in London's Royal Albert Hall is more up his alley these days.

But let's give credit where credit is due; if it weren't for Vidal, we might still be wearing rollers above our John Kloss negligees, and just think how far that would have set the sexual revolution back. He also eliminated hair spray from our vocabulary with the debut of his precision blunt cuts, which was a wonderful change from the stiff and sticky.

If Howard's not available, don't pout. All Vidal's stylists receive a rigorous in-shop training and the results are worth it. At Sassoon you know that the cut will be good. In fact, they refuse to even wash and blow-dry your hair if they haven't cut it for fear that someone will blame them for a bad one if they see it emerging from the Sassoon front door.

They've imported their entire men's department from Bonwit's, so there's always the chance that you'll run into Kirk Douglas or Dick Cavett on the way to the shampoo room.

There's just one little objection we've heard around town. When you walk up to Vidal's reception desk with five receptionists working madly away, does it sometimes occur to you that Sassoon moved into the General Motors Plaza to better study the assembly line?

SKIN

Alise Spiwak   20 E. 68TH ST.   10021
535-6878

When you're fed up with the formality of Elizabeth Arden—when you're tired of the red tape you go through behind that famous red door—go to Alise Spiwak for your waxing. But don't go without an appointment. So many New York models and film folk take advantage of her services that she is quite busy.

The real beauty of Alise is that she'll get you stubble-free without asking you to leave your hotel room. Of course you *can* visit her in her tiny offices, but if you don't feel like stepping out, just ask her to send Carol over for an hour. It's only double the price for house calls, but that won't bother a big spender like you!

Normal prices run $10 for half a leg, $20 for the whole leg, $3 for an upper lip, and $4 for an underarm. And normal hours run 8 to 6, just in time to have you ready for an evening of dancing at Régine's!

Christine Valmy	133 W. 57TH ST. 10019
	767 FIFTH AVE. 10022
	838-0775

The trouble with Christine Valmy's is that no matter what she does to your face—and she does wonderful things—she won't be able to have you looking as good as the salon itself! When Christine decided to do a showpiece to advertise her 700-odd salons across the country, she scrimped on nothing.

First you have to wade through that plush green carpet which leads to the skylighted, mirrored, reception desk (how cruel—reminding you how tired you look after a hard day trying on "important" stones at Harry Winston), where a nine-foot screen continuously presents demonstrations of the latest skin care techniques.

Next, into a consultation room where you'll meet the salon's director, Marina. If she hears that you're coming, perhaps Miss Valmy herself will stop in. Next into the treatment room, where colored lights will be changed to a tone soothing to your particular temperament. There you'll reap the benefits of a marvelous array of modern electronic apparatus and professional skin care products.

Though Christine Valmy does everything from complete makeup (ask for Joel) to foot massage (at $25 an hour), her main claim to fame is the "living cell" skin treatment she has developed for tired skins. (She also has a complete set of treatments devoted to post-plastic-surgery care).

On your way to the treatment rooms, you'll pass the glass-walled laboratory where living-cell masks and cosmetics are prepared. Here they're mixing up batches of Embryo-Val, the main ingredient in Christine's $25 facial treatment.

Miss Valmy's basic idea is that it's better to reveal the natural glow of a healthy, well-functioning skin rather than to try to conceal flaws with cosmetics. So while she doesn't totally eliminate makeup, she'll help you to establish a new set of priorities to produce that "natural" look.

Georgette Klinger   501 MADISON AVE.   10022
838-3200

Cleanliness... cleanliness... cleanliness. It might sound a bit repetitious, but then what can you expect from a girl who got a terrible case of acne after winning her first beauty contest. While it eliminated Georgette's chance for winning the title of Miss America, it *can* prove to be helpful to you if you'll only take advantage of the things which she learned while curing it.

Of course, these days, Georgette isn't the same young girl who worried about acne, but her mania with cleanliness remains the same. If you take a trip to Klinger, you can expect to be steamed and peeled down to the cheekbones.

Once you're down to your natural skin, Georgette will treat you with her special Revitalizing Facial Treatment, as well as a lengthy massage of the shoulders, neck and face. Masks will be chosen for your individual skin condition, and a final dosing with herbal sprays and treatment vials will leave you looking like a new woman. An hour and a half spent with Georgette Klinger is as good for the ego as it is for the skin!

Follow it up with at-home treatments which plan makeup remover, moisturizer, cleansers, drying lotion and masks specifically for your use. Scalp care is included, too.

By the way, one last secret about Georgette Klinger's clientele. Some of the most faithful customers are New York men. They're aware of the good life too!

Janet Sartin   480 PARK AVE.   10022
751-5858

667 MADISON AVE.   10021
832-9360

Having trouble getting into the "Eye" column of *WWD?* Can't even get them to run a two-line blurb—much less an 8x10 glossy?

THE NEW YORK BEAUTY SCENE 251

How's the world going to know that you're in New York if that keeps up?

As you might have suspected, we've got a solution. Just go to Janet Sartin and have your complexion analyzed. Not only will you emerge looking ever so photogenic, you'll probably step out the door next to Babe Paley or Betsy Theodoracopulos; and a day that passes without those girls being snapped by *WWD* is a dull day indeed.

For years we've considered the possibility that skin by Janet Sartin is actually a requirement for mention in a column. After all, every photographed face shows up in her soothing beige consultation room at least twice a year. There they are: the Duchess of Windsor next to Countess Marie-Hélène de Rothschild, Mary Martin, Betsy Bloomingdale, and Chessy Rayner. Tsk tsk ... we almost forgot Gloria Vanderbilt Cooper. Janet Sartin worked with Ernest Laszlo, and ever since his death, Janet's been the heir apparent for the Beautiful People's pores.

The only problem with going to Janet Sartin is that you'll have to make your plans months in advance. And though you *can* get a skin analysis in her new Park Avenue salon, no one in the New York Social Register would consider taking their tired faces anywhere but to the original Madison Avenue branch and availing themselves of the expertise of Janet herself. She's crisp, blond, and professional, and you'll have confidence the moment you see her in that terrifically clinical clean white smock. Of course it *is* a bit ruthless of her to look for flaws with the help of operating room lights—heavens, after all the trouble we've taken to be seen only by candlelight, it's a bit of a shock. Just keep telling yourself that it's for your own good.

A consultation with Janet is usually the result of a recommendation by one of her valued private clients. It will take about half an hour and will cost you $50. Without it you might as well forget the idea of using Sartin products at all. Only with an analysis will you gain the little yellow membership card that lets you buy her cleansers, moisturizers, and skin paste.

Following your consultation, Janet will expect you to be there for six treatments of $1\frac{1}{2}$ hours each. Using her own combination of electrical impulses, she will work toward returning the potency of atrophied muscles, as well as stimulating the circulation and cells. Now don't scowl when she hands you a bill of $75 per treatment. You know how horrid frown lines look!

From then on, being a Sartin believer is easy. She'll give you a one-month checkup your first time through, but from then on, she won't expect to see you more than twice a year. Home maintenance treatments are planned to be simple, too. You'll walk out carrying a six-month supply of her treatments (average total $60 to $80) in that status black and yellow shopping bag. It's an easy program: just a basic cleanser, moisturizer and makeup. With everything so pared down you can rid yourself of all those messy jars cluttering the bathroom now. Makes it ever so much easier for the maid to keep it clean, doesn't it? As if that's not help enough she's even written everything down in a little yellow pamphlet so you can double-check yourself from time to time.

Janet says that relaxation from stress is so important, and it's soothing to know that she believes that it's the skin that counts and not the name. Of course we believe her. But we also wonder how many faces she has seen that don't have "countess," "baroness," or "princess" attached to them.

If you haven't booked your appointment in advance, do visit her beautiful new salon on Park Avenue—and treat yourself to a consultation by one of her well-trained assistants.

Orlane Facial Institute 680 FIFTH AVE. 10019
757-4200

How long has it been since you let yourself be pampered by Orlane? As long as your last trip to Paris? Well, wait no longer. The French touch has come to New York. And while Orlane New York is considerably smaller than her Paris sister, she's still large enough to come to the aid of skin that has been assaulted by pollution, smoke, air conditioning, and steam heat. Even if your skin hasn't yet become completely parched from all of that, it's worth noting that an Orlane facial includes a certain amount of cuddling into clean, crisp sheets and an hour of relaxation on one of their comfortable, cushioned tables.

Margit Pinter is the acting director of the New York salon, and she'll personally insist on mapping out your skin care program. The basics of cleansing, toning and moisturizing produce a cared-for skin that ages more slowly and has fewer problems. It doesn't require much time—a monthly or bimonthly visit will be fine when teamed with your own home-care program.

The most expensive treatment Margit offers (well, you do want to go for the best, don't you?) is her B21 facial at $35. It's an hour and twenty minutes of hand massage teamed with heating pads, and reportedly has rejuvenating qualities which leave you with a restored elasticity which alleviates those bothersome lines that have been staring you in the face every time you look into your mirror at the Regency. Be sure to take along their night cream (just $85 for 1.76 ounce) to dab on whenever you're feeling a bit low.

If you're not feeling quite that low, you might try one of their shorter, less expensive facials, which range anywhere from $15 to $30. Their Rafermilane firming treatment is popular, as is the corrective treatment for troubled skin and their quick pick-me-up facial; so perfect if you have a half hour to kill before meeting him in the Palm Court.

Because Orlane is so small—just one makeup room, two rooms for facials, and a waxing area—smart travelers book appointments a week in advance. Particularly if they want a consultation with Marion Miller, their makeup expert. It's lovely to know that with each facial you're entitled to a complete makeup, which makes perfect sense. After all, what's the good of having wonderful skin if no one notices you?

TOILETRIES

Boyd Chemists   655 MADISON AVE. 10022
838-5524

Evermond from England, Garraud from France, Fenjal from Switzerland, and Renoir from New York. No, it's not the attendance list from the last Cannes festival in the South of France—it's a partial listing of the special brands which Bebe Boyd carries in order to make you more beautiful. They produce a complete line of lipstick, eye makeups, scents, and bath products.

The results can be seen on the Ford girls (Christine and Charlotte, that is—not the ones who left the White House), and Lee Radziwill. There are even boxes addressed to Princess Grace of Monaco leaving Boyd's. No wonder it's known as the Beautiful People's drugstore!

Where else would you find combs of French horn? At your local Rexall? Hardly! Boyds can pamper you with cleansers slowly extracted from French wildflowers, hypoallergenic makeup, bottles of tiny lash hairs to be mixed with wet mascara, or rejuvenating French breast oil. There are pure flower oils for fragrance and brow brushes of tortoise shell from France (just $2). And where else would you find a liquid eye makeup remover made especially for those of us who wear contact lenses?

Even Estée Lauder shops at Boyds, and who should know better? She can choose from skin treatment in mint or a mask made of tropical fruit and plant extracts. She can buy foam eye shadow applicators or Evermond's theatrical-looking mascara ($7.50). There are beautiful lemon-scented astringents ($5) and luxuriously invigorating wheat germ oil bath gel by Rolo ($15). Or perhaps Estée uses her own cosmetics and simply stops in to pick up one of Boyd's own expandable French envelope-shaped cosmetic cases at $6.95.

The Kennedys swear by Boyd's, as does Lynn Revson. And especially after you slim down with her cellulite cream that comes complete with its traveling bath brush and removable handle, we're sure you will too!

Cambridge 702 MADISON AVE. 10021
Chemists   838-1884

Isn't it lovely to know that you can get Culpeper sachet without going as far as Bruton Street? At Cambridge Chemists on

Madison Avenue you'll find not only the famous Culpeper soaps and clove pomanders, you'll be able to treat yourself to Floris perfumes and bath oils, Innoxa makeups, and the best selection of Kent brushes and pure badger shaving brushes we've seen in years.

Everything is clearly on display, and the atmosphere is European enough to appeal to regulars who range from Carol Channing to Jules Stein to Happy Rockefeller. They might have stopped by to pick up that wonderful German mascara, Ecarte. Or that slightly richer European version of Nivea Cream. Or that wonderful little vitamin A tablet, Slyvasun, which helps prevent sunburn. Or even to avail themselves of the Andrews Liver Salts which Cambridge keeps on display.

X. THE SPORTING LIFE

AND THEY TOLD YOU the biggest sport in New York was cab hunting... tsk, tsk. Why, New York is known for all sorts of outdoor life. Of course the majority of it has to be conducted indoors—it does get a bit nasty hitting a tennis ball past snowdrifts, you know—but still, it's done with the spirit of the great outdoors.

Naturally we want you to look good while you play. Though with the price per hour for the use of a tennis court in mid-Manhattan being what it is, you may have to finance the racquet on the installment plan; but we know you wouldn't dream of showing up courtside with less than the best!

Interested in a $2,500 deep-sea fishing reel for that next Bahamas vacation? Been hankering after a custom-made pair of hunt boots? Or perhaps it's a pair of flashy ice skates you had in mind. No matter, they're all available in New York (really, don't you know by now that you can have anything for a price!).

And by the way, if you're not quite ready for an hour on the racquetball court, that motorized bicycle in the corner is a mere $350. A month or two of living-room pedaling activity should put you into fine shape!

Abercrombie & Fitch	MADISON AVE. AT 45TH ST. 10017 682-3600

Abercrombie is by far the most famous sporting-goods store in the world. You can outfit any individual sport you can imagine, from skiing to skeet shooting. Where else but Abercrombie &

Fitch would you find a $60 telescopic fishing pole that fits into any busy executive's attaché case? Brown Bess, a limited-edition bicentennial rifle made from original 200-year-old plans, is $17,500. Boehm blackbirds, $5,400 the pair. A $175 Oregon Trail knife. A five-foot totem pole for $350. Angora long underwear, $38.50 the set.

Others have tried to copy A&F, but there's no duplicating it. It took too many years to build that reputation of offering a dazzlingly varied choice of sporting equipment. Today you can schedule your own safari to Kenya on the sixth floor at Adventures Unlimited, get a perfect Holland & Holland rifle on seven, buy a $16 pith helmet on five, and get safari-printed luggage to take it all with you. If you think you'll have spare time you can order the bicentennial chess set to take along for only $18,000 (George Washington is king).

Don't go in expecting to uniform your son's Little League team, however; you won't even find a baseball mitt at A&F. Convince the boy to take up deep-sea fishing and surprise him with a fighting chair at $2,300 including two rods. He should save up to buy the reels, however; $2,500 each will blow your entire budget.

Four floors are devoted to men's and women's apparel, but if you're looking for anything but action sportswear, we suggest you go elsewhere.

The exercise machine section is a treat. The Tuntari motorized bicycle is $350, a bargain for the shape it will keep you in. You can spend that much for a weekend at a spa. Don't miss the skateboards at $31.95, and for diehard joggers, you can get a treadmill for jogging indoors in inclement weather. Those adults with less energy will enjoy the motorized tricycle that goes 10 miles an hour. What a terrific way to get around Palm Beach!

The World of Golf   147 E. 47TH ST.   10017
242-2895

So, you finally got that coveted invitation to play at Piping Rock. Pity you didn't know five weeks sooner—it's going to take that long for the World of Golf to finish your custom clubs. Of course you could settle for being fitted from their stock of major brands, but wouldn't custom clubs look better peeping out from your Gucci golf bag?

Frank Malara is just the man to design them. A PGA pro, he's been in business since the late sixties with Ann Brahan, whose golf-addicted husband inspired her to buy a shop which made custom clubs. Today they've added to their custom club business (around $500 per set) all sorts of goodies that will give you the game that Jack Nicklaus displays on his good days. Their sensitized paper sticks to the face of your club and leaves a betraying black mark against you when your hit is off center. The hourglass Time Right clicks to let you know when the head of your club has gained enough speed to give you a good powerful swing. As for clothes, Ann leaves them to the experts. Ask for a pair of slacks, and she'll bundle you right off to the sports department of Saks Fifth Avenue.

Because really, their specialty is the custom clubs they do so well. To fit the clubs to the individual golfer's arc and tempo Frank uses a swing recorder machine. Make an appointment for an hour's analysis (just $35) and by the time you leave, you'll know which type of clubs are most appropriate for you, as well as how to improve your weaknesses and benefit from your strengths.

To make sure that you don't forget his good advice, Frank even gives you photographs to remind you of the tips he so carefully explained to you. Be sure not to forget them when you head out to Piping Rock. With the improvement Frank's made in your game, you're sure to have requests for autographed pictures before you're off the eighteenth green!

Hunting World   16 E. 53RD ST.   10022
                   755-3400

Some say that the next best thing to a safari is Hunting World's latest catalog. We say it's even better—not so much danger from those loose lions, you know. Just those dangers you're accustomed to facing every time you walk East 53rd Street! Besides, a conversation with owner Bob Lee is so close to the real thing that you can almost live an entire week's trip vicariously.

If you absolutely insist on going anyway, he's ready to sell you boots or jodhpurs, safari jackets, or pith helmets, even that perfect elephant-hair bracelet to add a fashionable ring of authenticity to your dress.

If you don't absolutely insist on going, you'll still enjoy the delicious smell of fine old leather and the very mannish look of it. Hunting World—the only thing that's missing is a white hunter in your tent! Would you settle for a Wall Street banker instead?

H. Kauffman & Sons 139 E. 24TH ST. 10010
Saddlery 684-6060

Planning on a few chukkers with the Potomac Polo Club? Well, before you start that trek to Maryland, you'd better make a quick trip to the Saddlery. Be it Meadow Brook, Purchase, or Potomac, you'll find just that perfect mallet in their stock of English and western riding gear. Of course there has been a bit of competitive shopping since *Vogue* announced that field boots were all the rage with Calvin Klein trousers, but you can always fall back on custom-made to guarantee that you get what you want.

Those good high polo boots will cost you $115, a paltry sum for a five-goal player like yourself. But if you'd rather be ready to hunt, plan on setting aside $250 for custom-made hunt boots. Of course they'd look silly if you didn't order the coat, too. You can have it for just $300 and a one-month wait.

Although Swaine, Adeney & Briggs, and Passier, Steuben, Barnsby and Pariani saddles are in stock, the Saddlery has been known to do everything from sewing Gucci reins on their bridles to designing the world's smallest saddle for a chihuahua. Since they have both a saddle maker and a tailor on the premises, nothing's too great a task for them.

Though you'll have a difficult time getting extravagant

orders filled around the November Madison Square Garden Show, a friendly word placed with Charles or Ron could do the trick. After all, it would be a shame to buy that yearling from John Kinney at the Saratoga/Keenland sales and not have racing silks ready for the day when he's going to run!

M. J. Knoud   716 MADISON AVE. 10021
              838-1434

You say you've only been in the city for a few days and already you're longing to be back on a horse? Trot on down to M. J. Knoud and speak to Bonnie Wright—she'll find a place for you.

While you're at Knoud, do look at the hunt garb. They carry some of the finest in the world. The firm is renowned for its wares for both horseman and horse. In fact, they saddle the entire Olympic team and most of the best stabled horses in the country. The Barnsby saddle, which is Knoud's exclusive brand, runs about $400 and is made to specification in England.

Once you've become socially acceptable in town, you'll no doubt go to Millbrook. We warn you: dress appropriately. A fine hunt jacket will be about $200 or a frock coat, $550, but isn't it reassuring to know that Knoud's will change the collar, cuffs, buttons, and color so that you blend right into the hunt of your choice? Your britches will take six to eight weeks; perfect tailoring does take time. Made-to-measure boots can be had for no less than $190, but we suggest you choose the very best at $270. Now, remember, Knoud's is strictly for hunt clothes. If you want something to wear while you ride your walking horse, you'll have to fly down to Lexington, Kentucky, and get properly attired at Myers.

After a particularly good hunt weekend the gift you send your hostess might just determine if you're asked back. Let Knoud's come to your rescue again. Ask Bonnie's father, David, to recommend something special. Most hunt gifts run the gamut through Knoud china, glassware, and placemats, so do try to be creative. If it really was a special time we might suggest the German crystal jewelry in 14- or 18-karat gold. The fox motif will run about $5,000, but is any price too high for a good hunt?

Sky Rink 450 W. 33RD ST. 10001
695-6555

So you're determined to cut a few figures in Rockefeller Center under the Christmas tree. You'd like to whiz across the ice stylishly enough to impress even the most jaded New Yorker. What a marvelous finale for your trip! But hardly the thing for a novice. Best that you get a few pointers at Sky Rink before you step out in front of the crowd. The Sky Rink Skating Club's instructors include double gold medalist Peter Dunfield and his wife Sonya Klopfer Dunfield, also a double gold medalist. If *they* can't get you doing a double axle, you might as well forget it!

They'll both tell you to stop in at Peck & Goodie for your new custom skates before you step out on the ice. White suede, fit to perfection so that your ankles won't topple—or at least so they'll topple less. Then on to Sky Rink, aptly named because it perches on the sixteenth floor of a Manhattan office building. The indoor rink is beautiful, surrounded by the flags of many nations, and when your ankles finally give out (despite those new skates) you can relax on the sundeck or munch a hard-boiled egg and some cottage cheese to renew your energy.

If you're planning on staying around, you'll want to join the Sky Club. It is private, but entree is readily accessible once you're recommended by one member and seconded by another. Dorothy Hamill skates at Sky Rink—perhaps she'll recommend you. Until she says yes, though, you'll have to do your figure eights during the public hours; since the hours vary according to the season, be sure to call the club before donning your skating skirt.

Live organ music aside, please bear in mind that the skating at Sky Rink is a very serious business and worthy of your utmost attention. Isn't it worth an investment of $9 per half-hour for Peter's instructions? You wouldn't want to see that six-year-old who was just lacing up her boots skate circles around you, would you?

Midtown Tennis Club	341 EIGHTH AVE. 10001 989-8572

You've seen it, we're sure. Enclosed in a bubble near Madison Square Garden and just minutes away from anywhere in Manhattan. You can finish your Madison Avenue shopping and be double-faulting in no time.

The Midtown Tennis club is a two-story affair with four downstairs courts and four upstairs courts. The lighting is nonglare, the courts are green clay, and the heat is kept at a comfortable temperature year round. As if that isn't enough to tempt you they also have showers, lockers, saunas, a tennis shop, and a club room complete with fireplace, and four pros, ready to make you into another Rod Laver for just $30 an hour.

The Midtown Tennis Club, however, is not a private club. Heavens, you could find yourself playing next to just anyone there. Also, you'll have to battle with the madding crowd for your reservations: $28 for prime time and $25 during the off hours early in the morning or late at night. So call well ahead, and do ask for a downstairs court. That nasty echo from the upstairs bubble has been known to throw some people's timing off for a week!

Tennis Port	51–24 2ND ST. LONG ISLAND CITY 11101 392-1880

For our money, Tennis Port, which opened in 1974, offers the best of both worlds. It has the exclusiveness of a membership club, plus the advantages of 25 courts, both indoors and out. It's got deluxe facilities which include a sun terrace, snack bar and fireplace for your off-the-court comfort. Thrown in as an extra added attraction is the occasional presence of Robert Redford and John Lindsay. But be careful: watching Redford play can be quite distracting—better that you turn the other way and study Jacob Javits. We respect him immensely, but must admit that his profile is far less likely to destroy your backhand.

Tennis Port is a fifteen-minute limousine ride from Manhattan, located at the end of the midtown tunnel in Long Island City. Fred Boutour and his ex-wife Marge run it. They've thoughtfully provided three pros, one of whom is Bill Talbert's son Peter. They've also thoughtfully provided both year-round and summer-only memberships, so if you'd rather spend those cold months skiing, you can cut your membership fee from $800 to $400.

Tennis Port has a resort atmosphere, in which post-game pros can relax and enjoy the magnificent view or have lunch on the spacious lawns. If you happen to be one of those doers we've heard so much about you'll also be glad to hear that the club has barbecues, dances, and tennis movie nights. (But really... when you could be at Le Club?)

Bring a good supply of those shocking green Wilson three dots: you're likely to see your mis-hits roll into the middle of a game between Walter Cronkite and Roger Mudd; by all means don't claim them. After all, if you do, the next thing you know you may be hearing that your game is off on the six o'clock news!

Tennis Lady	765 MADISON AVE. 10021
	535-8601

Tennis Lady confirms one of our dearest beliefs... it's not so much how you play, it's how you look. So while Tennis Lady stands ready to help you look absolutely smashing in a T-shirt and skirt, there isn't a racquet or ball to be found on the premises. How often must we repeat it—who needs a backhand when you've got good legs!

The Empress of Iran has Carol and Adrian put together her tennis wardrobe. That scores a few points for the store. And while we've heard her service leaves something to be desired, no one suggests that she looks less than athletic. With T-shirts running between $10 and $25, skirts from $18 to $25, and dresses from $30 to $60, she can afford a change for every set.

When the empress is not there, you might spot Dustin Hoffman or John Lennon shopping for their wives. Or are they just stopping in for another look at Tennis Lady's leggy, short-skirted young clerks?

NEW YORK...
We Don't Want to Say Goodbye

WE'RE ALWAYS so upset by the idea of leaving New York. Just about the time we become accustomed to the changing of the seasons in our new Ferragamo boots and resign ourselves to all those trying decisions like whether we'll go to Régine's or Le Club after the next theater opening, it's time to move on to Rio de Janeiro or the south of France. Oh well, nothing is forever...

If you're dejected by the thought of leaving the big apple without giving the city something to remember you by, how about throwing a smashing going-away party? Of course it is a bit difficult to give a going-away party in New York; it's such a big city, and you make so many friends. But we finally came up with the perfect solution: rent Shea Stadium. Really, it is just the right size. Seating for 55,000 without a bit of crowding! Where else could you manage to fit in all those new acquaintances you've made during the trip?

Naturally, it takes some planning. There *are* a few fans who'd be incensed if you planned your going-away party when one of the Mets' games was scheduled—you know how touchy people get when they're bumped out of their season seats. But if you're careful not to conflict with the home team, no one will be upset.

The arrangements are simple enough to make. Just phone up Jim Thompson, vice-president and business manager of the Mets, and book a date. Of course, he'll tell you that between rental of the stadium and necessary expenses (you know, electricians, 250 security guards, 200 ushers, a ground crew for clean-up and an insurance policy guaranteeing $10,000,000 in liability coverage, not to mention 40 ticket takers) the bill will be in the neighborhood of $75,000. But giving up that Harry Winston ring you had in mind will take care of that paltry sum.

Now don't forget those little extras... you know, things like hiring Executive Jet Aviation to fly in those friends who've been out of town and a helicopter service for the ones who are spending the weekend in the city. You wouldn't want 55,000 people going hungry, so you'll have to phone Glorious Foods and ask them to cater a lap dinner (let's see, with an order for 55,000 you'd better call them at least a week or two in advance!). And then of course you'll want to commission Steuben to do a little something in crystal for personal mementos. Good heavens! With all of this going on, you hardly need to put on a show!

But do it anyway... it's simple enough to find an act that will please 55,000. Jethro Tull sold out Yankee Stadium the last time he visited; he might be just the perfect entertainer. And if he's not in the country, maybe Barbra Streisand's free.

It all sounds like so much fun, but you say you prefer more modest gatherings? Don't worry, we have something a touch more modest up our sleeves for those of you who are still developing an extensive guest list. It's New York's version of the bateau-mouche.

As luck would have it, there's a very close cousin to Paris's bateau-mouche right in New York Harbor. The cabaret can accommodate up to 250 people, with the cost per person varying according to the type of menu you want (yes, caviar does run up quite a tab), the liquor service and entertainment. But the basic cost for a four-hour cruise around New York Harbor is just $2,000. Call World Yacht Enterprises (14 West 55th Street, 10019; 246-4811) and you might just be able to please all your new friends and keep the Winston diamond, too. And if that doesn't make leaving New York a bit easier to take, we simply can't imagine what would!

Index

Abercrombie & Fitch (sporting goods), 256–57
Adolfo (designer, boutique), 124, 135, 147
A La Vieille Russie (antiques), 217, 221–22
Alfredo's Settebello (restaurant), 22–23
Ambergris (antiques), 218, 219
Andus, Judith (antiques), 220
Antecacche (antiques), 218, 219
Antique Market, The, 219–20
Antiques Center of America, The, 217–19
Anton, Tony (boutique), 167
Arden, Elizabeth (beauty salon), 235–37
Arpels, Helene (shoes), 153–54
Art Bag Creations (handbags), 148
Arthur's Dress Shop, 148–49
Artwear (jewelry), 183–84
Aubry, Katia Perret (body toning), 238–39
Aujard, Christian (designer), 130
Austin Zuur (boutique), 149

Baccarat (crystal), 199–200
Bach, Lydia, and Berk, Lotte (body toning), 240–41
Bailey-Huebner (boutique), 132
Balducci's (fancy fruits and vegetables), 102
Ballato (restaurant), 23
Balmain, Pierre (menswear), 176–77
Barrie, Scott (boutique), 128
Barton, Peter (designer), 132

Basile (designer), 134
Battaglia (menswear), 172
Beauty Checkers (beauty salon), 133
Beene, Geoffrey (designer), 135, 162
Bendel, Henri (department store), 124, 131–33, 155
Bergdorf Goodman (department store), 125–27
Betsey, Bunky & Nini (boutique), 149–50
Betsy's Place (bakery), 103
Blass, Bill (designer, boutique), 128, 131, 135, 151, 162
Bloomingdale's (department store), 124, 127–30, 155
Blum, Joanne (antiques), 218–19
BodyWorks Salon (gym), 126
Bonté (bakery), 103–4
Bonwit Teller (department store), 124, 130–31, 155
Bottega Veneta (boutique), 136–37
Bouquets à la Carte (florist), 196–97
Box Tree, The (restaurant), 23–25
Boyd Chemists (beauty supplies), 253–54
Buccellati (jewelry), 183, 185–86
Bulgari (jewelry), 183, 186–87
Byrnes, Evelyn (boutique), 151

Café Carlyle (restaurant), 28
Café des Artistes (restaurant), 25–27
Café Orsini (restaurant), 131
Cambridge Chemists (beauty supplies), 255
Caravelle, La (restaurant), 21, 27–28
Carey Limousine, 5–6

INDEX

Carina Nucci (shoes), 142–43
Cartier (jewelry), 183, 188–89
Castelbajac (designer), 154
Caswell-Massey Co., Ltd. (boutique drugstore), 210–11
Cerruti, Inc. (children), 180–81
Chauffeurs Unlimited, 3
Cheese of the World (gourmet shop), 111–12
Cheesecake Elegant, Le (bakery), 104–5
Chez Pascal (restaurant), 28–30
Chloé (designer), 131, 135, 162
Christ Cella (restaurant), 21, 30–31
Cinandre (beauty salon), 243–44
Cirque, Le (restaurant), 31–32
Clock Hutt, Limited (antiques), 220
Club, Le (private club), 22, 96–97, 99
Coach House, The (restaurant), 32–33
Colette French Pastry (caterer), 119–20
Colleck, Philip (antiques), 225
Collector's Antiques, 218, 219
Colonial Nut Shoppe (candy), 116–17
Connoisseur Inc. (antiques), 222–23
Connoisseur Suite (boutique), 135
Continental Enterprises (antiques), 219–20
Côte Basque, La (restaurant), 21, 33–36
Country Host (gourmet shop), 102
Coup de Fusil, Le (restaurant), 36–37
Courrèges (boutique), 150
Creative Cakes (bakery), 105–6
Cremaillère, La (restaurant), 95–96
Cross, Mark (leather), 205–06
Crysteno, Inc. (menswear), 173
Cygne, Le (restaurant), 21, 37–38

Daly's Daffodil (restaurant), 38
Daly's Dandelion (restaurant), 38
Dave-el Livery (car service), 3–4
Davian (beauty salon), 244
David, Jean Louis (beauty salon), 133
David K's Chung Kuo Yuan (restaurant), 39

De Noyer, Jean (boutique), 140–41
De Steno, Dominick (menswear), 173
diCamerino, Roberta (boutique), 135
Doubles (private club), 97–98
Dumas Patisserie (bakery), 106–7
Dunhill Tailors, 173–74

E.A.T. (gourmet shop), 112–13
Elaine's (restaurant), 40
Elmer's (private club), 98
El Morocco (private club), 97, 99–100
Emmerich, André (gallery), 228–29
Empire Diner (restaurant), 40–41
Executive Jet Aviation, 1–2, 266

Falchi, Carlos (designer), 132, 158
Fauchon Boutique (gourmet shop), 135
Ferragamo, Salvatore (boutique), 143–44
Ffolio 72 (stationery), 215
Fioravanti, William (menswear), 173
Fiorentina Shoes, 166
Four Seasons, The (restaurant), 42–44
Frank Kay, Ltd. (antiques), 223
Fraser Morris (gourmet shop), 113–14
French and Company (antiques), 220–21
Fried, Bernice (antiques), 220

Galanos, James (designer), 131, 151, 161, 162
Gazebo, The (boutique), 211–12
Gino's (restaurant), 44
Givenchy Nouvelle Boutique, 126
Glacier, Le (ice cream parlor), 77
Glorious Food (caterer), 120–21, 266
Godiva Chocolates, 117
Golden Nonsense (jewelry), 191–92
Goodman, Alaine (boutique), 147
Good's Antiques, 218, 219
Goulue, La (restaurant), 44–46
Grand Café, The (restaurant), 46–47
Greenberg, William, Jr. (bakery), 110
Grenouille, La (restaurant), 21, 47–49
Gucci (boutique), 137–38

INDEX

Halston (designer, boutique), 124, 128, 151–53, 162
Hammacher Schlemmer (department store), 212–13
Hammer Galleries, The, 229–30
Harp, Holly (designer), 132, 133
Harvey Limousine Service, 4–5
Healthworks (restaurant), 49–50
Horn, Carol (designer), 133
Hornby, Judy (designer), 167
House of Poncee (antiques), 218, 219
Hunting World Boutique, 130
Hunting World (store), 258–59

Island Helicopters, Inc., 6–7

Jackie's Pizza Parlor (restaurant), 139
Jacomo, Ltd. (handbags), 160–61
Jaeger (boutique), 139
Jag (designer, boutique), 140, 155
Julie Artisan's Gallery, Inc., 230–31
Julio (boutique), 155–56

Kahn, Ben (furs), 127, 178–79
Kahn, Manya (body toning), 239–40
Kamali, Ltd. (boutique), 156–57
Kaplan, Leo (antiques), 224
Kauffman & Sons Saddlery, 259–60
Kenneth (beauty salon), 244–46
Kenzo (designer), 154
Klein, Anne (boutique), 128
Klein, Calvin (boutique), 128
Klinger, Georgette (beauty salon), 250
Knoud, M. J. (sports equipment), 260
Koos van den Akker (boutique), 157–58
Kounovsky, Nicholas (body toning), 241–42
Kron Chocolatier (candy), 118–19

Lady Continental Shoes, 159
Lagerfeld, Karl (designer), 135
L'Antiquaire Inc. (antiques), 222–23
Lapidus, Ted (boutique), 145–46
Lauren, Ralph (boutique), 128, 132
Lehr, Henry (boutique), 154–55

Leighton, Fred (jewelry, boutique), 190
Leonard Baking Co., Inc., 107–8
Léron (linen), 208
Liebow, Mrs. (antiques), 220
Linen Pavilion (boutique), 135
Little Bits of the Sixties (children), 181–82
Lombardy, The (hotel), 10–11
Lonia, Inc. (boutique), 159
Lord & Taylor (department store), 133–34
Lorris Azzaro (boutique), 159–60
Love, Diane (florist), 202–03
Lucky Arts Enterprises (antiques), 220
Lutèce (restaurant), 21, 51–52

McCallagh, Valerie (antiques), 218, 219
David McCorkle/Frank Davis (caterer), 122–23
McFadden, Mary (designer), 162
Madame Romaine de Lyon (restaurant), 52–53
Madrigal, Le (restaurant), 21, 53–54
Magnificent Doll, The (antiques), 203
Maia, Ronaldo (florist), 198–99
Maison Glass (gourmet shop), 102
Manet, Claude (boutique), 137
Manganaro's (caterer), 122
Manhattan Art and Antique Center, 217
Mann, Robert Edward (antiques), 220
Maria (antiques), 220
Mario of Florence (shoes), 161
Martha, Inc. of New York (boutique), 161–62
Matthews, Ruth (boutique), 162–63
Maximilian (furs), 179–80
Maxwell's Plum (restaurant), 21, 54–56
Mayfair House (hotel), 11–12
Meatique (gourmet butcher), 102
Medallion Fruit Market, 102

INDEX

Meledandri, R. (menswear, tailor), 174–75
Midtown Tennis Club, 262
Miss Grimble's Bakery, 108–10
Missoni (designer, boutique), 128, 130, 147
Mr. and Mrs. Foster's Place (restaurant), 57–59
Mr. Jennings (ice cream parlor), 131
Miyake, Issey (boutique), 128
Monsieur Marc (beauty salon), 246–47
Montenapoleone (lingerie), 163–64
Moon's (restaurant), 56–57
Mori, Hanae (designer), 162
Muir, Jean (designer), 132

Nanouchka (baby boutique), 135
Nassau, Lillian (antiques), 224–25
Nazlen, Henry Gerskum (autographs), 218, 219
Nena's Choice (gallery), 127
New York Hilton, 8–9
Nicola's (restaurant), 59–60
Norell, Norman (designer), 162

Objets d'Art (antiques), 218, 219
Odd Ball Antique, The, 218, 219
Oh-Ho-So (restaurant), 60–62
One If By Land, Two If By Sea (restaurant), 62–63
Orlane Facial Institute, 252–53
Orsini's (restaurant), 63–64
Oyster Bar, The (restaurant), 64–65

Pace Gallery, The, 231–32
Palace, The (restaurant), 67–68
Palm, The (restaurant), 68–70
Palm Court (restaurant), 15
Palm Too (restaurant), 69
Parioli Romanissimo (restaurant), 21, 70–71
Pat-Rick Children's Store, 182
Pearl's Chinese Restaurant, 72–73
Peretti, Elsa (designer), 152, 153
Petite Ferme, La (restaurant), 74–75
Pfeifer, Philip W. (antiques), 226

Hotel Pierre, 12–14
Pietro's (restaurant), 73–74
Pilates, J. (gym), 242–43
P. J. Clarke's (restaurant), 66–67
Plaza Hotel, 14–15
Plumbridge Confections and Gifts, 119
Port of St. James (antiques), 220
Porter, Thea (designer), 162
Porthault, D. (linen), 206–07
Pratesi Shop (linen), 209
Primavera Gallery, 232–33
Private Island (boutique), 135

Quo Vadis (restaurant), 75–76

Rajah's (ice cream parlor), 76
Régine's (private club), 22, 99, 100–1, 156
Renta, Oscar de la (designer), 134
Revillon Salon (furs), 136
Rhodes, Zandra (designer), 131, 162
Riffs Men's Boutique, 142–43
Rita Ford Music Boxes (antiques), 226–27
Rive Gauche Boutique (men), 177–78
Rive Gauche Boutique (women), 128, 169–70
Rogers, Ethel (florist), 197–98
Rogers, Jackie (boutique), 138–39
Rollston Livery Service (car service), 5
Rollston Motor Services Ltd. (car service), 5
Rose Lash International (boutique), 165–66
Rottenburger, Joseph (body toning), 237–38
Russian Tea Room (restaurant), 77–78
Rykiel, Sonia (designer, boutique), 128, 132

St. Laurent, Yves (designer):
men's boutique, 177–78
women's boutiques, 128, 162

INDEX

Saks Fifth Avenue (department store), 134–36, 147
San Francisco Clothing (boutique), 144–45
Sanchez, Fernando (designer), 133
Sant'Angelo, Giorgio (designer), 130
Sardi's (restaurant), 78–79
Sartin, Janet (beauty salon), 251–52
Sassoon, Vidal (beauty salon), 247–48
Schweitzer, Alice (boutique), 147–48
Sea Fare of the Aegean (restaurant), 79–80
Seine, La (boutique), 141–42
Serendipity (restaurant), 80–82
S'fari Room (boutique), 130
Shezan (restaurant), 83–84
Shields, Alexander (menswear), 175–76
Shoe Biz (boutique), 132, 133
Silent Woman Antiques, 218, 219
Simon Pure Better Diet Shop (gourmet shop), 114–15
Simpson, Adele (designer), 131
Sky Rink (skating), 261
Smith, Willi (designer), 133
SoHo Charcuterie and Restaurant, 84–85
Soup Bar (restaurant), 133
Spiwak, Alise (beauty salon), 248–49
Stair & Co. (antiques), 217, 227–28
Stavropoulos (designer), 131, 162
Steuben Glass, 200–01
Strong, Mrs. John L. (stationery), 215–16
Studio Galleries, 233
Stupell, Carole (home decorations), 201–02
Sulka, A. (menswear), 170–71
Sylbert, Viola (designer), 132

Tabletopping (boutique), 132
Tavern on the Green (restaurant), 86–87
Tearston, Sylvia (antiques), 228
Tender Buttons (antique buttons), 213–14
Tennis Lady (clothes), 263–64
Tennis Port, 262–63
Three Guys From Brooklyn (fancy fruits and vegetables), 102
Thylan, Ben (furs), 179
Tiffany & Co. (jewelry), 183, 193–94
Tomotsu (designer), 159
Trigère, Pauline (designer), 151, 162
Tuscany Hotel, 17–18
21 Club, The (restaurant), 87–90

Uncle Tai's Hunan Yuan (restaurant), 90–92
Ungaro, Emanuel (designer), 162
United Nations Plaza Hotel, 18

Valentino (designer, boutique), 134, 162, 168–69
Valentino, Mario (shoes), 142
Valmy, Christine (beauty salon), 249–50
Van Cleef & Arpels, Inc. (jewelry), 126, 183, 194–95
Veau d'Or, Le (restaurant), 92–93
Veneziano Boutique, 167–68
Vuitton (boutique), 134

Waldorf-Astoria (hotel), 19–20
Weatherill, Bernard (menswear), 173
Webb, David (jewelry), 189–90
Wildenstein Galleries, 234
Windows on the World (restaurant), 93–94
Wing Woh Lung (gourmet shop), 102
Winston, Harry (jewelry), 124, 183, 192
Winters, Harriet (designer), 159
Woolworks (needlepoint), 204–05
World of Golf, The, 257–58
World Yacht Enterprises, 266

Yves St. Tropez (boutique), 170

Zabar's (gourmet shop), 115–16
Zoran (designer), 132